D1602392

THE BEST OF THE SATURDAY BOOK

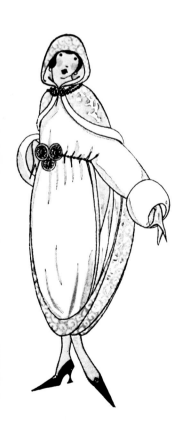

The drawing on this page is from the *Gazette du Bon Ton*, 1920. The figure reproduced in the frontispiece is by the Staffordshire potter John Astbury (1688–1743) and was in the collection of the late Captain C. B. Kidd. The silk Stevengraphs on the title page depict Stephenson's first train, 1825, and a train of 'The Present Time'.

THE BEST OF

The Saturday Book

EDITED BY JOHN HADFIELD

★

HUTCHINSON

LONDON MELBOURNE SYDNEY AUCKLAND JOHANNESBURG

HUTCHINSON & CO. (PUBLISHERS) LTD

An imprint of the Hutchinson Publishing Group
3 Fitzroy Square, London W1P 6JD

Hutchinson Group (Australia) Pty Ltd
30–32 Cremorne Street, Richmond South,
Victoria 3121

PO Box 151, Broadway, New South Wales 2007

Hutchinson Group (NZ) Ltd
32–34 View Road, PO Box 40-086, Glenfield,
Auckland 10

Hutchinson Group (SA) (Pty) Ltd
PO Box 337, Bergvlei 2012, South Africa

First published 1981
This compilation © John Hadfield 1981

Printed in Great Britain by George Over Ltd
London and Rugby, and bound by
Wm Brendon & Son, Ltd, Tiptree, Essex

ISBN 0 09 145990 7

Foreword

J. B. PRIESTLEY

I CAN ALWAYS ENJOY a good mixture, eating it, smoking it, or reading it. THE SATURDAY BOOK was a good mixture and I for one was very sorry when it vanished. However, not all has been lost, for here we have an enduring reminder of its excellence. Having seen a synopsis of its contents, I for one am now waiting impatiently to read my copy of THE BEST OF THE SATURDAY BOOK. There must be a good many of us who will be giving a hearty welcome to this particular volume.

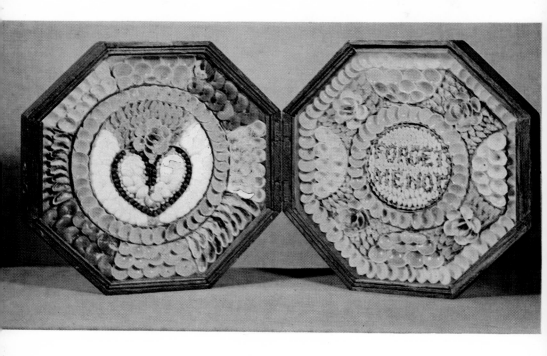

Introduction

CASTING MODESTY ASIDE, there are three points to be made about *The Saturday Book*. First, there is nothing else quite like it. Second, it defies description. Third, it enjoyed a longer life than any other annual miscellany.

Bibliographers might try to dispute the last point, but they would probably fail. The famous *Yellow Book* of the 'nineties was a quarterly, not an annual; and it ended after thirteen issues. To find close competitors one has to go back to the early nineteenth century, the Golden Age of the miscellaneous annual. Contributors then included writers of the stature of Coleridge, Byron, Keats, Scott and Tennyson. The most famous of all, *The Keepsake*, was started in 1827, but ran for four years less than *The Saturday Book*. *Friendship's Offering, or The Annual Remembrancer*, which started in 1825 and ended in 1844, ran us closer than most.

What *was* the essential nature of *The Saturday Book*? In his Introductory Note to the first issue, published in 1941, our first editor, Leonard Russell, was modestly negative in describing it. "The storm of the times', he wrote, 'is absent from this miscellany. If anything it looks backward, and nostalgia for small pre-war pleasures emerges from the pages. Here, then is a tranquil book, without a thunderclap of any kind."

That first issue, much more beautifully printed than most books in those

7

THE SATURDAY BOOK'S founder, LEONARD RUSSELL, with his dog Coco, in his house in Albion Street, off the Bayswater Road, photographed for No. 10. Coco, named after the famous circus clown, was a poodle, needless to say, of irresistible charm, who became a notable figure in the Hyde Park Parade.

days of war-time austerity, was mainly a collection of what used to be called *belles lettres*, by well-known critics and journalists, together with a long-short story by H. E. Bates. The illustrations were all from wood engravings by Agnes Miller Parker. It was very different in character and composition from the issues of the 'fifties, 'sixties and 'seventies though, surprisingly, it reproduced (in monochrome only, of course) a painting by René Magritte (whom the present editor thought he 'discovered' in 1958!). In that 1941 issue the distinguished art critic Eric Newton announced that "Surrealism is obsolete. The Surrealists' day is over."

That first *Saturday Book* was a prodigious success. It was just what war-weary readers wanted. Then, appearing to change his policy, Leonard began his second number with a brilliant series of war pictures by such photographers as Cecil Beaton and Bill Brandt, and narratives of war experience. The *belles lettres* occupied only the second half of the book. But every one of 10,000 copies were sold, and it is now very scarce.

It was not until Number 3 that the pictorial treatment of social history, which became a familier *S.B.* element, was adopted. In that issue, and the next three, there were pages of ingeniously contrasted photographs under such general headings as 'Manners and Customs of the English', 'Yesterday and Today' and 'The Social Register'. Many of those photographs have become familiar since then in other illustrated books, but Leonard was first in the field, and he made a 'corner' in a collection of Victorian and Edwardian photographs by Paul Martin.

It was not until No. 4 that colour illustrations appeared: a series of paintings from Temple Newsam and elsewhere, chosen by Philip Hendy, who later became Sir Philip, of the National Gallery. In No. 5 an acknowledgement was made to the design and illustrations provided by Laurence Scarfe, who continued to design the book until No. 11, and whose bold draughtsmanship and quirky eye gave the *S.B.* much of its distinctive character during its first decade. No.5 also introduced that cockney 'character,' Fred Bason.

In the fifth number acknowledgements were made also to Edwin Smith and Olive Cook, who provided another colour-plate section. In the sixth number Edwin Smith contributed the first of those pictorial miscellanies of rare, odd and beautiful objects which continued thereafter to be the most individual of all *S.B.* features. From then on colour increased, and the partnership of Edwin Smith and Olive Cook (who married) became the visual foundation stone of the book. It can reasonably be claimed that it was they, under Leonard Russell's influence, who put Victoriana on the map of British popular taste. During the last four years of Leonard Russell's editorship there was profligate indulgence in colour and, at a guinea, the book became fantastic value for money. Hence the enormous sale.

The contributors included such notable writers as James Agate, Edmund Blunden, Walter de la Mare, Robert Graves, Graham Greene, Richard Hughes, Compton Mackenzie, Bertrand Russell and Osbert Sitwell. But what gave the book its special appeal was the visual element. Unkind critics said it was a book to look at rather than read, and there is some truth in the statement that it was the originator of the 'coffee-table book' of today.

By then, however, the *S.B.* had developed a distinct personality of its own. Leonard said that everything that appeared in it was simply to please and instruct himself. The publishers let him do as he wished, and he had no advisers apart from Olive and Edwin and Laurence Scarfe.

People have often asked why it was called *The Saturday Book*. In 1948 Leonard recalled that when he was seeking a name he found himself humming a song which he had heard in a London music hall sung by Florrie Forde or Victoria Monks—'Sweet Saturday Nights'. That gave him a title with the right air of week-end relaxation.

The present Editor first contributed to No. 9—an illustrated essay on Toby jugs. And for No. 10 he was asked to write the first critical commentary on Laurence Whistler's engravings on glass.

In 1951 Leonard Russell relinquished the editorship, as he was heavily engaged at the *Sunday Times*, and he nominated the present Editor as successor. The new man thought he might last three years. He lasted twenty-three.

FRED BASON IN WALWORTH   OLIVE COOK AND EDWIN SMITH

I had no wish to alter Leonard's general conception of the book, though I took over the whole design and layout myself, which made it *look* rather different. I continued to make the utmost use of Edwin Smith's photography and his wife's wide-ranging knowledge of architecture and the arts. They made by far and away the greatest contribution to the book between 1945 and Edwin's death in 1971. Olive remained a contributor and a dear friend. The only reason why there is not more of their joint work in the present volume is because they themselves put together a pictorial anthology of their contributions in 1955 called *Collectors' Items from the Saturday Book*. This itself is now a collector's item.

The title of that book indicated a slight shift of emphasis under the new editorship. There was less purely literary content—though more poems; there were fewer short stories, and more attention to collectable arts and curiosities. One section was usually called 'A Cabinet of Curiosities'. Politics, economics and religion were always excluded, but nothing else was too out-of-the-way or eccentric to qualify. Reviewing the final issue in 1973 in *The Times*, Bevis Hillier referred to the *S.B.* as "a sampling-flask of the nation's subconscious".

It never sought to become a literary influence, like *The Yellow Book;* but it was by no means without its effect on public taste in other areas. In his first issue, in 1952, the present Editor devoted a large section to an assessment of "The Twenties". This was a year before the first production of *The Boy Friend*. In 1962 a big feature on Art Nouveau, then quite unfashionable, sparked off an international revival of interest in this period; and in 1972 the same thing happened with Art Déco. A feature on Aubrey Beardsley, in 1956 a largely forgotten figure, led to exhibitions of his work in London and New York and countless art students attempting to copy the Beardsley style. L. S. Lowry himself admitted that the spectacular rise of interest in his work dated from Howard Spring's appreciation of him in the 1957 *S.B.* And two years later the work of René Magritte shot back into international favour partly as a result of *S.B.* attention.

In minor fields of public interest the book has not been without effect: for instance, features on vintage cars, the poet McGonagall, and 'Cardinal' paintings—all somewhat recondite subjects in 1953, but now familiar to all. And new fields of connoisseurship were opened up by scholarly reassessments of early gramophone records in 1955, picture postcards in 1963, and cigarette cards in No. 32. John Moffatt, Peter Bull, Peter Scully and Ronnie Barker were among pioneers in these fields.

In trying to represent the contents of thirty-four issues of the annual— amounting to over ten thousand pages—in the 320 pages which is all we have available today, much, regretfully, had to be left out. I decided to include no short stories, although many masters of the short story have been represented. But their work had not any particular *S.B.* character. And I have had, purely for reasons of space, to omit some of the most substantial pictorial features, notably the splendid series on 'The Changing Face of Childhood' (in No. 22) and 'The Male Image' (in No. 29) by Madge Garland, and a whole sequence of visual commentaries, combing scholarship and wit, by that quintessential *Saturday Book* contributor, James Laver, who moved from 'The Natural History of the Chorus Girl' (in No. 14) to 'The Art of Seduction' (in No. 29), and put Victorian narrative pictures right back into fashion with the delightfully titled 'Every Story Sells a Picture' (in No. 16).

James Laver possessed what came to be known as 'a *Saturday Book* mind', in much the same way as one uses the phrase 'a John Betjeman building' or a 'Charles Addams character'. It was a joy to work with him, as it was with Edwin Smith and Olive, the ebullient Charles Gibbs-Smith, that pioneer of industrial archaeology Tom Rolt, that Anglo-Irish charmer and lovely artist, Robert Gibbings, and—needless to say—our present Poet Laureate.

Indeed, if one were to try and sum up the *ambience* of *The Saturday Book* one might compare it with a gathering of congenial friends, all scholars or experts in some particular sphere, in an elegant room containing an assortment of bric-à-brac, a few really fine works of art, and some intriguing curiosities. You, dear reader, are the fly on the wall, listening to the conversation. One of the knacks of achieving good conversation is to get people with distinguished minds mounted on their hobby horses. Our list of contributors has indeed been distinguished. And what a Saturday parade of hobby horses there has been!

J.H.

Contents

IN SEARCH OF THE PICTURESQUE

VERSE—AND WORSE

IN RETROSPECT

Illustrations by Edward Ardizzone, Zelma Blakely, Salvador Dali, Erté, David Gentleman, Charles Keene, Ronald Searle, and Leslie Thompson.

The decorative initial letters were drawn by William McLaren, who also designed the jackets for Nos. 19, 20 and 22. The endpaper drawings are by Michael Felmingham.

The famous Velasquez painting above is in the National Gallery, in London, and is known as 'The Rokeby Venus'. The 'Sleeping Odalisque' below, by Ingres, is in the Victoria and Albert Museum. Both appeared in No. 15.

THE

LOOKING

GLASS

OF

TASTE

The fashion drawing by Erté above was one of the illustrations to the opening feature in No. 32 entitled 'Fifty Years Ago', in which James Laver looked at fashions of 1923, John Foster White wrote on 'Suburban Nights Entertainments', Martin Battersby summed up Art Déco, G. N. Georgano recalled motor cars of 1923, Kenneth Allsop Jazz of 1923, and Richard Boston the 'Silent Comics' of film.

ASPECTS OF ETIQUETTE

For a woman to receive a man in her bedroom at an hotel is to
break an important convention. It places both in a false position.
—*Lady Troubridge*

The Perfect Gentleman

JILLY COOPER

TIQUETTE in other countries always seems fairly absurd. One thinks of the Japanese removing his shoes before entering the drawing-room, or the Eskimo offering the run of his unwashed wife to distinguished guests. No less foreign to our casual Western society today seems a slim volume written a hundred years ago entitled *The Complete Etiquette for Gentlemen*. Oh, the traumas of bettering oneself in those days! How one's heart bleeds for the poor tyro setting out like Christian on a tightrope journey towards social acceptability. How many Mr Salteenas must have bought the book hoping to transform themselves into the perfect gentleman—described thus:

> Quietness in all things is an essential element of a well-bred person. He shuns all outward display of his personality, he cares not to be seen or heard, and rests content with being felt as a power in the land. He thus not only eschews all noisy and grandiloquent talk, but all showy and noticeable costume. His voice is low, his words simple, his action grave, and his dress plain. He holds himself so habitually under constraint that his nerves never seem to vibrate with emotion. He becomes, as it were, an impassible being [could the author have meant 'impossible'?] upon whom no external cause seems capable of making an impression.

Your perfect gentleman, in fact, is a perfect pain in the neck, one of those stodgy deadpan puddings who gazes rigid and unsmiling out of Victorian photographs. Imagine too how neurotic your tyro would become if, as well as trying to be grave, controlled, impassible, and truly well-bred, he has to follow the instructions for walking:

> With your chest thrown out, your head erect, your abdomen receding rather than protruding, a self-poised and firm but elastic step, and altogether a compact, manly, homogeneous sort of bearing and movement.

Compact, manly, homogeneous, grave, his abdomen firmly receding, our tyro embarks on his first ordeal: outdoor etiquette, where he has to be permanently on his toes like St George, to protect damsels in distress.

> Towards ladies the most punctilious observance of politeness is due from gentlemen. Walking with them one should, of course, assume the relative position best adapted to protect them from inconvenience or danger, and carefully note and relieve them from the approach of either.

The well-bred gentleman must also remain constantly on the look-out:

> Should ladies whom you know be observed unattended by a gentleman, alighting from or entering a cab or carriage, especially if there is no footman, and the driver maintains his seat, at once advance, hold the door open, and offer your hand, or protect a dress from the wheel, and bowing, pass on, all needed service rendered.

Not a word is exchanged, rather like the silent films.

An absolute ballet is involved when you meet a lady and a gentleman together:

> Politeness requires that the hat should be raised as they approach, and bowing first to the ladies, include the gentleman in a sweeping motion or a succeeding bow, as the case permits. Should you stop, speak first to the lady, but do not offer to shake hands with her in full morning costume, should your glove be dark coloured or your hand uncovered. And as you part, again take your hat quite off, letting the party pass you, and on the wall side of the street, if that be practicable.

If one doesn't wish to stop as a male friend approaches, a more hearty response is recommended:

> Recognise him as you advance with a smile, or 'Hope you are well, sir,' or more familiarly, 'Ah Fred [daft if he were called Nigel]. Good morning to you.'

Approaching ladies is a trickier problem; the well-bred gentleman slides up like Grandmother's footsteps:

> Be careful in hurrying forward not to incommode her, and do not speak so hurriedly or loudly as to startle her or arrest attention, and should you only have a slight acquaintance with her, say as you assume a position at her side [with elastic step and abdomen receding], 'With your permission, Madam, I will attend you', or 'Give me leave to join your walk, Miss . . .'

Of course, no well-bred man ever risks the possibility of intrusion in this way, or ever speaks first to a lady to whom he has only a passing introduction. In the latter case, you look at a lady as you advance towards her and 'await recognition'.

But don't stop walking for an instant, for a page later the author descends like a ton of bricks on anyone who looks at ladies while standing still:

> If occasion demands your remaining stationary or in the portico of a public edifice, make room at once for ladies who may be entering, and avoid any appearance of curiosity regarding them . . . make no comment even of a complimentary nature in a voice than can possibly reach their ears . . . and when walking in the street, if beauty or grace attract your attention, let your regard be respectful, and even then not too fixed.

Having more or less mastered outdoor etiquette, probably at the cost of a thumping nervous break-down, our Mr Salteena now embarks on a spot of socializing. 'Among the minor obligations of social life,' says the author sternly, 'perhaps few things are regarded as more formidable by the uninitiated than ceremonious visits to ladies.' The procedure sounds rather like 'Come Dancing':

> When you are shown into the Drawing Room of a private residence, if the mistress of the house is present, at once advance towards her. Should she offer her hand, be prompt to receive it, and for this purpose take your hat, stick and right hand glove in your left hand as you enter. On no account place your hat on the chairs or table.

But alas the poor reader, at this most crucial point the author rats on him again: 'There is a graceful way of holding the hat, which every well-bred man understands but which is incapable of definition.' And 'Never remain seated in the company of ladies with whom you are *ceremoniously associated*.' The language throughout the book is that of a toast master presiding over a Rotary Club Function, exhorting gentlemen in charge of ladies whose corsages groan with maidenhair fern to be 'upstanding for their President'. 'Never remain seated', but plunge into a frenzy of activity. 'Follow them to any object of interest to which they may direct your attention' (one hopes it might be a bed). 'Place a seat for them . . . ring a bell, bring a book. In short, courteously relieve them from whatever might be supposed to involve effort, fatigue or discomfort of any kind.'

We move now on to the dress of a gentleman for occasions of ceremony, which include a

> stylish well-fitting cloth coat of some dark colour and of unexceptional quality, nether garments to correspond . . . the finest purest linen, a cravat or neckerchief, and vest of some dark or neutral tint, according to the physiognomical peculiarities of the wearer and the prevailing mode.

'Evening dress', we are told firmly, 'is never worn on Sundays, because, of course, there are no dinner parties on that day, the usual costume in all circles is a black frock coat, coloured trousers and black scarf or neck-tie.' Coloured trousers seem a bit wild for the Sabbath, particularly when the truly polite gentleman is told *never* to wear a coloured shirt because 'figures and stripes do not conceal impurity'.

> An English gentleman [is also] never seen in the morning (which means all that portion of the twenty-four hours devoted to business, out-of-door amusements, and pursuits, etc.; it is always morning until the late dinner hour has passed) in the half-worn coat of fine black cloth that so inevitably gives a man a sort of shabby genteel look; but in some strong-looking rough, knock-about clothes, frequently of nondescript form and fashion.

He had also to tread a fine line between hippy and skinhead:

> If you wear your beard, wear it in moderation – extremes are always vulgar. Avoid all fantastic arrangements of the hair, either turning it under in a roll, or allowing it to straggle over the coat collar, or having it cropped so close as to give the wearer the appearance of a sporting character.

(What vapours the author would have had over today's long-haired sporting characters kissing each other after goals are scored!)

Dining out must have struck terror in the most confident student of society—rather like taking one's finals.

> Nothing more plainly shows the well-bred man than his manners at table. A man may be well dressed, may converse well but if he is after all unrefined, his manners at table will expose him. If he is *au fait* at dinner he has passed one of the severest tests of good breeding.

All the things one had to remember *not* to do: one mustn't evidently eat ice cream with a spoon (what happened if it melted?) or asparagus with one's fingers, or drink one's soup noisily, or put butter on one's vegetables, or gape at others, or twist about, or 'give too insanguined pieces of meat to ladies' (rather like Americans offering the 'white meat' instead of breast).

It was also evidently a breach of etiquette to repeat the name of any person with whom one was conversing. Think of the clangers Tennyson dropped in 'Come into the garden, Maud'. Conversation must have been a nightmare too: 'One is sure', says the author smugly, 'to show good or bad breeding the instant one opens one's mouth.' Well-bred people, it seemed, never discussed politics or anything remotely highbrow ('with ladies, agreeability rather than profundity should be your aim') or last night's party, or any of one's friends ('gentlemen never assail absent ones in mixed parties'). One couldn't, obviously, talk about sex:

> Anything that will crimson the cheek of true womanhood is unworthy and unmanly to a degree of which it is not easy to express sufficient abhorrence.

'Good jokes and merriment', however, were 'always in order'. God knows what they found to make them about.

> But all strained attempts at facetiousness by one who has not a natural talent for it, are sure to end in making him ridiculous. Therefore, let no man venture upon gay sallies at dinner, unless they so press forward to his lips as to escape almost in spite of him.

It is not surprising gay sallies pressed forward at dinner bearing in mind the amount of drink everyone knocked back. 'Always hurry the bottle round five or six times . . . and if either lady or gentleman is invited to take wine at table, he or she must never refuse.' The ritual of taking wine is straight out of Rotarian Ladies' Night:

> You should politely say: 'Shall I have the pleasure of a glass of wine with you?' You will then either hand him the bottle, or send it by the waiter and afterwards fill your own glass, when you politely and silently bow to each other as you raise the wine to your lips.

All very gracious and decorous and manly, which makes it all the more of a shock when, in the next chapter, the author suddenly plunges into a panegyric rivalling the most unbridled flights of women's romantic fiction:

> Are there any good reasons why the subject of love should be shrouded in mystery, for it is the one which occupies more than all others the human thoughts.

At last our tyro may get a chance to embark on gay sallies, in his fashionable vest of some dark or neutral tint.

> A young man entering society at the age when young men begin to be desirable members – which is not until they are capable of the tender passion – is likely to be attracted by one or more persons. [Sounds a bit promiscuous.]
> The first attraction of a very young man is likely to be a lady of mature years, and this sentiment when it can be indulged without ridicule or scandal, and has for its object a woman of taste and character is great good fortune. Such a woman is just the teacher and friend a young man needs to polish his manners, refine his taste, improve his understanding and ripen his heart.

At this point one suddenly begins to suspect that the author is no gentleman at all, but a rather sour, middle-aged lady of mature years, whose husband spends too much time at his club, and who rather fancies the idea of young men languishing after her. One sees her as a sort of Tabitha Twitchet, permanently worrying how the fine company will react, and terrified that wild, boisterous, kittenish people are going to rush in and spoil the dignity and repose of her tea party.

Her rash fierce blaze of riot doesn't last, anyway. Poetry and drama may be filled with the passion of love, but our well-bred truly polite tyro isn't going to be so lucky. 'A love affaire ought to be conducted with caution and delicacy, there should be no rashness or mistake', we are told, and when you have been accepted and the engagement announced, 'Be discreet in your raptures, and begin preparing with all diligence and dignity for the change that awaits you.' (Rather like going into the church.)

Nor is anyone going to get the chance to marry a smasher. 'A career of idleness and irresponsibility' (with men charging about fetching books, ringing bells, carrying shawls for her, one doesn't see how she could have had anything else) 'is no desirable prelude to the quiet duties essential to the home happiness of a man of moderate resources and retired habits. It may be questioned whether a woman who has long been used to the adulation and excitement of a crowd will be content . . . with the simple pleasures which alone will be at her command thus circumstanced.'

The gates of the prison house begin to close:

> However gay and frivolous a man may have been before his engagement, he should conduct himself with the utmost propriety after that event. A sense of what is due to a lady should repress all habits disagreeable to her, smoking if she dislikes it, frequenting places of amusement without her, paying attention to other women. Nothing is so disgusting as the flirtations which some men carry on after they have pledged themselves to one alone.

Shades of *The Desert Song*! Then the old double standard emerges again. 'Women may have some excuse for coquetry, but a man has none.' The husband, however, gets his own back on the day of the wedding:

> The etiquette of the wedding breakfast varies considerably in good circles. The bride may appear at the breakfast or not, but the latter procedure is generally preferred.

Presumably while the husband is getting sloshed with all his friends and relations the bride is expected to sit alone in her bedroom contemplating the horrors of the impending night.

Once they are married, one of the 'quiet duties' of the bride will surely be shopping, and there is stern advice on the subject. 'It is seldom indeed that a lady of any refinement delays long in making her purchases.' In her husband too, one of the most heinous crimes is chatting up shop girls:

> It is remarkable how little some men can be, how childish, although adorned with hirsute appendages and looking, as far as the outer man goes, intelligent. Yet their talk is all lisped nothings. Their eyes sparkle as they lisp the silliest things; they laugh and make merry, and cause people to turn in wonder that any human being could make himself so thoroughly ridiculous; and they 'chaff the girls' to use their own vulgar phraseology, until it has occurred to them that a change of scene would be productive of new delights.

On to the ballroom, where fatties and clodhoppers go to the wall:

> It is far preferable to be a passive spectator than a clumsy performer. It may be said, also, that while a knowledge of dancing adds to the attraction of a figure naturally

symmetrical and agile, it serves but to render still more conspicuous those who are incurably ill-shaped, heavy, or insensible to any graceful motion.

For a gentleman waltzing with a lady, there is skittish advice. He should beware not to press her waist: 'You must only lightly touch it with the palm of your hand, lest you leave a disagreeable impression, not only on her ceinture, but on her mind.' Waltzing is also 'proper and agreeable as the pleasant exercise of a morning, where in a family group' (the men presumably in strong-looking knock-about clothes of nondescript form and fashion) 'the piano forte is opened and the dance occupies the pauses of conversation' (a hell of a lot of them, one would think, when there is so little subject matter) 'and gives life and motion to those who so often grow languid and ill for want of it.'

> A gentleman of feeling [we are told] will not fail to lead out a lady who appears to be neglected by others, but he will not do it ostentatiously.

One is reminded of Mr Knightly saving Harriet from humiliation, when Mr Elton refused to dance with her. Mr Knightly is probably the only really attractive man in nineteenth-century fiction that the author would have approved of. Mr Rochester and Heathcliff wouldn't have stood a chance, nor Will Ladislaw skulking in the laurels, and certainly not Sidney Carton, nor Mr Darcy, spurning Elizabeth Bennett at the Assembly rooms.

A gentleman, too, should take it like a man if a lady turns him down.

> We cannot always fathom the hidden springs which influence a woman's actions, and there are many bursting hearts within white satin dresses; therefore do not insist upon the fulfilment of established rules.

We then move on to mannish pursuits, the gentleman in his club, where we find Old Stuffed Shirt: 'The well-bred man of the world who has seen everything and done everything, who is surprised at nothing, and believes only in stern facts.' One rubs shoulders with some reprehensible types: 'The rather boisterous youngster who has just commenced to mix with men', and 'the sallow-skinned Anglo-Indian who is reserved by reason of his liver' (perhaps it was the *Plat du jour*).

To watch the entrance of Stuffed Shirt, we are told, is always a profitable study; as usual, he never puts an elastically-stepping foot wrong. We notice his 'quiet dignity' as he walks to his accustomed seat, nodding to a friend here and another there, as he is perceived. And when he wants a drink 'this is done in the quietest possible way' (all well-bred men seem to be members of the Noise Abatement Society). 'No rapping on the table with a stick or coin; the bell is pulled without violence but just so that it can be heard. It is the height of rudeness to let everybody know you are about to partake of refreshment.'

One is also advised to temper stinginess with altruism in Forsyte style:

> If your guest prefers claret to champagne, let him have claret by all means. To say to him 'have something better' implies that he has only been accustomed to drink which is inexpensive, and that on this occasion you will give him a treat.

In the smoking-room, it goes without saying, the conversation should be carried on so as not to disturb your neighbour:

> As a rule middle class Englishmen rarely offend in this way . . . so much cannot be said for our continental friends, notwithstanding the name they have earned for politeness. Their presence is felt and their tongues are heard on the threshold of the place, and they talk and gesticulate the whole evening, as though their affairs were the only ones of importance in the world. It is well for us that we do not imitate them, otherwise there would be neither decorum nor comfort to be found anywhere outside one's bedroom.

Decorum in the bedroom? However did Victorian couples produce a Tertius, a Sextus or even an Octavius?

But if the Victorians would have been shocked by the sexual freedom of the twentieth century, equally shocking to us today is the way the Victorians sanctioned the making of money. The author praises 'Acquisitiveness' as a most gentlemanly virtue.

> To acquire and gather wealth, to create riches by industry, to accumulate a wealth of beautiful things is a high right and duty of every person. To be honestly rich, to be rich with a full recognition of the rights of others is noble and praiseworthy in all respects.

It sounds like a credo for the Forsytes. Presumably in their spare time they trained camels to jump through the eye of a needle. *The Complete Etiquette for Gentlemen* is in fact a book in praise of bourgeois gentility. The upper classes are continually being cut down to size.

> There is no more common or absurd mistake than to suppose if people are of high rank they cannot be ill-bred . . . even the lower classes (whatever their own practices may be) keenly appreciate and gratefully acknowledge the slightest consideration shown to them by their superiors.

One suspects more than a touch of resentment towards all those grand unmanageable people who couldn't give a fig about etiquette and went round doing exactly what they liked.

[1975]

Drawing by Charles Keene for *Punch*, June 13, 1885

The Perfect Lady

ARTHUR MARSHALL

'CAN ANYTHING in the world be nicer than a really nice girl?' asked Mrs Humphry ('Madge' of *Truth*). Well, various possible answers spring to mind, but Mrs Humphry, who wrote about *Manners for Women* towards the close of the Victorian age and whose praiseworthy aim it was to keep ladies firmly on the acceptable social tracks, clearly expected by way of reply a resounding, deafening NO. The modern girl, lolloping her way down the King's Road in clothes plainly filched from her great-grandmother's wardrobe, may care to profit from Mrs Humphry's explanations as to what, at the turn of the century, constituted a really nice girl, and a girl, moreover, about to burgeon into glorious womanhood, marry and become a perfect lady. Etiquette books of the period are numerous and provide valuable signposts to a leisured life of refinement and good taste.

First, the voice. You'll probably have to change it. Nothing even faintly shrill will do. Sweet and low is the best. The thing to aim at is a mellow contralto, the muted boom of a pocket Clara Butt with the vocal chords revolving sluggishly in a sort of gear-box of liquid honey and producing a restricted range of ear-caressing tones. And with the voice, the laugh. This needs practice. Don't imagine for a single solitary moment that your laugh is all right. It isn't. But courage! Help is at hand. Genial Mrs Humphry leaps once more to the rescue and urges us to follow the example of the actress, Miss Florence St. John, who every morning 'sings a descending octave staccato with the syllables Ha! Ha! Ha!' Mrs Humphry doesn't say *where* she does this but you'll soon find a secluded spot – the small billiard-room, the second sitting-room or the orangery would all be quite suitable. Close the door, clear the throat and let fly 'with a ripple of silvery notes that form the perfect laugh.' Tight-waisted corsets, though showy enough in their way, are at this moment no sort of help. Either loosen them or ring for your maid and totally remove them and start again.

After approximately three months of Florence St. John and ditto of Clara Butt, we are just about ready to speak and, indeed, to laugh, should a tasteful opportunity present itself. Yes, but speak about what? Here we desert Mrs Humphry, if it be but temporarily, and fly for aid to 'A Member of the Aristocracy' who, having fallen maybe on evil and impecunious days, produced an admirable volume entitled *Society Small Talk*. In no time at all it had sold 80,000 copies and unleashed, up and down the country, thunderclaps of excited, breezy chatter.

Don't, counsels Our Member of the Aristocracy, attempt too much too soon. Nothing is to be gained by haste. Girls cannot run before they can walk. Eschew, naturally, the vapid and vacant manner, and be all lively attention, with the eyes opened wide and the lips freshly moistened, but limit yourself, until you find your feet, to either 'Really?' or 'Indeed!' Then ring the changes. After a month or so of 'Really?' and 'Indeed!' you are ready for bigger things. Nothing too ambitious, you understand, but, for once, a direct statement. Choose a cosy-looking lady and, for pity's sake, keep the voice down. 'I always think it is a good plan to go to the sea in November. The sunny mornings are so invigorating and cheering, are they not?', which may well lead on to a spirited exchange of opinions concerning the rival residential merits of Eastbourne and Scarborough (on no account mention Brighton if there is any risk at all of being misunderstood). Why Our Member plumps for the month of November, or just where she finds her sunny mornings, it is not for us to question.

Before passing on to other invaluable conversational ball-rollers, Our Member gives a most helpful list of Remarks To Avoid, helpful because they are all just the kind of thing that one might have clumsily, as they say, come out with. For example, 'How painfully dissipated and extravagant your son appears to be. What a wasted career his is.' The lady thus addressed may well find herself, while reeling from this body-blow, the victim of a follow-up attack: 'What a very unbecoming colour green is to you. I wonder why you wear it.' And then, by way of laying her flat on the canvas: 'How drawn and pale your husband looks. Is he quite well?'

Back to jollier matters and the sort of chit-chat one will be likely to find in the upper-crust world in which one is, of course, most at ease. How's this for starters? 'I understand Lord Lynton's illness was entirely owing to drinking iced water. It gave a very severe shock to his entire system and he is recovering in Baden Baden.' A sympathetic mumbling sound will suffice by way of answer, and then it's your turn: 'What really gorgeous diamonds Mrs Chetwynd wore last night, but who was the woman with the black pearls?' Who indeed? But there is no time to discover her identity, for dinner has just been announced and the procession of pairs is forming up. You need something to say while parading to the dining-room? Very well then. 'We must take care not to tread upon the Duchess's smart train. We do not want to bring the wrath of the fair wearer down upon our heads! She is in great looks *ce soir*, is she not?'

Before passing on to a really magnificent sheaf of lively opening remarks, Our Member, reminding us that both yawning and glazed expressions are not in good taste, gives excellent advice on how to extricate yourself from a boring dinner-table conversation with the man on your right, thus: 'Your friend opposite appears to be relating something amusing. What is he saying?', and while the bore is trying to discover what the jape was, swing round to the man on your left with 'Where are you quartered just now?'

But to our openers, and what a feast of ingenuity they are, ranging from shorties such as 'Have you a leaning towards spiritualism?' and 'What have you to say in favour of stimulants?' to more robust stuff: 'What wonderful strides oculists have made in late years. The aurists are very much behind in their discoveries in the sister art! How trying it can be to talk to deaf persons . . .', which leads comfortably on to a discussion of ear-trumpets and the new and vastly improved Luxivox 'Stentor' silver-plated model. After this, the pace quickens excitingly: 'Have you been to the Academy? I hope we are to hear you sing later. I see that the next tempting *entrée* is sweet-breads! Do you paint on china? Do you model in soap? Are you fond of balls?'

'When friendship outsteps its prescribed limits', coyly announces our informant, 'it enters upon Cupid's domain.' Dan Cupid is by no means skimped in her social survey and finds his fullest expression among the dreamy waltzes ('Do you reverse?') and the glossy palms of the ballroom. 'How well the rooms are lighted', says the girl, with perhaps a romantic wish for less dazzling illuminations, while the man, inflamed with claret-cup, counters meaningfully with 'Yes, they are lighted by the light of beauty's eyes, and you are lending your share?' The girl flaps her fan a little (she isn't going to swoon *yet*) and cries, 'Now, Captain Anstruther, that was a deliberate compliment!', to which the obvious riposte, and one hardly needs to set it down, is 'I envy that butterfly perched so daintily on your hair close to that shell-like ear. What secrets would I not whisper were I so near. Happy butterfly!'

Before Cupid's darts start to find their mark, what has been going on at the dinner-table itself? The guests are assembled there, after all, mainly to eat. Let us follow the fortunes of the lady who has, we trust, succeeded in not impeding the Duchess's sedate progress foodwards. She seats herself where instructed, hastily whips off her gloves, placing them carefully on the table without disturbing the fronds of virginia creeper that have been spread tastefully here and there, unfolds her napkin, places the piece of bread it contained at her *left* hand, fires off an opener ('I understand that the Bishop has supplied our Vicar, fortunate man, with a new tricycle)', and is now all ready to tackle soup and, mind you, just the half ladleful ('To fill a soup-plate with soup would be in very bad style', warns Our Aristocrat.)

The process of munching, the manipulation of cutlery and the general eating accoutrements all bristle with traps and problems. 'However hand-some a cruet-stand may be, it should never be placed on the dinner-table.' There now! and one had been going to place it bang in the middle and cover it with smilax.

With the arrival of the meat and vegetable course, Our Member becomes very agitated and communicates her anxieties to her readers. There is so much here that can go wrong; one can hardly hold the knife for nervous trembling. *'Don't* overload the fork. Convey meat and vegetables to the mouth *separately'*; don't arrange them on the fork in a compact form. The hand and the mouth 'should act in unison. The mouth should *not* be kept open in expectation of the well-laden fork's arrival. The mouth should only be opened to receive the contents of the fork at the moment when it has reached the lips.' Safe at last, you think? Not at all. 'To place the fork directly opposite the mouth is a most ungraceful way of eating, and bending the wrist round to accomplish this feat is similarly so. The fork should be simply raised to the mouth, and the hand should *not* be turned round to face it.' All this, and conversation too! ('Which are your favourites among the grasses and ferns of Great Britain?')

Let us mark time for a moment and return to the good Mrs Humphry to garner an assorted bundle of useful hints to help one along Life's Highway. Are you recently a widow? If so, you may now wear linen collars a month after your bereavement—previously you would have had to wait six months for linen collars; so, while sorrowing, be grateful for small mercies. Is your daughter about to be married? In that case, on no account order too *heavy* a cake, 'heavy' in the sense of sheer weight ('They have been known to bring down both the table on which they rested and the ceiling of the room beneath'). If you *must* bicycle, do beware of 'the promiscuous acquaintanceship for which the handy steeds are frequently responsible': don't set out awheel unless fully kitted up—inability to mend punctures gives a man a chance to pounce and indulge in almost any sort of familiarity ('Can I lend you my pump?'). When yachting, fight down that urge 'to don lace-trimmed white petticoats', and for punting, heel-less prunella shoes just will not do: 'neat patents' are the thing. Oh, and in the Casino at Deauville do remember that men, and foreign men at that, with their bold, unbridled, challenging glances, may be standing behind your chair: so avoid too generous a *décolletage*.

And now, for all these splendidly varied activities, what are you going to *wear*? There is no end to the exciting range of possibilities for girls just 'out' and for ladies of riper years—married ladies, of course (it is sad but true that nowhere in any of the books is the smallest attention paid to spinsters. As a class, they do not, however well-born, exist). Fancy-dress balls are all the rage, so why not startle your circle of friends by going as a hot-blooded Bacchante in mauve accordion-pleated chiffon, your bodice prettily draped with grapes and vine leaves, and pearls and beads wound into your *coiffure*. And that is not all. Mrs Eric Pritchard, a mine of information on this and other subjects, advises that the costume be completed 'by the skin of a lynx arranged on the front of the dress. This gives a wild and fantastic touch.' Yes indeed. Best to order half a dozen lynx skins and keep them handy. You never know when they'll be needed.

There's not the faintest need to look dowdy while motoring, so why not a threequarter-length *Directoire* coat in puce velvet, your beaded bag jammed with smelling-salts in case of a spill from the De Dion Bouton, and on your head a bright green beaver toque trimmed with black braid cockades? For rail travel (and hold on to that bag in case of a derailment at Devizes) a smart tailor-made is the ideal thing, 'with a beautifully cut waistcoat of white leather with the bolero coat turned back with revers of green and gold embroidery and with a short basque over the hips. There is a certain studied simplicity about this garment', muses Mrs Pritchard, 'which renders it particularly striking' (she does not, alas, inform us about what would, in her view, constitute a complicated garment). For country walks 'the *trotteuse* skirt is still *de rigueur*, accompanied by the neatest and smartest footgear', while for the bridge table get your *couturière* to run you up a Josephine robe in Liberty velveteen and Indian muslin.

A few years behind Mrs Humphry, but spiritually at one with her—two cherries on one stalk—proudly marches Mrs Massey Lyon, with a positive cornucopia of wide-ranging instruction for those tip-toeing cautiously about in society's upper reaches. If invited to a Royal garden party, don't for good-ness' sake go and plonk yourself down in the special 'Durbar' tent and start wolfing the cress sandwiches (they are intended for the Royal teeth). If Royalty comes to dine with *you*, do remember that the sovereign and consort are the only ones allowed finger-bowls at dessert. (Why?) And if the German Emperor comes to stay, your house will have to absorb a retinue of not less than eighty people, thirty of whom will expect private sitting-rooms.

In a thought-provoking chapter entitled Little Things That Count, Mrs Massey Lyon prefers 'May I have the salt, please?' to 'May I trouble you for the salt?', and '*Au revoir*' makes a pleasant change from 'Good-bye' and shows that the week-end at Boulogne was not wasted. In country houses, where morning and evening prayers are said in the private chapel, always attend unless (rather mysteriously) asked not to. It is good form for men to take off their hats in hotel lifts if ladies are present but they should keep their hats *on* in hotel corridors. Dont' say 'Pray assist yourself to whisky', and a handy sentence for almost any English occasion is 'Escaped the 'flu fiend, I trust?' Oh, and do get names pronounced correcly. 'Beauchamp' is 'Beechum', 'Lygon' is 'Liggon' and 'Pontefract', as with those delicious cakes, is 'Pomfret'.

Well now, I think that's everything. All set, Jennifer? O.K., Mrs Budi-bent? Off you go then, and good luck. As you see, there's really nothing to it.

[1975]

Madam, your Achilles Tendon is Showing

OGDEN NASH

Hem go up, hem go down,
Sing the bells of Paris town,
Haute couture is in the doldrums,
Needs a touch of folderoldrums.

Monday, ankles are forbidden,
Ankles are demurely hidden;
Tuesday, hear the *dernier cri*,
Hems ascend above the knee.
Well dressed women in disdain
Drop Monday's dresses in the Seine;
No such furore since pants with cuffs
First were seen in Council Bluffs.
More lethal than a pistol loaded
Is a woman with a hem outmoded.
I somehow think, when from the Ark
The weary crew did disembark,
Said Mrs Ham to Mrs Shem,
I wonder where he's put the hem.
When Xantippe screamed in shrewish fashion
That her newest chlamys was out of fashion
Though Socrates' foes with poison filled him,
'Twas the hemline, not the hemlock, killed him.

Hem go up, hem go down,
Sing the bells of Paris town,
Sing the golden anthems famous,
Sing Te Dior Adoramus.

[1954]

Beauty in the 'Twenties

Photographs and Commentary by

CECIL BEATON

ERHAPS I AM RARE among my contemporaries in finding that the 'twenties were, on the whole, remarkable and vital. To me the fashions of the 'twenties are infinitely alluring. Looking through a fashion magazine of 1926 or 1927, one is struck by the simplicity of line with which the illustrators sketched those longer-than-life ladies who, with their short, tubular dresses, cigarettes in long holders, cloche hats, bobbed hair, plucked eyebrows, bands of diamond bracelets from wrist to elbow, and earrings hanging like fuchsias, symbolised the visual aspect of the period. For all the deleterious values that are associated with the decade of *The Green Hat*, bath-tub gin and gangsters, it was also a period of immense creativeness. The architects Le Corbusier and Frank Lloyd Wright have never been excelled; the Barcelona chair remains the most satisfying piece of modern furniture. Picasso's influence is apparent not only on canvas but in ballet *décor*. Chanel revolutionised fashion.

The photographs which follow were taken in the late nineteen-twenties or the beginning of 1930. When the Editor of THE SATURDAY BOOK suggested reproducing them, as a little portrait-gallery of notable beauties of their period, he also suggested that they might be accompanied by comments on the sitters which I had written at the time or not very long afterwards. He chose passages for the most part from my first book, THE BOOK OF BEAUTY, published in 1930, and a few from THE GLASS OF FASHION, published in 1954. Apart from sometimes—alas—having to change the present into the past tense, they appear substantially as they did then.

[1968]

N LONDON during the 'twenties Miss Ponsonby (later Loelia, Duchess of Westminster) was one of the instigators of a new type of gala. She would, on an impulse, arrange a last-minute party and ask her friends to contribute an essential ingredient: some benevolent godfather would supply a band, other guests provided supper, all brought champagne. Nancy Mitford and a bevy of new personalities just down from Oxford, Lord Kinross, Evelyn Waugh, Harold Acton and Oliver Messel, were the nucleus of a group who were either of the aristocracy or entertained the aristocracy by their talents. They had a splendid zest for life and an ability for expressing that zest. Friends provided impromptu cabarets with their imitations and impersonations; elaborate and ingenious treasure hunts were organised, and hoax picture-exhibitions arranged. The spirit of masquerade reached new heights, and almost every night there was some excuse for putting on fancy dress.

Above: Oliver Messel and Anne Messel (later the Countess of Rosse)
Opposite: Nancy Mitford

 HE HONOURABLE Mrs Reginald (Daisy) Fellowes, half French and half American, was much publicised as the best-dressed woman in the world. Such a title would seem to imply frequent changes of wardrobe; but, on the contrary, she earned the distinction more for the brilliance of her studied simplicity. Daisy Fellowes always had a scrubbed classical look, an unparalleled air of slickness, trimness and cleanness. She had the air of having just come off a yacht, which she very likely had!

THE INFLUENCE of the theatre was far from negligible. All sorts of men suddenly wanted to look like Noël Coward— sleek and satiny, clipped and well groomed, with a cigarette, a telephone or a cocktail at hand. Gertrude Lawrence was the distaff personification of this new charm. Though not a great beauty, she possessed the flavour and personality of the age to a high degree. Her mellifluous voice was yet rather curdled. She smoked cigarettes with a nuance that implied having just come out of bed and wanting to go back into it.

ADY ASHLEY (subsequently Mrs Douglas Fairbanks) was the final justification for the young lady of fashion of 1930, with her tall willowy figure, long Dresden-china neck and arms, and sloping shoulders. No photograph does her justice, for no photograph shows the colour and texture of her beauty. Only she herself could reveal her pathetic delicacy and helplessness, her mild, childish lisp and naïve naturalness that were so beguiling. She had always been pretty, with starry, lidless, naked eyes, but developed a style to which her many imitators could never approximate.

NITA LOOS was an amazing specimen, so absolutely of her time, a cute little Venus that only twentieth-century New York could have produced, a pocket Venus with a perfectly proportioned body on a Lilliputian scale—a Venus like the pertest child or most impertinent ventriloquist's doll, whose clothes, although not always fashionable, were of an audacious chic combined with a sense of humour, whose hairdressing was that of an urchin playing in a backyard, with a difference.

ADY CUNARD'S DAUGHTER, NANCY, had the same eyes as her mother, more exaggeratedly serpent-like, and the effect was increased by her painting them heavily with dark liquid pigment inside the sockets, as the Arab women do. Her appearance was very Egyptian, with Nefertiti's long upper lip and slightly pouting mouth, which she painted like a crimson scar across her face. Her hair was metal blonde, her cheek bones pronounced. She resembled a robot woman in a German film, but this inhuman effect was completely shattered by her voice, so full of humour, warm sympathy and human understanding.

ALLULAH BANKHEAD is a wicked archangel with her flowing ash-blonde hair and carven features. Her profile is perfectly Grecian. Her eyelashes, built out with hot liquid paint to look like burnt matches, weigh down the lids over her enormous snake-like eyes. She is Medusa, very exotic, with a glorious skull, high pumice-stone cheek bones, and broad brow. . . . Hers is the most easily recognisable face I know, and it is the most luscious. Miss Bankhead's cheeks are like huge acid-pink peonies, and her sullen, discontented, rather evil rosebud of a mouth is painted the brightest scarlet.

Pin-ups of the Past

RAYMOND MANDER AND JOE MITCHENSON

IN-UPS, as they are now universally known, can be said to date back to the advent of commercial photography, although this title probably did not come into vogue until the First World War. Society beauties, ladies of the town, actresses from both the legitimate and the musical stage, were photographed and their pictures displayed for sale in the shops and even dispensed by slot machines for a modest price. Firstly they were a small *carte-de-visite*; later the larger cabinet-size pictures took over until the introduction of the picture post card at the turn of the century.

The *Pose Plastique* or *Tableau Vivant* is an age-old stratagem to exploit the nude. It was used from the days of Emma Hamilton to those of The Windmill. Provided no one moved all was well. In mid-Victorian days Madame Warton titillated the town at Saville House (the site of the Empire in Leicester Square) and later Charles Morton at the Palace Theatre of Varieties found himself in trouble with the authorities over his *Tableaux Vivants*. Famous paintings were the usual excuse. *The Repentant Magdalene* by the seventeenth-century Orazio Gentileschi, at one time court painter to Charles I, must be held responsible for the 'pin-up' above.

'How would you like to swing with me?' An 'eighties Gaiety Girl, her shiny satin costume and boots remarkably foreshadow the kinky outfits of a later era. The first Gaiety Theatre where 'The scared lamp of Burlesque' was lit by John Hollingshead in 1868, and was later sustained by George Edwardes, until he 'invented' muscial comedy in the nineties, became legendary as the home of the 'Gaiety Girl'. These ladies of the chorus, show girls in modern parlance, have remained to this day the epitome of the naughty 'nineties. Darlings of the stage door Johnnies, they never stepped over the boundary of good taste into the world of the *demi-mondaine* but they and their theatre were still taboo to middle-class morality.

The ladies of Burlesque and *Opéra Bouffe* were always a target for the puritan reformers. Their reputation is tacitly acknowledged in a drawing by Alfred Bryan, published in 1889, which depicts the unmistakable back of Edward, Prince of Wales, examining a playbill displayed in a pastrycook's window advertising the 'Best burlesque in London' while the shop itself is designated as a 'Noted shop for tarts'.

As Burlesque and *Opéra Bouffe* followed the transvestite tradition, the ladies played the male parts and *vice versa;* their pictures were certainly not fit for the Victorian drawing-room! Across the Atlantic Lydia Thompson, in 1868, introduced to Broadway her 'British Blondes'. Lulu Mortimer, who appeared with the rival Millie Alexandrina's 'Troupe of Blonde Beauties', is here seen in a Burlesque of the Orpheus legend being seduced by Zeus in the form of a bee.

'Praise', 'Gentleness' and 'Reflection'—Edwardian book-mark post cards. These three innocent little maids could certainly be introduced into the drawing-room without bringing 'a blush of shame to the cheek of modesty', maintaining the respectability insisted upon by W. S. Gilbert (to say nothing of Sullivan) which they had introduced into the world of light opera.

The invention of the cheap picture post card, late in the 'nineties, opened the doors to a flood of 'pin-ups' from all over the Continent, both of celebrities and unknown models. The use of a classical pose or costume goes far back into portraiture and has always provided a convenient excuse for any innuendo!

AZERAC
PARIS

DE PÉBREL ★

Gerlach

Nina Barkis
as Salome

A 'Parade of the Nations' has been a standby excuse for a 'Leg show' since it was probably devised by Augustus Harris (aided and abetted by his designer, Wilhelm) when he rehabilitated Pantomime at Drury Lane in the latter years of the last century. The lady above, probably at the Folies Bergère in Paris in around 1905, represents Germany, complete with Kaiser Wilhelm on a gold Deutsches mark.

Oscar Wilde, who literally 'invented' Salome in 1892, had a lot to answer for. In the early nineteen-hundreds every dancer (the play having been banned) decided that the head of John the Baptist on a charger

47

was a passport to success and the *Dance of the Seven Veils* proved irresistible. Maud Allen, from America, was a sensation at the Palace in London and was banned by the Watch Committee of a provincial town. Her innocence was defended by the Prime Minister of the day, Mr Asquith, who invited her to tea at No. 10! The lady on the left, Lena Barkis, looks, as Dickens would have said, 'willing'! It only needed Strauss to make Salome operatically respectable in 1905.

We now enter the realm of the 'Pose'. This rather wooden Berlin lady of 1904 (above) appears to be riding side saddle on the stump of a studio tree. A curious occupation at any time but undoubtedly provocative!

Further south, in Italy, in a warmer climate, the photographer has draped his model in tulle and given her a tiger skin on which to recline. It may be said she has given the world her 'tits' for posterity!

The Greeks certainly had a word for it, but France captured the world market! Robinne as Diana, a beautiful photograph by Reutlinger, a highly reputable Parisian photographer in his day, turned into a post card for universal distribution as a *Carte postale, Cartolina postale, Tarjeta postal, Levelezolap, Postkarte* and *Briefkaart*.

The phallic innuendo of the quiver could not be mistaken even by the most innocent of recipients! [1975]

Bring on the Fiends

P. G. WODEHOUSE

OD BLESS MY SOUL, I don't know when I have been more pleased than when I read in the paper the other day that Mr Sax Rohmer had sold the radio, television and film rights of his famous character Doctor Fu Manchu to a motion picture company for four million dollars. It is not that the price is particularly high—*The Saturday Book* will pay me about that for this article—the significant thing is that it shows that another of those trends has popped up. What so braces me on learning that Fu Manchu has hit the jackpot—apart from my esteem for Sax Rohmer, who, when we were both younger, endeared himself to me by writing a story about a lift attendant who was born at Downham and educated at Uppingham—is that it shows that the bad days are over and Fiends In Human Shape are back in the money again.

I can remember the time when you couldn't open a magazine without flushing half a dozen fiends in human shape. Then for some reason the bottom dropped out of the racket, and they were down in the cellar, with no takers. Now the bull market in fiends has apparently started once more, and the man cheering and waving his hat is me. You can't, in my opinion, have too many of these admirable characters about the place. Come right down to it, they are the only really satisfactory villains—or heavies, if you prefer it—for what used to be called 'thrillers' and are now labelled 'novels of suspense.'

The great problem confronting those who write stories of that type has always been the selection of a convincing louse to do the dirty work. The detective was easy. You could make him almost anything from the frivolous detective who made wisecracks to the dull detective who unmasked the criminal by means of his special knowledge of toxics and things. And there was always the Scotland Yard man and the tough Private Eye.

But the heavy was a different matter and one that called for more thought. For a long time heavies in suspense stories were divided into three classes, all silly: (a) Sinister men from China or Assam or India or Tibet (or practically anywhere except Ponder's End and Oswaldtwistle) who were on the track of the jewel stolen from the temple. (b) Fellow with a grudge which had lasted as fresh as ever for thirty years. (c) Master Criminals.

If I had a son who was thinking of writing novels of suspense—and if I had a son of pen-holding age that is certainly what he would be doing nowadays—I would advise him to try anything rather than (a). Sinister jewel-trackers reached saturation point round about the beginning of the century. Besides, what I might call the heavy-supplying nations have grown so absurdly touchy these days. Make your murderer a Mexican now, and within a week of your story's appearance letters start pouring in to the publisher's office signed *Disgusted Peon* and *Mother of Five (Mexico City)*, denouncing the unfair libel. Go elsewhere and you run up against *Indignant (Tibet)* and *Fair Play (Java)*. It is not worth it.

And yet the idea of falling back on (b) is not agreeable. The age we live in is so practical and matter-of-fact. We are no longer able to believe as readily as our fathers did in the man who cherishes a grudge for thirty years. It was all very well in the old days, when there were fewer distractions, but what with golf and tennis and crossword puzzles and filling in our football pools it seems incredible that a man would have the leisure to keep his mind on some unpleasantness which happened in the early spring of 1926.

Which brings us to the last class, the Master Criminals. I suppose the first M.C. I ever came across was Professor Moriarty, and I remember in those days thinking him about as nasty a piece of work as one was likely to meet in a month of Sundays. As a boy, he thrilled me. (I don't mean when he was a boy, I mean when I was a boy.) He curdled my blood on the printed page, and he curdled it again in William Gillette's stage version of the Sherlock Holmes stories. (Gosh, that 'protruding face, for ever slowly oscillating from side to side in a curiously reptilian fashion!') But more recently I must confess, I have come to the conclusion that the Prof. was not so hot.

Sherlock Holmes, you will recall, comes to visit Doctor Watson and speaks of this Moriarty in high terms. ('He is the Napoleon of Crime, Watson, the organizer of half that is evil and of nearly all that is undetected in this great city. He has a brain of the first order.') He then tells Watson that he is on the point of dishing the Professor—'I have woven my net round him until it is now ready to close'—and explains that Moriarty, taking umbrage at this, is using all the resources of his vast organization to destroy him.

'Watson,' says Holmes solemnly, 'on my way here I was attacked by a rough with a bludgeon!'

A rough with a bludgeon! Gad, sir, if I were a Master Criminal with a brain of the first order and an oscillating face I would think up something a little better than roughs with bludgeons.

The psychology of the Master Criminal is a thing I have never been able to understand. I can follow the mental processes of the man who, wishing to put something by for a rainy day, poisons an uncle, shoots a couple of cousins and forges a will. Conduct like that is based on sound commercial principles. We all like to salt away a piece of money; and inserting strychnine into a rich uncle is probably the simplest and pleasantest way of doing it. But the Master Criminal does not need cash. He has already got all any reasonable man could want. What with the Delancy emeralds, and the Duchess's pearls, and those shiploads of bullion his minions are always stealing, he must be a millionaire several times over. So what on earth does he want to go on for?

Why not retire and enjoy himself?

The way I look at it, it's no good sitting motionless like a spider in the centre of its web and organizing thefts of jewels and secret treaties (which is where the big profit is these days: no income tax)—if you don't get anything out of it. When I set up as a Napoleon of Crime and the stuff starts rolling in, I shall call it a day and do myself well. A house in Mayfair, another in Leicestershire (so that I can get a bit of huntin'), a shooting box in Scotland (for the shootin'), a stretch of water on the Test (for fishin' purposes), a yacht, a racing stable, some decent cigars and a new razor blade every morning . . . all that sort of thing. But no Master Criminal I have ever heard of would dream of launching out and making a splash.

I have just been reading a story about one of these poor half-wits. This one lived in a cellar on a smelly wharf on the river, posing as a lodging-house keeper. All he did with his time was chop wood in the back yard. And, at a conservative estimate, after paying salaries to his staff of one-eyed half-breeds, pockmarked Mexicans and knife-throwing deaf mutes, he must have been worth between fifteen and twenty million. One scarcely knows whether to laugh or weep.

How different is the case of the fiend in human shape.

Yes, I know what you are going to say. You are going to remind me that Fu Manchu, as up-and-coming a fiend as ever snarled out of the side of his mouth, used to pig it in the bowels of the earth, far below the level of the Thames, under Sam Pak's, a Limehouse resort of evil reputation.   True. But there was a reason. His job necessitated keeping a lot of furnaces going day and night which had to be fed with human flesh; and for that you need privacy. Just try doing that sort of thing at the Ritz or Claridge's and see what happens. You will scarcely have shovelled on your first torso when there will be stiff telephone calls from the management, and you will either have to close down the furnaces or move elsewhere.

The great advantage of the fiend in human shape as heavy is that his motives are sound and intelligible. Like the Master Criminal, he does not spend much money, but that is because money means nothing to him. If you tell him that there is little or no profit in dropping cobras down people's chimneys, he replies that he is not in the business for what he can get out of it, but for the quiet satisfaction, the sense of something attempted, something done, that cobra-dropping gives him.

'There is such a thing,' he says coldly, 'as Art for Art's sake.'

Fu Manchu, I know, holds that view. If he puts on false whiskers and stands outside the hero's house on a chilly night, pumping poison gas through the keyhole, it is because that is his way of expressing and fulfilling himself. It means nothing to him that there is no percentage on the deal—on which, as a matter of fact, he is probably down, for cobras and poison gas cost money. He is like the baby in *Alice in Wonderland*; he simply does it to annoy because he knows it teases. Making a profit is the last thing he thinks about.

That is why, as a heavy, he is so superior to the man with the thirty-year-old grudge and the Master Criminal. To the man with the moth-eaten grudge we say, 'But, my dear fellow, consider. If you stick that knife into Sir George, what of the future? What will you do in the long winter evenings with no dream of vengeance to nurse?' To the Master Criminal we point out that he is giving himself a lot of trouble and discomfort to add to an income which is already absurdly large. But the fiend in human shape we pat encouragingly on the back with a cheery 'Good luck, Fiend, old man.'

Especially if he is Chinese, as Fu Manchu is. To be a Grade A fiend in human shape Chinese nationality is almost a 'must,' for then you start with the advantage of having slanting eyes which are horribly filmed (like most of the motion pictures I have been seeing lately) and can snarl sibilantly. Reading the Fu Manchu stories, one can understand why the United Nations are so reluctant to have Red China joining the party. Let Red China into the U.N., and first thing you know its representative is popping a wire cage over you and dropping rats into it. ('Cantonese rats, Doctor Petrie, the most ravenous in the world. You know my partiality for dumb allies. You have met my scorpions, my death-adders, my baboon men . . .')

Obviously that sort of thing would ruin the cosy atmosphere of Security Council meetings.

'What is that curious object crawling along the floor, Pierson? A scorpion?'

'Looks to me more like a death-adder, my dear Lodge.'

'And isn't that a baboon man over there?'

'Yes, you're right. It is.'

'Very unpleasant.'

'Most. I always said it was a mistake giving Red China a seat.'

Nor do fiends, if Chinese, stop at scorpions and death-adders. I have met one who could open double-locked doors just by looking at them and another who could take a ginseng root, rub it a little and turn it into a homunculus which went scuttering all over the place. You don't want things like that distracting your attention when you are trying to listen to Russia registering its three hundred and forty-fifth veto.

But in novels of suspense we welcome these splendid chaps. There are moments, as the expression is, when a fellow needs a fiend. So I'm glad you're back, Fu, with your Cantonese rats and the rest of the troupe. Heaven speed the cobras you drop down the chimney, and if you want to destroy the world with that Death Ray of yours, go to it, boy. It's not much of a world, anyway.

[1957]

Stanley Matthews

ALAN ROSS

Engraving by David Gentleman

Not often *con brio*, but *andante, andante,*
   horseless, though jockey-like and jaunty,
Straddling the touchline, live margin
   not out of the game, nor quite in,
Made by him green and magnetic, stroller
Indifferent as a cat dissembling, rolling
A little as on deck, till the mouse, the ball,
   slides palely to him,
And shyly, almost with deprecatory cough, he is off.

Head of a Perugino, with faint flare
Of the nostrils, as though, Lipizzaner-like,
   he sniffed at the air,
Finding it good beneath him, he draws
Defenders towards him, the ball a bait
They refuse like a poisoned chocolate,
   retreating, till he slows his gait
To a walk, inviting the tackle, inciting it.

Till, unrefusable, dangling the ball at the instep,
He is charged—and stiffening so slowly
It is barely perceptible, he executes with a squirm
Of the hips, a twist more suggestive than apparent,
    that lazily disdainful move *toreros* term
      a Veronica—it's enough.
Only emptiness following him, pursuing some scent
Of his own, he weaves in towards,
    not away from, fresh tacklers,
Who, turning about to gain time, are by him
    harried, pursued not pursuers.

Now gathers speed, nursing the ball as he cruises,
Eyes judging distance, noting the gaps, the spaces
Vital for colleagues to move to, slowing a trace,
As from Vivaldi to Dibdin, pausing,
    and leisurely, leisurely, swings
To the left upright his centre, on hips
His hands, observing the goalkeeper spring,
    heads rising vainly to the ball's curve
Just as it's plucked from them; and dispassionately
Back to his mark he trots, whistling through closed lips.

Trim as a yacht, with similar lightness
    —of keel, of reaction to surface—with salt air
Tanned, this incomparable player, in decline fair
    to look at, nor in decline either,
Improving like wine with age, has come far—
    born to one, a barber, who boxed
Not with such filial magnificence, but well.
'The greatest of all time,' *meraviglioso* Matthews—
    Stoke City, Blackpool and England.
Expressionless enchanter, weaving as on strings
Conceptual patterns to a private music, heard
Only by him, to whose slowly emerging theme
He rehearses steps, soloist in compulsions of a dream.

[1957]

This is one of a series of three poems on sporting themes written by Alan Ross (no mean fast-medium bowler) for No. 17. He had contributed a vivid essay on Sardinian bandits to No. 13, and he wrote of the Golfo dei Poeti in No. 19.

Girl under Fig-tree

LAURIE LEE

Slim girl, slow burning
quick to run
under the fig-tree's
loaded fruits.

Skin-cold like them
your wet teeth spread,
parting pink
effervescent lips.

When I hold you here
valleys of fruit and flesh
bind me
now wet, now dry.

While on your eyes, the cool
green-shaded lids
close on the
wells of summer.

Slim girl, slow burning
quick to rise
between question
and loaded promise.

If I take you, peel you
against the noonday dark,
blind wasps
drill my hands like stars.

[1969]

The Death of Painting

EVELYN WAUGH

ROM TODAY painting is dead,' cried Paul Delaroche in 1839, when first shown a daguerreotype. He spoke too soon. For two generations there was life—vigour, sometimes—in the stricken body. Even today in odd corners painters may still be found plying their ancient craft for the pleasure of a few impoverished private patrons. But for the professional critics, the public committees, the directors of galleries, the art is indeed dead, picked white; not a smell survives. It is noteworthy that a Frenchman first saw the significance of this French invention. France was the scene of the death agony. Delaroche's prognosis was sound enough. But it was based on a false diagnosis.

Nearly twenty years later an Englishman wrote: 'Photography is an enormous stride forward in the region of art. The old world was well nigh exhausted with its wearisome mothers and children called Madonnas . . . its wearisome nudities called Nymphs and Venuses . . . Then a new world slowly widens to our sight, a very heaven compared to the old earth . . . There will be photograph Raphaels, photograph Titians. . . .'

That was the prospect Delaroche feared. Here were a box, a lens, a bath of salts and with them the common man could effortlessly accomplish all that the great geniuses of the past had attempted. For until the present century the whole history of European painting was determined by man's striving to reproduce and arrange visual appearances. The critics of the last fifty years have been busy in imputing quite different motives to the Masters and in identifying quite different achievements. There is no evidence of these preoccupations in the rather sparse documents. Most of the letters and recorded precepts of the Masters deal with prices, models, and technical devices. When they speak of their aims they are unanimous. Leonardo da Vinci wrote: 'That painting is most praiseworthy which is most like the thing represented' and: 'When you wish to see whether your picture corresponds with that of the object presented by nature, take a mirror and set it so that it reflects the actual thing, and then compare the reflection with your picture.' Nicholas Hilliard wrote: 'Now knowe that all painting imitateth nature or the life in everything.' Piero della Francesca: 'Painting is nothing but a representation of surfaces and solids foreshortened or enlarged.' Poussin: 'Painting is nothing but an imitation of human actions . . . one may also imitate not only the actions of beasts but anything natural.' In the court of Louis XV it was disputed whether two perfect painters, observing the same scene, would not produce identical pictures, painters by inference differing only in their faults. There were certainly at different periods some differences of opinion about the rights of selection of the artist, about the modifications he might make in his model in the interest of ideal beauty, what details he might eliminate in the interest of grandeur. Painters represented things they had never seen, such as cherubim on the wing. Some, such as Bosch, portrayed pure fantasy but all the objects were imagined as concrete, visible and tangible and painted as such. It was never questioned that the painter's prime task was to represent. Actual illusion was never achieved except in amusing toys—dog-eared papers apparently pinned to the wall so that the fingers itch to remove them—but there is no reason to doubt that had a full-scale *trompe l'oeil* ever been effected, it would have been applauded.

Today high honours and high prices are given to the practitioners of 'non-representative art.' Patronage is in the hands of people who no longer seek joy in possession; the directors of public galleries conceive it as their duty to instruct by exemplifying 'movements,' however repugnant they may find the task. In the early days of the Post-Impressionists there were ingenious journalists who tried to demonstrate that the new painters were logically developing the discoveries of the Masters; that true aesthetic emotion had always existed in some unexplored subconscious area and was only at that moment (*circa* 1911) becoming articulate; that all original artists had begun by shocking the Philistine. As the scrupulously accurate drawing of Holman Hunt and the early Millais looked 'deformed' to Dickens, so a few years were needed before the common man could see Léger with new eyes. That particular bit of humbug has not worn well. In the last fifty years we have seen the drawings of savages, infants and idiots enjoying fashionable favour. The revolutionaries have grown old and died. No new eyes have grown in new heads. The division between the painting and sculpture of this century and its predecessors has become more pronounced, as more observers in other spheres recognize the evils of the time. There have been no sensational recantations of the kind prevalent among political writers, but the critics on the whole now admit that while Giotto and Tintoretto and Rembrandt and Degas were all in their enormously different ways practising the same art, the activities—call them what you will—of Léger belong to an entirely different order. Can this revolution be attributed to photography?

That invention certainly failed in the claims originally made for it. It has been a humble assistant to the Arts. There are mosaics and frescoes so placed that they can be seen imperfectly and then only with great fatigue. Photography has disclosed new beauties in these. The camera can reveal certain things that are invisible to the naked eye, such as the hitherto unrecognisable stains on the Holy Shroud at Turin. As in the classic hypothesis of the apes typing eternally until they write the sonnets of Shakespeare, the millions of plates exposed have inevitably, but quite fortuitously, now and then produced an attractive composition. But in its direct relations with painting, photography has never been a rival. The allegorical groups and costume-pieces produced in the '50s and '60s—such as Rejlander's celebrated *The Two Ways of Life* and Mrs Cameron's illustrations to *The Idylls of the King*—are what Delaroche feared, and they proved to be wholly ludicrous. The mortal injury done to painters was something quite other; it was both technical and moral.

In technique it was the instantaneous snapshot, not the studio exposure, which proved revolutionary. Movements which before had eluded the eye were arrested and analysed. The simplest example is that of the galloping horse. Draughtsmen had achieved their own 'truth' about the disposal of its legs. The camera revealed a new truth that was not only far less graceful but also far less in accordance with human experience. Similarly with the human figure. In posing a model a painter was at great pains to place her. His sense of composition, her sense of comfort, the feasibility of maintaining and resuming the pose, were important. It was a frequent complaint of young artists that their elders were content with the repetition of art-school clichés. They struggled to build up from sketches entirely novel attitudes. Then came the camera shutter to make permanent the most ungainly postures. The 'slice of life' became the principle of many compositions at the end of the nineteenth century. At the same time 'gum prints' were invented by the photographers, a process by which the surface of painting was imitated. For a decade or more painting and photography were very close. There are 'gum prints' by the Parisians Demachy and Bucquet made at the turn of the century which at first glance may be mistaken for photographs of Impressionist canvases. How far the founders of Impressionism worked from snap-shots is conjectural. Their followers were quite open in the matter. Sickert used to translate photographs into paint in just the same way as Victorian ladies translated paint into needlework—and in both cases with very pretty results.

Many early photographers, among them the herald of the 'photograph Titians' quoted above, were unsuccessful painters. There was a fair livelihood to be made out of the new device, especially by a man with the air of an artist; nothing comparable, certainly, to the splendid earnings of the popular painters, but the photographer did not have to work for it, as they did. Perhaps no painters in history worked so hard as the eminent Victorians. They knew little of the easy student days of *Trilby* or of the versatile apprenticeship of the renaissance. Painting had become a profession, respectable, rewarded, specialized. They trained as hard as for the law or for medicine, and they kept in training through the long years of rich commissions and hereditary honours. The physical exertion of covering their great canvases was immense. They used 'assistants,' but very furtively. Not for them the teeming studios of Rembrandt or the factory of Alan Ramsay. The English patron who was paying two or three thousand pounds for a picture demanded that it should be all the artist's own work.

Photography provided the ideological justification for sloth. The camera was capable of verisimilitude; it was not capable of art; therefore art, the only concern of the artist, was not verisimilitude. Verisimilitude was what took the time and trouble. Art was a unique property of the spirit, possessed only by the artist. You could be awfully artistic between luncheon and tea. So the argument ran.

In 1877 Ruskin denounced Whistler's pretentious 'Nocturne in Black and Gold' with the felicitous expression: 'a coxcomb flinging a pot of paint in the public's face.' The prospect of enlarging this opionion in court was 'nuts and nectar' to him. 'The whole thing,' he wrote to Burne-Jones, 'will enable me to assert some principles of art economy which I've tried to get into the public's head, by writing, but may get sent over all the world vividly in a newspaper report or two.' Alas, that great projected trial came to nothing. Ruskin was too ill to appear. Whistler was given contemptuous damages without costs; Ruskin's costs were paid by public subscription. But it was not the hoped-for triumph of high principle. The pert American scored some verbal points and gentle Burne-Jones reluctantly gave evidence that Whistler's work lacked 'finish.' This clearly was not the point at issue with the early and life-long adulator of Turner. What a tremendous occasion had Ruskin at the height of his authority and eloquence stood up to warn the world of the danger he acutely foresaw! Something as salutary as Sir Winston Churchill's utterance at Fulton, U.S.A., and perhaps more efficacious. By a curious aberration of popular history the trial was for more than a generation represented as a triumph of Whistler against the Philistines. Today, it is reported, there is an honoured American painter who literally does 'fling' pots of paint at his canvas. What would Whistler have to say about that? Ruskin, we may be sure, would be serenely confident in his early judgment.

The German demagogues of the '30s attempted an exposure of 'decadent' art, so ill-informed and ill-natured and allied to so much evil that honourable protests were unheard or unspoken. The art dealers were able to appeal to a new loyalty; if one hinted that Klee was the acme of futility one proclaimed oneself a Nazi. That phase is ended. Today we need a new Ruskin to assert 'some principles of art economy.' First, that the painter must represent visual objects. Anatomy and perspective must be laboriously learned and conscientiously practised. That is the elementary grammar of his communication. Secondly, that by composition, the choice and arrangement of his visual objects, he must charm, amuse, instruct, edify, awe his fellow men, according as his idiosyncrasy directs. Verisimilitude is not enough, but it is the prerequisite. That is the lesson of the photographer's and of the abstractionist's failure.

[1956]

A Collector's Piece

GEORGE SIMS

BOUGHT my first Shakespeare letter on July 4, 1954. I have the date noted down in a little book as it was quite an occasion and I think a record of such things adds to their interest. I bought this little treasure from J. M. Turner, Gaumont Parade, Sandside: his shop is the one next to the cinema in the High Street. A modest-looking place and probably to the stranger rather unpromising. Up to the war Mr Turner stocked only Western magazines, Penguins, *Black Stocking*, the kind of thing that sells well during the season here. But at the end of the war he decided to branch out into old books, sets of *Punch*, the *Illustrated War Magazine*, etc.

This venture on his part coincided with my urge to collect. I decided that with my 'demob' money I would get together a good library. And within a year I had two editions (the 9th and 10th) of the *Encyclopædia Britannica*, a Gazetteer of the World dating back to 1905, and one of the earliest Bibles known, with the date in Latin, printed about 1780.

I don't know how I turned to collecting letters and documents, but it is true that this collecting is like a mania. I remember that Mr Turner sold me a rare edition of Byron's poems, a copy from which the title-page had been torn by the poet 'in a rage with his youthful work,' as Mr Turner put it. Some weeks after this he told me that he might be able to find an original letter from the poet about the book. And I did not have long to wait before I had the letter and could insert it in the book. It cost 7s. 6d., so it was with not a little fear and trembling that I carried it home. My wife says that I get more pleasure out of it than one would think possible. '*Dear Mr Morgan, I have decided to tear out the title from some books of early poems as I am in a rage with all my early work. Please let me hear from you sometime. And oblige. Yours faithfully, Lord Byron.*'

Once I had that letter I really got the 'bug,' as they say. I was always pestering Mr Turner to keep his eye open for other such literary relics. As he said at the time they are not to be found growing on trees, but within six months I had letters from Livy, Dante, Spenser, Shelley and Keats.

But I am digressing from the Shakespeare letter. I had kept it a secret until the Editor of *The Saturday Book* persuaded me to tell the story because, as Mr Turner says, it's no use making other collectors jealous. And there are so few Shakespeare originals about it might cause bad blood. Naturally, I am proud of having one of them. In fact, a letter from the Bard was my first request after the Byron treasure came to light. Mr Turner told me of their scarcity; in fact he told me the whole story, of how Will suffered from 'writer's cramp,' and how he burnt nearly all his goods including his manuscripts and his bed.

Week after week I haunted the shop only to be met with the same reply 'nothing by him on the market.' And then one day, when I had more or less given up hope, I arrived home to find my wife had a message from Mr Turner. He had been round 'in quite a state.' You can imagine how I felt as I went down the High Street. What with not eating I felt quite faint and nearly had one of my turns outside the shop.

The blinds were pulled in the windows and the card about the repair of fountain pens was in the door, so I thought he had got tired of waiting. But he opened the door, his face quite white and his hands trembling. Apparently he had heard a rumour of a Shakespeare letter being found somewhere in the North Country and had investigated carefully. The letter had been found but the price had been forced up and up until he had paid £5!

So there was the problem, but he was not going to persuade me to buy. The decision was mine. I sat down in the rather dusty 'inner sanctum,' quite an honour in itself. He pulled a curtain and one bright shaft of light (I can still see it) lit the table on which the letter lay.

Now it was my turn for trembling hands as I opened the envelope. No stamp, as they had not been invented then, but the special mark which Mr Turner told me stood for coach delivery. The letter was rather stained and torn, but what matter such trifling defects. I can sense your impatience: you want me to get to the letter itself. It is fairly long but of such interest that I want to have it printed in full here. I do not know the copyright position but hope that a tyro in such matters will be forgiven for any unknowing breaches.

Dear John,
   How are things with you? Things here are very quiet and I often long for the old days. The pleasures of the boards and all the merry throng. But it is no use to repine. I have my work here. 'Hamlet' is going quite well and in the evenings I often get out 'Macbeth' and tinker with it, ever polishing and revising it. Still I miss news of the court and the pleasures of Londinium.

All the best,
Will Shakespeare.

Fellow collectors will be interested to know that under the signature there is the mark some scholars take for the initials F.B. So that old problem remains. But I am hoping to take my studies further by examining other letters which are known to be on the market. It is possible that manuscripts too may be found. But that is another story.

[1956]

Making Them Laugh

PAUL JENNINGS

T IS A DREADFUL confession for a writer to have to make, but when you call to mind any great comedian you do not think first of jokes he made, of songs he sang, of words at all. Obviously these follow—marvellous, utterly characteristic words truly inseparable from your memory of the man, of the sound of his voice. But the first impression is not even visual either. It is of a presence, a spirit, a man: a man standing up there (or, if these are early memories and you were still up in 'the gods', *down* there) able to do something both to you personally and to everyone else.

He is able to make a mysterious communication with the audience—that tiger; to make it lie down and be tickled, helplessly, asking for more.

Like all great artists, the great comedian can make all other considerations—your past, your personal life, your worries and hopes, the whole fabric of life and cities, the entire outside world—vanish into unreality. Just for this timeless moment of laughter you are in—ah, not just *his* world, that's the beauty of it—you are in a shared paradise, almost in that state of lost innocence, before the mere adult intellect stepped in, where the laughter of happiness is the same thing as the laughter of humour. He may *begin* with this (as it were) secondary laughter of humour, but as the act proceeds that kind of self-conscious 'appreciation' of individual jokes gives way to a kind of generalised happiness on an altogether higher plane. In just the same way, now and again at a concert the real thing happens; it is no longer a matter of appreciating particular turns of phrase but of actually living in the music, *being* it. So with laughter.

To be traitorous for just one more paragraph to the sacred cause of words and articulation, I can think of several occasions when I have entered, or rather been brought into, this magic world of total, helpless laughter by purely visual means. There were the two clowns in Bertram Mills' circus before the war who, with a step ladder and some hundred buckets of water, provided a delirious ten minutes simply because each had the transparent design of pouring a bucket into the trousers of the other. There was the sublime scene in *Duck Soup* where Groucho, aware that Chico and Harpo were made up to resemble him exactly, performed a wonderful pantomime, all the time attempting to find out if the figure reflecting him was a real person or a real reflection. There was that wonderful troupe of acrobats, with doleful Edwardian moustaches and long thin shorts, who filled the stage of the Palladium with endless preparation and cries of 'Hup!' and never actually *did* anything. . . .

But of course it is words that give the thing its final completion, its total humanity. Much as I admire the greatest mime in the world, Marcel

Marceau, after twenty minutes I get tired of his arbitrary silence; I want to hear him speak. I can't picture those clowns doing anything *else* but pour water; and God knows Groucho never kept quiet for long.

All the great stand-up comics stood up and *spoke*. And they spoke their own words, not those of script-writers. Their words were a perfection, an extension of themselves. If there was collaboration it was with a partner, not a writer. I remember Murray and Mooney, for instance. Murray (or it may have been Mooney) would attempt a long dramatic story or poem, which Mooney (or Murray), sucking a fag-end mysteriously as alight at the end of the act as at the beginning, would constantly interrupt:

"'Ere, do you know, when I was born, I weighed one pound, one ounce.'
'Did you? And did you live?'
'Did I live! You should see me now.'

Two more lines of recitation, then:

"'Ere, do you know, I 'ave found a way to catch fish without any bait.'
'Well, how do you catch fish without any bait?'
'I have a calendar, an alarm clock, and a lawn-mower. I go down to the river an' I set orf the alarm clock, an' it wakes the fish up, an' they come up to look at the calender to see what day it is, an' then I cut orf their 'eads with the lawn-mower.'

There was a thin, not altogether distinguishable line between the self-spoken words of these great men and actual ad-libbing. Certainly it sounded like ad-libbing, although doubtless it was the well-rehearsed spontaneity practised by speakers in more serious spheres, such as Winston Churchill, trying out his gestures and quips before a mirror.

There are comics about today who retain the technique of inspired ad-libbing; one thinks instantly of Ted Ray and Tommy Trinder. But these are men who learnt in the days when there were music halls all over the country in which to practise their art (and as a curious side-note to this, many of the last—and sometimes I think mournfully it is *the* last—generation of post-war comics graduated not from music hall but the Windmill Theatre in London. Harry Secombe, Jimmy Edwards, Tony Hancock, John Tilley, Eric Barker and others must have sharpened their wit on some of the dreariest audiences in the world; whatever they came for—what am I saying? We *know* what they came for—it wasn't laughter, so if you could make *them* laugh you could make anybody laugh).

Getting the bird on TV is such a time-delayed and confusing process, with so many other people—producers, cameramen, script-writers—involved, that the comic can't possibly learn the direct lessons from it which he absorbed the night they threw tomatoes in Burnley. In the true performance there has to be this underlying possibility of failure, this feeling that *now* is a unique occasion, for the great triumph, the great resounding wave of continuing laughter, to be possible.

It is significant that one of the best ways for a young unknown comic to get known today is to include in his act impressions of better-known showbiz people. It's as though audiences, distrusting the whole idea of comedy anyway, and not quite sure by what standards to judge the man before them, had said to themselves: 'At least we know what Sammy Davis or Mick Jagger are like; now we can see if this chap's any good or not.'

In the days of the great stand-up comic it was the other way round. He had an audience of whom it could be assumed that, a comic idea once having been planted, they would want to sit back and watch it unfold. I know it was a film and not music-hall, but that mirror sequence from *Duck Soup* illustrates my point. Once the Marxes had set up the idea that Groucho wasn't sure whether he was facing his own reflection or another actual man, the variations followed as logically as in Euclid.

Harry Tate went about the country with his motoring sketch practically unchanged for thirty years. Nobody wanted him to change it. The more it was the same the more polished it became, the more its audiences savoured its inevitability; laughter can be more intense when you know what's coming.

Because of this, the great stand-up comics could be superlatively themselves. They didn't need script-writers or situation comedy. A man like Sid Field *was* a situation in himself. And I don't think the art declined through any inner weakness but because of radio and TV, especially the latter (for radio was a fertile soil for characters like Handley or Edwards, even though they also inaugurated the script-writer era). TV, now they've invented Ampex tape, likes to have everything cut-and-dried. And the only counter to such predictability is surrealism.

Ultimately audiences, and even their TV equivalents, for which I think it is time the word *vidences* was coined, will tire of the instant-joke act of one-line gags *and* the situation comedy and will find they hunger for something more sustaining; more human, in fact. The brilliant, unexpected, surrealist surprise is fine, but a half-hour programme of a succession of such instant jokes becomes wearying. And in nine out of ten situation comedies you can hear the gears grinding.

So where will they go for it? Well, the only place I can go to is Clacton Pier (where I've seen two unknowns who subsequently achieved national fame). But that'll be the day, when they hope to get on TV as a prelude to Clacton Pier!

[1971]

Except for the pictures of Sid Field and W. C. Fields, the photographs which follow are from the Mander & Mitchenson Theatre Collection.

Harry Tate, with his son Ronald, in his Motoring sketch

Every line in the body of George Robey (Commander of the British Empire, and eventually Sir) recalls an age when comics didn't have to hurry through a succession of one-line cracks. The personality flowered in his language: 'Kindly temper your hilarity with a modicum of decorum.' He was a character comedian—and the character, whether vicar, bridesmaid or pantomime Dame, always had a red nose, and addressed the audience in a conspiratorial whisper with 'honest vulgarity'.

Like many great comics, Billy Bennett was one who let the audience do all the smiling. ' 'Twas a dirty night, and a dirty trick, when our ship turned turtle in the At-lan-tic'; and, after a ponderous pause, 'Well, it *rhymes*.' He was billed as 'Almost a Gentleman' and all his parodies and monologues were interlaced with marvellously would-be cultured asides, or perhaps a few indescribably serious ballet steps. His fame coincided with the last phase of uneroded music-hall glory.

Will Hay was an amateur astronomer, but his schoolmaster sketches did not exactly give the impression of a giant intellect; indeed there seemed little to choose between him and the Old Man (Moore Marriott) and the Fat Boy (Graham Moffatt) who often appeared with him in unlikely institutions besides schools, such as police or fire stations (also seen in memorable films). He was superb at puzzlement, deadpan, and double-take. 'You boys gambling?' 'Yessir.' 'For money?' 'Yessir. Want a hand?' 'What, me? Gamble?' Pause. 'Orright.' He was Nature's, as well as the casting director's, choice for the part of Dr Smart-Aleck in the film about Beachcomber's famous school, Narkover.

Monsewer Eddie Gray in a rare attitude—smiling. For quite a lot of his act he would mutter gloomily as he juggled. Sometimes he would start with an impenetrable, involved card trick, introduced for some reason in pidgin French—'I cuttee the cards, vang-seess ici, vang-seess there-see.' Then he would abandon the whole thing for juggling ('this is the trick I usually broadcast'), later suddenly yelling 'Ten of diamonds!' He joined the Crazy Gang, often as one who interrupted their act from a box. 'I happen to be the Norwegian Ambassador. You have just insulted my country.' This when the others were clearly in Greek costume. 'But this is Greek.' 'Oh.' And he would sit down again, though not for long.

Sid Field was the brightest of the post-war comic stars, perhaps the last true
genius of the music hall. One view is that there have been three great clowns in a
hundred and fifty years; Grimaldi, Dan Leno, Sid Field. His death in 1950, aged
forty-five, was a tragedy. He had the supreme gift of being able to imply that he
himself knew the absurdity of a situation even while he played it with total con-
viction. In his golfing sketch, when Jerry Desmonde, as the professional, instructed
him to 'get behind the ball' he replied with lunatic logic: 'But it's behind all round
it.' As a soccer fan he would yell hoarsely: 'Use your own judgment!'

W. C. Fields is best known in England for his famous film performance as Mr Micawber; but the dyspeptic, child-hating ('Your line is *goo goo;* don't muff it'), alcoholic ('There is no such thing as a large whisky') character seemed to spill over from his vaudeville and film career into real life. It is said that, obsessed by the fear of dying in poverty, he opened bank accounts in many towns where he was playing, under such names as Mahatma Kane Jeeves, Cuthbert J. Twillie, Otis Criblecolis and Egbert Sousé. Some of his remarks ('I'd rather have two girls at twenty-one each than one girl at forty-two') have become folk-sayings.

Douglas Byng was not strictly speaking a music-hall comic, although as a *grande dame* of Dames he has appeared in pantomine. Cabaret and revue have been his forte, providing him with the right kind of audience to savour his appearance as 'Doris, the Goddess of Wind', 'Millie, a messy old Mermaid', or as a castle, complete with strategically placed drawbridge. He designs these costumes himself. A master—or maybe mistress—of *double entente*.

There are, of course, plenty of female names in the history of music hall or vaudeville, though most of them belonged to women who were primarily singers. But nobody would deny that Nellie Wallace was a mistress of music-hall comedy, a male-dominated field. Billed as 'The Essence of Eccentricity', wearing multi-coloured socks, elastic-sided boots, a stringy boa, and alway a hat topped by a nodding feather, she would project in a quavering but everywhere audible voice such songs as 'Next Sunday morning is our Wedding Day.'

Tommy Trinder, lantern-jawed, knowing, quick Cockney wit, came up the hard way. Working men's clubs in the early 'twenties, music hall, concert party at Shanklin. At one time he was doing, every day, two shows at Finsbury Park Empire, three at the State, Kilburn, two at the Holborn Empire, and a night-club stint at the Paradise Club; and he said to his agent, 'I don't seem to be doing anything in the mornings.' He is known as a brilliant ad-libber, not from an instant mental card-index of jokes, like some, but from real creative flashes, although his act is often peppered with prepared asides: e.g. as late-comer arrives in dinner jacket, 'Sorry, sir, we had to start without you. Trouble with the bike?'

It is not only Jimmy Durante's nose but his entire personality that seems larger than life. Quite as many stories are told of his off-stage life as of his lines in a long career in vaudeville and films. Almost everyone knows the one about his being woken before dawn by his week-end host to go shooting, and trailing behind the others slapping each tree as he passed it. Asked why, he said: 'While I'm awake, no boid's gonna sleep.' It is said that when he buys such things as shirts he buys six and gives the other five away. Interviewed after being guest of honour at a banquet, he said: 'Well, foist of all we had the *pâté de foie gras*.' 'Could you tell the listeners what that is, Jimmy?' 'Whaddya mean? It's enough I can say it!'

Norman Wisdom has perhaps suffered from perfecting a very good music-hall technique. By the time he arrived at Collins' Music Hall in 1945, after appearance in war-time concert parties, the sun was beginning to set on music hall, and some critics have tended to go on as though his acrobatic abilities were his only ones. But, even though not everyone can fall down as skilfully as he does, there have always been inspired moments in his films when it is clear that no one else can do what he does when he gets up, e.g. as humble worker answering phone in manager's office, drawn into delicious posh impersonation.

'I've got a Fireman's song, sir, with a real fireman's helmet.' Hostile manager from wings: 'It looks like it's been in a real fire.' Horace Kenney was an absolute original. Lugubrious to the point of genius, he was the supreme master of the straight, not to say acutely miserable, face. 'I went to visit a friend in the 'orspital. I read 'im the railway timetable all the way from Bury St Edmunds to Gravesend to cheer 'im up.' His mournfulness was increased by evident fear of the manager. 'Well, sir, I've got the Jolly Laughing Cobbler's Song . . . "I laugh ha ha, I laugh hee hee"—No, I said "ha ha" when I should have said "he he".'

Max Miller, the quintessential Cockney 'Cheeky Chappie', was not the diminutive that these words might suggest. He was a very large man, in even larger, outlandish suits, with big blue eyes perpetually surprised at the audience thinking 'filthy things'. In a non-stop rattle of patter he would run on past the point of the gag, then stop in surprise at the laughter. 'Ere's another thing: feller took 'is wife to Paris—there's a novelty, like taking coals to Newcastle . . .' Or he would come on with a black eye—'How should I know there was a handle *inside* the wardrobe ?'

Frankie Howerd has the air of a perpetually surprised horse, and in addition to variety, radio, TV and pantomine has appeared in Shakespeare, notably as a memorable Bottom and as Launcelot Gobbo. He brings his own style of pregnant pauses and heavy asides to the audience about 'them'. This can refer either to the management or the rest of the cast, and as he often appears in somewhat out-rageous shows like *Up Pompeii!*, the field is wide and there are depths of innuendo.

JAMES BLADES, from the film *We Make Music* (World Mirror Productions)

The Man behind the Drums

JAMES BLADES

MUSIC CRITIC once said that I lived by calculated violence done to a variety of instruments. To this intriguing description by John Amis of the professional side of an orchestral percussionist's vocation could be added the task of calculating periods of silence to a split second, for it is at times far more difficult to do nothing than to do something. A count of 209 bars' rest instead of Wagner's prescribed 210 preceding the entry of the first mighty clash of cymbals in the Mastersingers Overture—and you're for it!

Like most professional players I've often been asked what prompted me to become 'pro' and why I chose percussion. Well, I just wanted to play the drum, and I must confess that it was no classical masterpiece that inspired me to make music. No, it was the sound of a bass drum—the big drum in a Salvation Army Band.

At the age of seven or so, Sunday evening usually found me on Peterborough Market Place as near as possible to the man who played the big drum. He was an ex-Guards drummer named Jim Pack—a fine big man and a tremendous showman on the march, with his stick-twirling, etc. Exciting as was his pyrotechnic display, it was the soft sounds he made in the hymns that thrilled me most. Gentle rumbling like distant thunder, with sometimes a crescendo into the last verse which would nearly lift me off my feet.

In addition to the Salvation Army bass drum there was the lure of Uncle George's drumsticks. Uncle George did a bit of drumming in the Volunteers Band, and on Sunday mornings after service I called on Uncle George and Auntie Lydia hoping to be asked to stay to dinner. Whilst Auntie was busy in the kitchen, Uncle and I would get down to business in the front room: he tapping on a leather chair in time with his gramophone, and I trying to imitate Mr Pack's bass drum by thumping on a cushion. What a time we had!

When Uncle George returned from France in 1918 he began to teach me the necessary rudiments for the side drum: paradiddles, stroke rolls, etc., ensuring that I did plenty of Mam-my—Dad-dy practice—the accelerating two beats on each hand to produce the long roll.

The hallmark of an orchestral side drummer is a smooth well-controlled roll: the technical term for a sustained note or tremolo on all percussion instruments. To cultivate and maintain a smooth roll entirely free of rhythmical stresses requires assiduous practice. The same applies to the numerous rudiments which include grace notes, such as flams and drags. Some of the solos given to the side drum in the orchestral repertoire are particularly taxing. A touch of the 'pearlies' (a nervous tremble), and the solo to open Ravel's *Bolero* 'goes for a Burton'! Similarly the solo side-drum rolls which open the overture to Rossini's *La Gazza Ladra*—the first *forte* and the second usually played *pp* as an echo. No one was more aware of the concern of the side drummer at this point than Sir Thomas Beecham. If he was in a particularly whimsical mood he would start the player on the *pp* roll, and then turn to his leader and chat for what seemed to the side drummer the length of the overture! One of *my* most trying experiences was sustaining a roll for three minutes to cover a situation in a horror film.

I became something of a nuisance as a boy with my constant 'tip-tap', and I was given the pigsty as my practice den. Our pig was spared the infliction, having been eaten the previous winter.

Uncle George eventually arranged for two local players to take me in hand, and I soon qualified sufficiently to do an odd job in small dance bands, augmenting slightly my meagre wage as an apprentice engineer.

My musical chum at this time was a youth named Frank Hitchborn, a pianist. As we were not overwhelmed with paid engagements we decided to form an orchestra. For some reason or other no one seemed anxious to team up with us, so we formed a duo—piano and drums. The magnificence of this combination, and the fact that we were at liberty for weddings, dances, and suchlike occasions, we made known to all and sundry; but we remained un-accountably 'vacant'. Then something happened. Our town was to have a visit from Royalty: the Prince of Wales was to open the Agricultural Show. The great day arrived, and Frank and I obtained a good position near the show ground—just as we had planned—he with a melodion borrowed from his grandfather, and I with a small drum. As the procession, headed by the Prince and City Officials, passed us we struck up 'God Bless the Prince of Wales'. We were immediately grabbed by a policeman who jerked us to the back of the crowd and rebuked us in no uncertain terms. A night in jail would not have worried us; our object had been achieved. We made our way quickly to a stationer's shop and ordered cards to be printed—'Played before Royalty'!

My first job was in a circus band. I replied to an advertisement in *The Era*, and received an offer written on a piece of fish-and-chip paper which read: 'Start Monday, Ginnetts Circus, Henley-on-Thames, £3 a week and tent—Sam'. I got the tent, but never the three pounds! With the blessing of my family and Frank, and a sigh of relief from the neighbours, I made my way to Henley-on-Thames and found the band tent that was to be my home for the next three months. Sam—of the fish-and-chip paper—turned out to be the bandmaster. He eyed me up and down, and so did a lion in a nearby cage, but both turned out to be quite friendly. Sam told me we started at three o'clock and gave me some bits of music, which I must confess looked like Greek to me, particularly the opening march. But I was certain of one thing: at the start I was to play for two bars, then count two bars rest, and then start the drumming again.

At three o'clock Sam started us off by nodding his elbow (he played a cornet as well as conducted). I went: 'Pom-tiddy-pom-tiddy-pom-pom-pom' and counted softly 'one-two-two-two'. 'Stop,' yelled Sam to the other men—all three of them (second cornet, trombone and euphonium). Sam turned to me and shouted: 'What the so-and-so do you think you're doing?' I replied in a quaking voice: 'Two bars rest, sir.' He said: 'Now look here, my boy, circus drummers never ruddy well rest; from the time we start to the time we finish you flog them drums as hard as you can go.' That single experience taught me that the conductor is always right!

I survived my next engagement by sheer diplomacy. It was in a small silent cinema. The manager told me not to bother about the music but to watch the screen, and the conductor told me to watch the music and not to bother about the screen! For some time I found it easier to heed the manager. The conductor would angrily point at the music, to which I replied by pointing to the screen and the manager's office. In due course the drum music became less puzzling, and I neglected the screen occasionally and thereby pleased the conductor. Down would come the manager and point to the screen, and I would then point to the conductor. I kept the two of them at bay, practised hard, and saved enough money to buy my first pair of timpani.

The men in the orchestra impressed on me the value of getting experience by moving around. I got work in various parts of the country: Jarrow, Workington and Dundee. It was in Dundee that I had the interesting experience of officiating as an organ-stop. A rival cinema installed a massive Wurlitzer complete with all the gadgets. Our organ had no such accoutrements, so the manager (a resourceful man) decided that I should be installed in the bowels of the organ complete with glockenspiel, xylophone and tubular bells. Working from a red light which flashed when the organist pulled out a dummy stop, we kept the opposition in hand until we beat them with a larger Wurlitzer.

My experience as an organ-stop did me no end of good. The snippets I played on the glockenspiel, xylophone, etc., needed a good deal of practice, inasmuch as the majority of them had to be memorised. Until such composers as Bartók, much of the writing for the xylophone and similar instruments was repetitive and imitative, and consisted of short passages often memorised. In recent years there has been a marked change in the style of writing for the tuned percussion (glockenspiel, xylophone, marimba, vibraphone and tubular bells or chimes). The complex and often lengthy passages can be difficult to memorise. Today it is essential that the tuned percussion player is an able sight-reader. In most cases he is a specialist and is responsible for the more important of the parts given to the xylophone, etc. To watch the music, the instrument, and the conductor is no mean feat. On one occasion when conducting the BBC Symphony Orchestra Toscanini halted proceedings to congratulate Stephen Whittaker (a lifelong colleague of mine) on his expertise on the glockenspiel.

In comparison with Steve's prowess my efforts in the organ loft must have been pretty mediocre; but it was good groundwork for what was to follow. My chief concern was to get to London. Through the good services of the late George Black (of the London Palladium), for whom I had worked in the Newcastle area, I eventually got to London, the Crouch End Empire, then a silent cinema.

Having got to London, my aim was to get into the West End. Again George Black was helpful, fixing me at the Holborn Empire. Six months of twice-nightly programmes (fourteen acts, most of them with an effects cue sheet as long as your arm:—'Catch me as I fall', 'Motor horn when he taps me on the bottom', etc., etc.) convinced me that this was not altogether my sort of music.

Dance bands fascinated me, and they were considered good jobs too. An engagement of this nature came my way, admittedly out of London, but at quite a swell hotel: The Majestic, St. Annes-on-Sea, with Gerald Bright (later the famous Geraldo). Gerald Bright was a model of sartorial elegance, quite the most handsome leader I have met, and (omitting his sarcasm) one of the nicest. He took a ghoulish delight, however, in pouncing on me to play the opening of *Tales from the Vienna Woods* on my newly acquired vibraphone, knowing that the 'double-stopping' (chords), combined with the pedalling system—similar to the sustaining pedal on the piano—gave me a good deal of trouble. The vibraphone—an American invention—was at that time (1929) a recent arrival in England, functioning primarily in light music. It was not until 1934 that this instrument attracted serious composers. Berg is generally given as having first scored for it (*Lulu*, 1934). The bars of the vibraphone are made from a metal alloy. Unlike the xylophone and the marimba, where the tube resonators below each wooden bar merely strengthen the note, the resonating tubes on the vibraphone act as pulsators. The tube is opened and closed at the top by means of small fans or shutters which are revolved by motor mechanism. The breaking up of the air column alternately strengthens and weakens the sound of each bar: hence the vibrato.

Following my stay at the Hotel Majestic came two delightful years with Al Davison and his Claribel Band: the summers at the Villa Marina, Douglas, I.O.M., and the winters trotting round London providing musical interludes six times daily between the recently introduced 'talkies'. Al Davison was a superb musician and scholar.

Al did more for me than improve my knowledge of the progressions so necessary in the current style of improvising on the vibraphone and xylophone. He released me—with his blessing—from a contract at the Dominion Theatre, Tottenham Court Road, where the Claribel Band was accompanying Jeanette Macdonald in a spectacular stage presentation, to enable me to accept the offer of a West End 'plum'—behind the drums at the Piccadilly Hotel. Here, with Gerry Hoey and his six-piece dance band, I remained for ten years, every one of them full of excitement and hard work. Soon after settling down at the Piccadilly I became house-drummer at the Gaumont British Film Studios with Louis Levy. This led to similar positions at Denham (London Films with Muir Mathieson), Elstree Studios with Idris Lewis, and Ealing Studios, with the redoubtable Ernest Irving. Added to this was a fair number of gramophone sessions with such personalities as Tauber, John McCormack, Gracie Fields and Peter Dawson.

Most days started at or before 10 a.m. and finished in the small hours, an average week being sixty-five hours wielding the drum-sticks or keeping alert to do so at any prescribed moment.

Long as the hours were, there was no hint of boredom—one never knew what to expect next. On one occasion I returned home at about my usual time (3 a.m.) to learn that Louis Levy had phoned at midnight to say that the effect of a horse with a loose shoe was required for the morrow's film. That meant an hour or so in my workshop experimenting with coconut shells and so forth. The 'cloppidy-clink' worked wonderfully well on the recording, compensating for the reduction in my usual four and a half hour's sleep.

Life at the Piccadilly Hotel was equally exciting and surprisingly relaxing. What was required here was quiet 'mushy' dance music, known to the 'pro' as the 'West End drone'. Diversion came by way of two short cabarets and an occasional stunt to amuse the customers. The majority of these jokes were impromptu, but our New Year's Eve presentation was a carefully planned affair. On one occasion Gerry (the leader) suggested that we rig up our double-bass player as Father Time. Here was an excellent idea, and after a good deal of consideration it was agreed that Bill—complete with beard, wig and scythe—should be secreted inside a huge grandfather clock case that I managed to pick up in Shepherd's Bush market. It was arranged that the clock, complete with Bill, be shuffled to the front of the band rostrum at a little before midnight, and Bill would work the hours of the clock face from the inside. Midnight on the clock face was to be my cue to play the chimes of Big Ben, and on the twelfth stroke Bill was to emerge through the front door of the clock and announce the New Year. At rehearsal the whole thing went like a bomb, and we were all certain that we were on a winner. At a few minutes to midnight the lights were lowered and the clock was duly placed in position. 'Zepp', the head waiter, gave me the tip as the hour reached midnight. I chimed the four quarters and started to strike twelve; but then the trouble started. Instead of the door opening slowly as we had arranged I heard Bill scratching about inside the clock, and it was soon obvious that he had got hooked up somehow or could not find the catch in the dark. I slowed the strikes on the bells and hoped for the best. As I struck twelve, the door of the clock burst open with a terrific crash, and Bill shot out halfway across the ballroom floor, falling on his scythe and breaking it in half. Disaster!—or so it seemed. Bill, however, was a resourceful chap. Up he jumped, shouted: 'Out with the old,' and dashed the remainder of his scythe on the floor. 'In with the new,' he yelled, as he threw his beard and wig to the 'customers'. It was a riot. Bill took umpteen calls, I nipped in with a drum roll, and off we went into *Auld Lang Syne*, during which Mr Jacoby, the manager, grabbed Gerry's hand and said: 'Gerry my boy, this was the best ever—how did you think it all out!'

By the following New Year's Eve I was engaged with material of a sterner nature. I made two trips to France in October 1939 with the first Ensa troop of the war. The party was headed by Sir Seymour Hicks and included Gracie Fields and Tom Webster (of 'Tishy' fame). I left the Piccadilly Hotel to become a member of the London Symphony Orchestra. Ensa concerts with this famous orchestra, work in the film studios, and a tremendous amount of broadcasting more than filled each day. It fell to my lot to record the 'V' signal drum beats for the BBC. My association with this signal (possibly one of the most widely heard sounds in the history of radio), and the fact that I recorded the sound of the gong which is the audible signal of the Rank Organisation, have made me (somewhat against my will) something of a legend in certain circles.

On many occasions during the war I had sudden calls to fill a gap in many of our leading orchestras, conducted at that time by such notabilities as Sir Henry Wood, Sir Adrian Boult, the then Dr Malcolm Sargent, Albert Coates, George Weldon, Basil Cameron, and of course 'Sir Thomas'. On one occasion I had an urgent call to join the London Philharmonic Orchestra at Oxford. I arrived at the Sheldonian almost on the 'down-beat'! The principal percussionist, Freddie (Bonzo) Bradshaw, greeted me and said: 'We covered everything as well as we could at rehearsal. Take the triangle, tambourine and bass drum, and nip in on anything else you can as we are a man short.' He added: 'Not too close a roll on the tambourine in the 'Tame Bear' (*Wand of Youth Suite*) as it's supposed to sound like a chain.' 'Keep the triangle down in the *Enigma*, Variation II—it's the tinkle of the medal on Dan the dog's collar—and plenty of bass drum in the finale. Keep on eye on Sir Adrian, he won't let you down.' I kept an eye on Sir Adrian, and he kept one on me too—as he has done a few times since!

The playing of such instruments as the triangle and tambourine may appear to be a simple undertaking. Not in a symphony orchestra, by any means. Such instruments, and indeed every percussion instrument, is a solo voice, and nerves of steel are required at every entry, be it *ppp* or *fff*. Even more so with the timpanist—the maestro of the orchestral percussion section who, in addition to the demarcation of rhythm, joins the harmony of the orchestra. The orchestral timpanist is judged by his tone, intonation and technical command. The apparently simple parts given to the timpani in the works of such early composers as Bach, Haydn and Mozart are no less exacting than the intricacies in many *avant-garde* compositions, as pitch, tone and precision are vital in every instance. The timpanist's task is aptly described by Dr Gordon Jacob who says: 'A conductor is always thankful for the presence of a really reliable timpanist. His part in the orchestra is so telling and individual, especially in modern works, that he is looked upon as an important soloist in the orchestra and one who can contribute both rhythmical firmness and dramatic excitement to an interpretation.' These aspects are similarly necessary in the works of Beethoven, as for example the four gentle strokes to open the Violin Concerto, or the tremendous energy required throughout the Ninth Symphony. The works of Mahler are equally demanding, and this could be said of many of the works of such composers as Berlioz, Bartók, Stravinsky, Bliss, Walton and Britten.

Of all the instruments of percussion, none are more satisfying to play than the kettledrums, though all members of the orchestral 'kitchen' are involved in moments of excitement, and at times danger. I recall an occasion at the Royal Albert Hall, during the first of the Christmas series of carol concerts given by the Royal Choral Society. The massive choir was accompanied by the late Arnold Greir (organ), William Bradshaw (timpani and chimes) and myself (cymbals and other percussion), with Sir Malcolm Sargent at the helm. My great moment was a mighty clash on the cymbals at the beginning of 'The First Nowell'. It was a beauty, but, to my horror, what I thought was 'Nowell' proved to be an encore of 'Silent Night'!

Repartee with Sir Malcolm and such notabilities could be suicidal, though the 'baton' was not always the victor, as for example when a well-known oboist placed Sir Thomas at a disadvantage. The oboist (James McDonagh, father of the eminent Terence) had replied with his customary Irish wit to a thrust from Sir Thomas. 'Ah,' said Sir Thomas, 'we have a fool at the end of the oboe.' 'Which end, Sir Thomas?' replied 'Mac', pointing the bell of his instrument at Sir Thomas.

Chamber opera and chamber orchestras have taken a good deal of my time in the last twenty years. As a member of the English Chamber Orchestra, the English Opera Group and the Melos Ensemble, I have taken part in the premières of many of Britten's works—most of which demand much from the percussionist. Britten, however, was engagingly disarming. On one occasion, when presenting me with quite an involved drum part, he said: 'I know it will work, I tried the difficult passages on the table!' Britten's skill in culling the essence from percussion is especially evident in such works as *The Turn of the Screw*, *Nocturne for Tenor Solo*, the *War Requiem*, and his parable operas: *Curlew River*, *The Burning Fiery Furnace* and *Prodigal Son*. For each of the parable operas he enlisted my co-operation in creating percussion instruments to yield the novel sounds he had in mind. For the final opera of the trilogy he asked for an instrument, possibly a gourd, to give the effect of plodding feet on a monotonous journey. After due experiment I submitted a gourd, partly filled with small shot, which gave (I felt) the required shuffle. 'Let's consider it over lunch,' B.B. said. 'What I really had in mind was a left and a right foot.' With a gourd, conical in shape, the desired effect was produced. One treasures such moments as these, and such stimulating experiences as playing that 'pearl' of percussion, Stravinsky's *Soldier's Tale*, under the composer, or being directed by Walton in a performance of his *Façade*, or wielding the cymbals at the Coronation in 1953, under the batons of Sir Adrian Boult and Sir William McKie, and the invitation from Sir Thomas Armstrong to join the professorial Staff of the Royal Academy of Music. Equally gratifying could be the high compliment paid to me by a small schoolboy at the conclusion of one of my lecture-recitals, when he assured me that in his opinion I was 'nearly as good as Ringo'!

[1969]

In its early days THE SATURDAY BOOK *paid a good deal of attention to music, perhaps partly because of its Editor's family connection with Thomas Russell, of the London Philharmonic Orchestra, who contributed an essay on Beecham to No. 2. Indeed, in No. 4 there was an announcement of a* SATURDAY BOOK *Concert to be held at the Royal Albert Hall on January 6, 1945, for which the L.P.O. had been engaged. The same issue contained a critical essay by Desmond Shawe-Taylor on the work of Benjamin Britten.*

Despite being in at the birth of the first Aldeburgh Festival (albeit not in a musical capacity) the Editor who succeeded Leonard Russell did not perhaps do justice to music in the pages of THE SATURDAY BOOK. *But it was at one of the Aldeburgh Festivals that he sat down to dinner with "the drummer", James Blades, and realised that he was in the presence not only of a master of percussion but also a masterly raconteur. Hence the reminiscence that has preceded this note. It was expanded into a full-length book of memoirs,* DRUM ROLL, *in 1977.*

In case anyone deduces that Mr Blades is not a "serious" musician, since he admits to playing in cinemas and dance bands, let him enquire at his library for that extremely scholarly tome, PERCUSSION INSTRUMENTS AND THEIR HISTORY.

Sun and Fun

Song of a Night-club Proprietress

JOHN BETJEMAN

I walked into the night club in the morning,
 There was kümmel on the handle of the door,
The ashtrays were unemptied,
The cleaning unattempted,
 And a squashed tomato sandwich on the floor.

I pulled aside the thick magenta curtains
 —So Regency, so Regency, my dear—
And a host of little spiders
Ran a race across the ciders
 To a box of baby 'pollies by the beer.

Oh sun upon the summer-going by-pass
 Where ev'rything is speeding to the sea,
And wonder beyond wonder
That here where lorries thunder
 The sun should ever percolate to me.

When Boris used to call in his Sedanca,
 When Teddy took me down to his estate,
When my nose excited passion,
When my clothes were in the fashion,
 When my beaux were never cross if I was late,

There was sun enough for lazing upon beaches,
 There was fun enough for far into the night.
But I'm dying, dear, and done for,
What on earth was all the fun for?
 Draw the curtains, shut the sunlight out of sight.

[1952]

This was Sir John Betjeman's first contribution to THE SATURDAY BOOK. *It was followed by his spooky 'Lord Barton-Bendish' in 1956, for which John Piper drew decorations, and in 1971 by his scathing poem on retirement to the Costa Brava, which we accompanied with an engaging photograph by Lord Rossmore of the poet in the act of composition, on the site!*

The Golden Age of Jazz

HUMPHREY LYTTELTON

JAZZ HISTORY has a most convenient habit of arranging itself into decades. Starting from the half-true assumption that jazz began in the neighbourhood of 1900, it is quite easy for the glib historian to mark off the development of the music into periods of ten years, with a portmanteau chapter-heading—the Swing Age, the Classic Period, and so on—for each one. My title for this short essay on jazz in the 'Twenties is ready-made. The 'Golden Age' tag has been handed down by previous generations of chroniclers, and is generally accepted as being appropriate to the period. I have a suspicion that it was first applied early in the 'Thirties in a moment of bitter reaction against Swing Music; jazz lovers are quick to adopt a 'things-aren't-what-they-used-to-be' philosophy whenever the object of their affections shows a change of mood.

Nowadays, when we stand far enough away from the trees to see the wood in perspective, the tag requires qualification. During the last ten years, a revival of interest in the prototype New Orleans jazz has directed a critical onslaught upon the 'Golden Age', and most of the accepted doctrines of the period have been either modified or completely reversed. In order to give a true picture of the development of jazz in the 'Twenties the essayist must combine two themes—the True Golden Age, only lately discovered, and the Pinchbeck age which our predecessors took for gold. For, as I will show, jazz made its first world-wide appearance backwards, and standing on its head. The reason for this lies in the relationship between the people's music from New Orleans and popular music in general. In referring to jazz as people's music, I am not toe-ing a party line, but stating a plain fact.

Seen against the vast back-cloth of American music, the beginnings of jazz must seem to the layman to be unbelievably trivial. They can be reduced without too drastic simplification to a single circumstance. New Orleans in the 'Eighties and 'Nineties was a gay city which demanded music to accompany its festive moments. High Society had its trained bands and orchestras. Low Life had nothing. So Low Life took the law into its own hands, and provided music for itself. Untaught musicians, both black and white, provided rough and ready music for the parades, picnics, dances—and funerals—which were part of the life of the city. The fact that this music was untutored would not by itself have resulted in jazz. But the Negro musicians from the poor, uptown quarter differed from the whites in two important respects. They were not hamstrung by an ill-digested academic tradition; and they had behind them a tradition of their own which was improvisational in character, stretching back through plantation songs, spirituals and slave chants to the drums of Africa. It was the application of this vocal and rhythmic tradition to the raw materials of popular music which produced the jazz language. The Negro improviser in New Orleans carried over into his playing many of the idiosyncrasies of the Afro-American singing style—a thick, almost husky tone, a pronounced vibrato, and a habit of striking certain notes in the scale off-pitch. The use of just one of these digressions from conventional, academic usage would cost a straight symphony or dance man his job within five minutes.

It is important to emphasize here that New Orleans jazz was not the first syncopated dance music to find its way into the musical life of America. Long before it had made any mark outside its native city, there were syncopated songs and dances to be heard all over the country in the 'coon' and minstrel entertainments. By the publication in 1897 of two pieces, Tom Turpin's 'Harlem Rag' and the classic cakewalk 'At a Georgia Camp Meeting' by Kerry Mills, syncopation was firmly established in American popular music. It is a fallacy that the first time the American Negro put an instrument to his lips, jazz music came pouring out. Throughout the development of ragtime into what we now call straight dance music, Negroes with the talent and opportunity to learn to read and write 'music' were contributing their share, in conventional fashion, and there is no evidence that their style differed much from that of their colleagues in the white bands.

During the second decade of the century, America went dance crazy, and the emphasis in popular music shifted from the song to the dance. The mad, hectic era following the First World War has been retrospectively dubbed the Jazz Age. This is misleading, because jazz in the true sense was neither responsible for, nor inspired by, the post-war mood. The Roaring 'Twenties would have roared just as loudly had jazz music never emerged from New Orleans, for the dance music industry was by then a thriving concern, and could doubtless have continued to pour forth its stream of 'hits' without any assistance from jazz.

What happened, however, was that in 1917 the city authorities in New Orleans closed the Storyville brothel district, and the music which had hitherto been concentrated within the space of a few blocks in a single city, spilled out all over the world. By 1919 it had reached as far as London, which received its first inoculation at the hands of the Original Dixieland Jazz Band. But, of all the towns and cities which received it, only two are of direct importance to its development through the 'twenties—Chicago, the natural upriver terminus, and New York, the capital of the Entertainment World.

In Chicago jazz established a home from home. The tough, slap-happy mood of gangsterdom found in it a sympathetic accompaniment. And furthermore, the city South Side housed a large Negro population which had moved up from the Mississipi valley to find work in the factories, and which knew and understood the music of the Blues from which jazz had sprung. By 1920 many of the most renowned New Orleans men were living and working in Chicago, passing on the secret of their music to the young local musicians who came to hear them, and contributing to what was discovered, twenty years later, to have been a very rich period of New Orleans music.

The research into the early jazz which has taken place over the last ten years has raised doubts about the 'purity' of the music which was first recorded in Chicago. One school of thought asserts that, by the time King Oliver and his Creole Jazz Band cut the first Negro jazz records, there had already been a decline under the baleful influence of commercial dance music. The claim is supported by the musical evidence of a handful of old-timers who have never left the southern city, and who are therefore supposed to reflect the true, untainted spirit of old New Orleans. It is true that the recently recorded music of Bunk Johnson, George Lewis, Kid Rena and the rest is simpler and rougher than the jazz recorded in Chicago during the 'Twenties; but it is a rash critic who lays down the work of old and unpractised men as a standard for all time.

Without doubt, at some period in its development, jazz music acquired a sense of form and craftsmanship which it lacked in its primitive stages. There is good evidence to show that this maturing process took place long before the Chicago period; it was certainly maintained until well into the middle of it. The leading figures in recorded Chicago jazz during the 'Twenties—King Oliver, Johnny Dodds, Louis Armstrong, Jelly Roll Morton—were men who developed and organized the jazz language along personal lines. In most instances there was no question of commercialism. Their records were made for a Negro market which required no concessions, and the custom of recruiting their bands from New Orleans men is proof enough of the care which they took in preserving the character of their music. The jazz of King Oliver may have been more advanced than that of Buddy Bolden, but there is no reason for thinking that it was less pure.

The whole question of 'purity' in jazz is one which very easily topples over into absurdity. It is difficult to argue that any music can be pure which acknowledges influences from Africa, Spain, France, England and America. I have suggested already that jazz is more of a musical language than a complete music in itself. And as such it is capable of infinite extension and variation. When Louis Armstrong in his early Hot Five recordings (1926–28) expanded the traditional improvised break into a full length virtuoso chorus, he was merely stretching part of the jazz idiom to suit his own temperament. Likewise, Jelly Roll Morton's custom of transcribing his piano solos for New Orleans bands was a perfectly legitimate device wherein no precious 'purity' was sacrificed. On the other hand, it can be claimed that, when musicians without understanding of the jazz language started to prune away its characteristic features, and to replace them with great chunks of non-jazz material, the result was a hybrid which can fairly be called impure. And that is just what happened when jazz reached New York.

As early as 1916 two little groups from New Orleans, the Original Creole Band (under Freddie Keppard) and the Original Dixieland Band, had made a sensation on Broadway. New Orleans jazz had come to town. And its subsequent fate in the Big City holds the secret of the misconception which underlies the Golden Age Legend. New York was the headquarters of show-business, and the whole musical life of the city was devoted to the service of a great industry. When jazz hit Broadway it made an immediate appeal, not as music, but as a stunt. To borrow from the contemporary jargon of Tin Pan Alley, it had a gimmick. And Broadway was quick to exploit it. Soon every musician who had strength in his arm or breath in his lungs was clattering and blasting away in crude imitation of the men from the South. The fearful din which resulted inevitably brought on a reaction, and when the Original Dixieland Jazz Band returned to New York after triumph in England, they soon found that their magic had gone. The stolid tradition of straight dance-music, with its strict code of musical etiquette, had asserted itself in their absence, and 'ear-music' was beyond the pale.

The violent reaction which followed the pseudo-jazz craze in New York is significant to our theme, because it set up a prevailing atmosphere against New Orleans jazz which kept the music at bay throughout the decade. After the initial success of the Creole Band and the Original Dixielanders, New York set its face against this unruly music and refused to accept it unless it was dressed up in the decent clothing of 'musicianship.' Paul Whiteman, a big man with a big band, set the style with his symphonic jazz, a product which was innocent of the slightest taint of real jazz music. In the recording studios a group of musicians who had fallen for the Dixieland style and had developed a polite variation of it succeeded in cornering the recording market for 'hot' jazz. The partnership of Red Nichols and Miff Mole, which led this little clique, heads the Pinchbeck Age roll-of-honour. The former was a competent musician with a flair for imitation and a highly developed business sense, while the latter aroused the admiration of fellow-musicians with his formidable trombone technique. Neither of them ever got close to the heart of jazz. The drawing-room music which they and their various groups recorded so prolifically cuts an elegant but feeble figure beside the New Orleans original.

In Harlem, where one might have expected some sort of natural musical activity corresponding to that of the Negro districts in New Orleans and Chicago, show-business also had a crippling hold. For Harlem was a show-place for sightseers, and the large and flashy Negro bands were too busy providing 'Negroid' music for tourist consumption to worry about anything else. Nevertheless, the music of the Original Creole Band had made a deeper impression on Harlem than on Broadway, and had started a school of hot playing which was certainly superior to the refined effusions of Whiteman and Nichols. This was further boosted by the influence of New Orleans men who joined the big Harlem bands. In 1924, Louis Armstrong spent several months in Fletcher Henderson's Orchestra, and when he sickened of the platitudinous dance music which he had to play, and returned to Chicago, he left his mark on the style of the band. Listening to one of the records which Armstrong made with the Henderson Orchestra, one receives a vivid impression of the fundamental difference in language between New Orleans jazz and popular dance music. Armstrong's occasional solos leap out of the wax with all the vitality of a living music, while, of the rest, nothing is left but a collection of out-dated mannerisms. By the late 'Twenties Negro bands such as Henderson's, Luis Russell's and Duke Ellington's (all bolstered up with New Orleans men) had evolved a synthesis of jazz and dance music which retained the language of the former to a very large extent. Ten years later they called it Swing Music and it had a great vogue. But throughout the 'Twenties it was just Harlem jazz, lapped up by the tourist and Negro population, but offering no serious competition to the white orchestras on Broadway, to whom colour discrimination gave a head start.

As a general rule, then, we can say that throughout the 'Twenties jazz was appreciated in New York in inverse proportion to its authenticity. Even if we rule the pretentious concert-jazz of Paul Whiteman out of court altogether, we are still left with the fact that Red Nichols and his colleagues represented to the New Yorker the ultimate in 'modern hot style.' In itself, this reversal of values would have had very little effect on the course of jazz history but for one important and, for good jazz, disastrous fact. It was New York, and not Chicago, which was the nerve-centre of world-wide show business. And New York in the 'Twenties held the position in relation to jazz which Paris holds today in relation to feminine fashion. Largely through the medium of the record companies, whose largest studios were, of course, in New York, the city established itself as the arbiter of taste.

The effect of this upon the history of jazz appreciation in this country, to take one example, was quite devastating. Every phase of New York's complex reaction to jazz music was reflected in England, from the original jazz craze onwards. Jack Hylton became London's Paul Whiteman, and the imitations, by his 'Jazz Band', of Paul Whiteman's impressions of the Original Dixieland Band's version of the Negro music of New Orleans can still be found in the junk record piles outside the premises of second-hand dealers. Anti-jazz reaction in New York was echoed in London, and in its issue of November 1927 the *Melody Maker*, mouthpiece of the British dance music profession, had occasion to reprimand the Columbia Record Company for using the word 'Jazz' in its publicity material.

'I wonder if the Columbia record people know what this word conveys to musicians,' asked the record-reviewer, 'Needlepoint.' 'If not, let me hasten to enlighten them by saying that it signifies everything that is bad and everything that is old-fashioned. It is a word of sarcasm.'

The theme that jazz was old-fashioned runs through all the *Melody Maker* reviews of the period. It was based, with some justification, on the fourth-hand music which had been accepted as jazz in the early 'Twenties. But it led poor 'Needlepoint' into some unfortunate judgments. When a few recordings by Jelly Roll Morton trickled out into the English catalogues, they sounded to his untutored ear to be near enough to the music of the 'jazz craze' for him to pan them as being out of date. From our present-day vantage point, we can recognize that Morton's 'Blackbottom Stomp' was, even for 1927, very advanced New Orleans jazz, bearing as much relation to the stilted derivatives of 'Dixieland' as a Grecian vase to a cloche hat.

We need not dwell upon the contemporary attitudes to Negro performers betrayed by such *Melody Maker* comments as 'the nigger has a heart as big as his great woolly head,' beyond saying that it served as a further barrier to the acceptance of real jazz. A craving for respectability is one of the British dance-band musician's prevailing characteristics, and his efforts to dissociate himself from what he called 'coon' music flung him straight into the arms of Red Nichols, whose reputation grew to vast proportions. By the middle of the decade, Nichols had himself fallen under the spell of a young cornet-player who had come to New York with the Wolverine Orchestra from Chicago. The band was a failure, but Bix Beiderbecke emerged from it to take the leadership in the white jazz field. Although it is almost heresy to say it, Beiderbecke's example strengthened the anti-jazz forces. His own clear-cut melodic style was, in itself, a striking concoction of jazz and straight ingredients, highly enjoyable and commendable in isolation, but disastrous when accepted and imitated as being the real thing. Red Nichols and his associates were dazzled by Bix, and their music from 1925 onwards proclaims his influence from every bar. But as we have seen already, what New York thought at a given time was conveyed, through the sluggish channels of the gramophone industry, to the British critical mind two or three years later. And while Red Nichols was devoting himself to the slavish imitation of Bix's mannerisms, 'Needlepoint' was delivering the following judgment in the *Melody Maker* of September, 1927:—

In 'Riverboat Shuffle' and 'Ostrich Walk' . . . the laurels must go to Bix Bidlebeck, the trumpet player, who loses nothing when compared to the great Red Nichols.

It is not my intention to set up the *Melody Maker* reviewer of the time as an Aunt Sally. It is difficult to see how, under the circumstances, anybody could have approached much nearer to the heart of jazz when the channels of information were controlled and directed by New York. Indeed, but for the fact that the big record companies of the day decided to cash in on an un-exploited section of the public by issuing a series of 'Race' records for Negro consumption only, it is probable that the real jazz in Chicago would have remained in oblivion to this day. By the end of the 'Twenties the link with New Orleans had begun to wear thin, and one by one, the exiles succumbed to the demands of show-business. By 1926, King Oliver's New Orleans Band had been succeeded by a large orchestra in the Harlem pattern, and Louis Armstrong, while clinging to the hometown style in the recording-studios, was beginning to develop the virtuoso technique which was to bring him world-wide fame. Consistent with the topsy-turvy pattern of jazz appreciation in the 'Twenties, Armstrong's big-band work in the service of show-business completely overshadowed his finest playing in the New Orleans tradition. The now classic Hot Five recordings, made in Chicago for the Okeh Race lists, only found their way into the general catalogues by virtue of his popularity in the Swing field.

As the 'Twenties were drawing their last gasp, there began a movement away from the New York white school towards Negro jazz. But by then New Orleans music was in total eclipse, and the men of Harlem took the bows. It was not until ten years later that there began a determined attempt to unravel the threads of gold and Pinchbeck. For most jazz lovers the world over, the New Orleans Revival was not so much a revival as a revelation. It brought to light the treasury of jazz music which had been locked away in the obscure 'Race' record lists, and established in a position of due importance the musicians—many of them now dead—who were responsible for forging a real Golden Age of Jazz. How far that age extended back before the invention of the gramophone we can only guess. As for the future—who knows ? Events may be forthcoming which will make a 'Needlepoint' out of me.

[1952]

THE SATURDAY BOOK *can claim to have done well by Jazz, whatever short-comings it may have displayed in more orthodox musical spheres. In the very first issue Iain Lang wrote a long and comprehensive study of the origins of Jazz, and in No. 7 a sketch of Lead Belly, the blues singer. In our twenty-first celebratory issue Kenneth Allsop wrote on 'Twenty-one Years of Jazz'.*

Astaire

J. J. CURLE

In THREE LITTLE WORDS
(Metro-Goldwyn Mayer)

EXACT upon the beat,
machine-gun-fire staccato
tapping feet
exteriorise,
then STOP!—Slow smile
extending Laurel's mouth,
the gesture's style
dissolves from face to arm,
from arm to wrist:
the ordinary can again exist.

97

In BLUE SKIES
with Bing Crosby
(Paramount)

With light, flat voice,
cracked-edged,
with down-thrust hands
and slightly simian stoop
(the 'parachutist lands'
posture of set-to-go),

99

In LET'S DANCE
with Betty Hutton
(Paramount)

        the turning head
        moved square to camera,
        its features dead-
        pan, save the twisted-up
        self-mocking lips
        (a cartoon-scribbled face),
        frame without hips,
        (the waiter humbly glad
        of coming tips)
        he plugs half-bitter quips.

In YOU'LL NEVER GET RICH
with Rita Hayworth
(Columbia)

ND then—
the music takes him,
shakes him,
wakes him,
with its stark electric shock.
A force that drives
arrives ecstatic,
acrobatic,
breaks time's clock;

100

In TOP HAT
with Ginger Rogers (R.K.O.)

thrills to find,
to touch and grace
upon all nature's
tender face
the convolutions
lovers trace
in learning features
loving-long
(like hands
that mould them into song).

In THE BAND WAGON
with Cyd Charisse
(Metro-Goldwyn-Mayer)

 XACT,
percussive,
balanced,
swung,
his body is
the censer slung
upon a chain
that brings it back
(all movement reined
within its slack),
inevitable and precise,
a gyroscopic, centred force
that can be hurtled through two planes

102

In BROADWAY MELODY
OF 1940
with Eleanor Powell
(Metro-Goldwyn-Mayer)

but on a third holds changeless course.
About some point that flows in space
he moves, contained,
in whiplash grace,
an easy panther, pattering claws
through multiples
of motion's laws;
a man unfettered,
born to thrive
on simple zest
of being alive:

103

In EASTER PARADE
with Judy Garland
(Metro-Goldwyn-Mayer)

a force of nature
with a grin,
immune to death
and time and sin,
because where it
contrives to be
verges upon
eternity.

In THREE LITTLE
WORDS
with Vera Ellen
(Metro-Goldwyn-
Mayer)

ND WE who watch
observe a rite
in which we cannot
ever quite
explain to others
what we see.

This is art's central mystery;
to be at once
the means and end;
what facts achieve,
what they portend.
Here is an artist:
—if you care
that such exist
hail Fred Astaire!

In YOLANDA AND THE THIEF
with Lucille Bremer
(Metro-Goldwyn-Mayer)

[1970]

Laurence Whistler's Pictures on Glass

N 1950 THE PRESENT EDITOR was asked by his predecessor to write in *The Saturday Book* about the then little-known art of diamond-point engraving on glass that was being revived by the poet Laurence Whistler, brother of Rex. Indeed the present fame of Mr Whistler's exquisite work may be said to have originated in that first serious appraisal of it.

Leonard Russell quickly followed the example of the Queen Mother, Walter de la Mare, Sir Edward Marsh and Sir Duff and Lady Diana Cooper, and commissioned from Mr Whistler a set of six straight-sided rummers engraved with images of insects. These were exhibited in the Festival of Britain Exhibition on the South Bank in 1952.

In 1956 we printed a progress report on Mr Whistler's engravings, and over the years he also contributed poems and a story. Perhaps the most significant stage in his development as an artist was marked in No. 30 when *The Saturday Book* printed illustrations of a series of what Mr Whistler called 'pictures on glass'. (This was also the title of a book containing a fascinating discussion of his work published in 1972).

We have only space now to illustrate a few of these 'pictures', which link his glass engravings closely to his general view of life and nature.

In Laurence Whistler's view, though happiness can never be pursued for itself, it is still the purpose of being; but most often the reality is happiness longed-for rather than achieved, lost as soon as found, remembered or foreseen rather than tasted; and this is reflected in the meanings man reads into his surroundings, and the meanings he expresses in the works he makes.

In the illustrations which follow we see how Whistler's view is expressed in small pictures, about 3½ inches high and 6 inches wide, each engraved in reverse on the far side of a glass goblet, so as to invite the eye right into the concave world of the scene, suspended in transparency. But how to persuade an imagined landscape to convey a meaning? That is the problem of this artist. He takes a hint from the kind of effect we often meet in our surroundings and dismiss as accidental. An object, say a wood on a hill or a window in a wall, may appear too simple and too emphatic to be 'natural'. Ambiguities of shape occur. Outlines of hills seem to cross. Things seem to wear expressions, or to point at one another, or consciously to 'rhyme', resembling each other. A simple shape, say that of gables or lines of ploughing, seems to dominate a scene. Accidental it is, but it appears intended, breaking out from the profusion and mere randomness of things-as-they-are.

The notes that follow, based on conversations with the artist, may help to elucidate the significance of his work.

EXACT TIME: APPOINTED PLACE. A car waits at twilight beside a country road, with lights extinguished, for a rendezvous. The place is where the line of the road runs up into the spire, and the sides of a shed gable exactly meet and are extended by two crossing hills. The time is when the new moon just balances on top of the spire. These are like precise co-ordinates: there can be no other place and moment in the world like this. Thus the meaning is uniqueness, or the once-onlyness of experience.

THE ENCOUNTER. Here the meeting is explicit. Two figures approach one another down a gallery with no visible end, which at the same time appears to be a bridge. Urns of flowers mark the seasons. The wall opposite the sunlit windows is blank, but with a plain door.

MOUNT OF OLIVES (*left*). A figure looks out on the modern world through tree-trunks that assume demonic forms of mockery. The night sky is full of signs and wonders. In the circle of radiance round the bowl there is an allusion to Henry Vaughan: 'I saw Eternity the other night, Like a great ring of pure and endless Light.' Below is the same glass seen from the other side.

WET LANE TOWARDS EVENING (*right*). 'Towards' in both senses. Here the artist comes nearest to naturalism, but this imaginary scene is pinned to three bright points—the road, the sea, the valley—as if it were held in balance, while the light grows clear after the rain.

THE MAUSOLEUM. It stands, beflagged, on a hill-top with the land-scape seeming to extend from it: between the sterile and the fertile, and answered by the far country beyond them. [1970]

Disney Profiles

DILYS POWELL

REAT TALENTS have sometimes been defeated by the excess of their own qualities; Draco's penal code, for instance, left so little to chance that, had it been strictly applied, there would have been no survivors to administer it. Goofy's daring has induced in him a disregard of physical laws whose logical consequence in a logical world could only be a broken neck. Enthusiasm, resolution, contempt for the word impossible—these are the qualities which have guided not Goofy alone, but the Disney Trio in general. A man without the debonair and jovial confidence of Mickey Mouse might have lapsed into misanthropy. Less strongly armed with consciousness of moral rectitude, Donald Duck would long since have fled from the humiliations of public life. If Goofy were afraid of hard knocks he would give up sport. The Trio have never faltered. Disappointment, ridicule, the bleak hostility of the world of matter, all have been dared. It is in keeping with their curious story that in the family group only their dog, Pluto, quite escapes the melancholy shadow of the unaccomplished.

Fifteen years ago the eldest and the most internationally famous of the Trio made his debut in New York. In September 1928 visitors to the Colony Theatre were electrified by the apparition of a small acrobatic figure with globular head, protuberant ears and gay inquisitive nose, wearing patched short pants, outsize shoes and the air of a conqueror. The public were accustomed to quiet heroes. Mutt and Jeff, Felix, Valentino himself had operated in a silence broken only by the chatter of the cinema piano. For a year now the old ways had been changing. In 1927 a mort of things happened: Lindbergh flew the Atlantic, a Revised English Prayer Book was issued, Tunney beat Dempsey at Chicago and Al Jolson's voice was heard in *The Jazz Singer*. Now in 1928, year of the Kellogg Pact and the *Royal Oak* incident, the silent film suffered yet another defeat. Mickey Mouse appeared; and he was a musical Mickey.

The whole of the huge Disney family, in the pause between the wars, came to be connected in the public mind with music, much as the Barrymore name stood for the stage. Not all branches of the family boasted performers; perhaps some members who did perform would have done better to refrain; and his most devoted friends will scarcely claim for Donald Duck a sensibility to pitch. To Mickey, however, must go the credit for the introduction of synchronised sound in cartoons. In music, as in other spheres of human activity (for their humanism is the first, the inescapable characteristic of the Disney Trio), he immediately showed himself a resourceful as well as a cheerful executant. His emergence coincided with the years of high living and ballyhoo; and when in *Steamboat Willie*, beaming, he propped open the jaws of a cow and used her teeth for musical instrument, something in the public mood responded to the confident insolence of his gesture. Mickey the musician came, played and conquered.

Conquered: those were indeed the years of conquest for Mickey Mouse. First in black and white, then, from 1935, in colour, he fought a fantastic battle with a world of prodigies and portents. In 1929 the slump came to put, as an American moralist expressed it, honky-tonk in hock. Mickey went right on winning. He did not, of course, remain purely and simply the musician. A historian points out that between his first appearance and the beginning of World War II he had played 'gaucho, deck-hand, farmer, impresario, teamster, musician, explorer, swimmer, cowboy, fireman, convict, pioneer, taxi driver, castaway, fisherman, cyclist, Arab, football player, inventor, jockey, storekeeper, camper, sailor, Gulliver, boxer, exterminator, skater, poloist, circus performer, plumber, chemist, magician, hunter, detective, clock cleaner, Hawaiian, carpenter, driver, trapper, horseman, whaler, and tailor.' Never was the American manner of life, in which White House is approached by way of log cabin and the actor qualifies first as soda-jerker or elephant-tamer, better exemplified.

In his individual adventures, maybe, he was even at the first not always the victor. The hero of a score of tussles against overwhelming odds might be defeated by the trifling opponent; a canary and her brood, a family of young Mickeys in destructive mood might reduce to impotence the intrepid explorer, Two-Gun Mickey, the Klondike Kid. It was as the man of action that Mickey, above all in his black and white period, won an international reputation. Yet already in these moments of defeat the sharp-eyed observer might have divined the shadow of the frustrated future which awaited, not Mickey only, but to an infinitely greater degree his younger brother Donald. By an ironic coincidence, in their first public appearance together in colour, Donald, the most irascible, and fated to become the most often thwarted, of the Trio, was the instrument of Mickey's most notable reverse. Friends of the family never tire of recalling the incident. It was *Band Concert*, and the maestro was conducting the 'William Tell' Overture. Stirring, exultant, Rossini's martial notes sawed through the air. The music came abruptly to the end of a phrase; and in the momentary silence before the composer had set off on a new tack, Donald was heard continuing in the same key with a rendering of 'Turkey in the Straw.' The dovetailing of the two compositions was as perfect as Mickey's discomfiture was spectacular. This time Donald was the winner. But something in the obstinacy with which he filled in the pauses each time Rossini and Mickey stopped for breath might have warned the onlooker that here was a being doomed to perpetual struggle. The fanatic in modern society creates his own enemies, and Donald's persistence, his refusal to entertain the idea of defeat, were to arouse the opposition of the inanimate world. So far as he is concerned, things have, not tears, but malevolent laughter.

But before Donald joined Mickey in the life of public adventure the eldest of the brothers had won the respect of a humbler companion. Pluto has sometimes been taken for a member of the family. A certain facial resemblance links him with Goofy: the long muzzle, the pendulous ears are the same. But the careful observer will mark the differences. Goofy is rigged out in formal or sporting dress; Goofy walks upright; Goofy talks. Pluto, to whatever degree of family intimacy he may be admitted, remains the dumb animal. From the early days—for Pluto too was born in the black and white period—he was essentially a one-man dog. Silly, demonstrative, faithful, he followed the fortunes of his master Mickey with clumsy devotion, at once pet, servant and friend. His fidelity persisted into the age of colour. Still he caddied for Mickey, still valeted his owner; if the boss went shooting, Pluto

went too, scaring the game, struggling with noisy mimicry to learn the business of a sporting dog, falling a victim at last to the insolence of the birds who perched all over him as, transfixed, he pointed. In return Mickey has always showed a special tenderness for his pet. Those who know him best say his voice takes on warmth and (if one may apply the term to so fluting an organ) depth when he instructs or admonishes Mickey. If Pluto is a one-man dog, Mickey is a one-dog man.

Other pets have entered the domestic circle in which Mickey increasingly spent his later years: a parrot, for instance, or, a bitter pill for the favourite, a kitten. People who doubt whether dogs have a moral sense should remember two episodes in Pluto's life: his conscience-stricken dream of a Judgment Day presided over by a Rhadamanthine cat, and the battle between his higher and his lower self as the kitten in the bucket rattled down the well. Domestic cares, however, and the anxiety of bringing up a family have lain lightly on him. His chief enemy, a bulldog with whom he has had what he calls bone-trouble, he has defeated by superior dog-tactics. For the rest, he has been a happy-go-lucky creature, enjoying adventure where he found it. In his time he has done a good deal of miscellaneous swallowing. An electric torch and a magnet have continued to exercise their functions inside him; nothing comes amiss. Animals, they say, assume the characteristics of the human beings they frequent, and in this Pluto might be said to take after Donald, as a swallower himself no dope. Only the other day Donald swallowed an alarm clock; its illuminated dial ticked contentedly under his vest. But Pluto is no mimic of mankind. He knows his place, on the hearth, in the kennel, in the world; a casual worker but an exuberant friend, more often than not in hot water, but shambling clear on his huge awkward pads, touchingly confident of applause.

Donald's association with Pluto began early, but never threatened Mickey's ascendancy over his pet. The relation between Donald and Pluto was rather that of workmates: of workman, sometimes, and indolent mate. Donald, aloft, would clean the windows while Pluto snored on the sidewalk; Donald would signal for a pail of water, Pluto, still unconscious, would hoist a bucket of clinkers. Donald's conscience has never let him take life easy. In the first years of his career he was apt to be overshadowed by his brilliant elder brother. Mickey's dash and verve, the multiplicity of his adventures, his long and picturesque romance with Minnie, all combined to make him the darling of the public. Yet there is no denying that in the last few years the gay spark has rather withdrawn from the public eye. His appearances have been rarer and on the whole in less triumphant roles. The barriers placed in his way by sardonic circumstances have been more impenetrable. And as the hedonist has retired, the apostle of stubborn endeavour has advanced.

Donald in some curious way has won fame, not as a success, but as a failure. Outwardly his career has followed the lines of his brother's. Like Mickey, he has been a rolling stone, in his time fireman, bill-poster, blacksmith, bell-boy, trapper, agriculturist and caravanner. In some of these pursuits he has been the companion of both Goofy and Mickey, for the Disney Trio, despite their occasional personal disagreements (and their curious lack of family likeness) are a united family, enjoying work as well as recreation in common. But there the resemblance stops. Donald might venture into romance with Donna. He might, in a flourish of frivolity, take up golf, hockey, motoring, fox-hunting or autograph-hunting. With transparent optimism he might engage in occupations as rich in disappointment as gardening, chicken-farming or going to bed early. It would be no dice. Donald lacked both his elder brother's bonhomie and the resilience of his younger brother. His tyres would go flat and the fox would fool him. The prairie marmot would eat his melons at fabulous speed. The cock would picket the eggs and the folding bed would fold up on Donald. Nothing if not a tryer, he would tackle each new hobby, each new job with the brisk enthusiasm of a man unacquainted with failure. He even sang at his work. 'Early to bed, early to rise,' he crooned hoarsely, tunelessly to himself, 'With a cluck-cluck here,' 'A-hunting we will go.' But only too soon the enthusiasm would turn to fury and the contented droning would swell to a torrent of abusive squawks. Animal, vegetable, mineral, everything was against him; even the garden pump played him tricks.

With the passage of time Donald has grown more defeated and more inclined to the morose. Occasionally emotion has been known to unman him. When Admiral Byrd sent him a young penguin, Donald, under the impression that his new pet had eaten the goldfish, punished the little creature; convinced of error, he apologised: 'I'm sorry, Tutzie,' he cried. 'Aw, be a sport, Tutzie!', and the episode ended in expiatory tears. The public still applauds his uncontrollable rages, his endless battle with the blank hostility of inanimate matter. With war a new interest came into his life. A sturdy moralist, he finds in the war an outlet for his patriotism. Bitten by a new enthusiasm, Donald wanted to fly. And, together with every other American caught in the draft, he discovers a fresh enemy in his sergeant. Those who had wished for Donald a taste now and then of success were gratified when, by enthusiastic use of camouflage paint, he became the Invisible Private. The Invisible Man, we know, lost his reason. This time the Sarge it was who went to the psychopathic ward.

In some ways the youngest is the most mature of the Disney Trio. A comparatively late arrival, Goofy, first known as the Goof, went through an apprenticeship of some years before Mickey and Donald would allow their kid brother to make a solo appearance in public. With them he went whaling or holiday-making in Hawaii. With them he cleaned clocks, built boats and— a responsibility sustained with genial calm in circumstances of peculiar danger—drove the car for the trailer. Donald was his favourite brother, and the pair shared certain pursuits from which Mickey was excluded; it was, for example, with Donald as huntsman that Goofy enjoyed his first recorded adventure on horseback. This was the prelude to the experiences in the sphere of sport which were presently to rivet public attention. In 1939 Goofy went for the first time outside the circle of the immediate family, taking as his partner in a joint fishing venture a distant cousin, Wilbur. Another two years were to go by before the youngest of the Trio could be said to stand on his own feet. In 1940 the public still was not Goofy-conscious. But in 1941 the young man appeared, modestly but with an unshakable confidence, as the pupil pilot of a glider. Suddenly the world understood that here was a portent among sportsmen, a character never to be deterred by difficulties or dangers from attempting the ultimate proficiency. The great Goofy Instructional series had begun.

From that moment no field of sport was closed to Goofy. Ski-ing, fishing, swimming, baseball—again and again enthusiasts were admitted to an intimate view of the champion's progress from tyro to expert. Ignoring the risibility of interested parties, he pursued the art of self-defence and the varied activities of the Olympic Champ. Fish went into convulsions of gaiety over his fly-casting, and when his horsemanship suffered a mischance his mount lay down and laughed till it cried. Still he was the Mark Tapley of sport; radiant, he tackled the impossible, and after each rebuff his voice, rich, unctuous, was heard recommending yet a farther step. Failure left no mark on him, and frustration has so far left unimpaired the endeavours of this pioneer in the struggle against the law of gravitation.

In their personal circumstances and characteristics the brothers are strangely dissimilar. Mickey, the only one of the three to marry and enjoy a settled establishment, is yet the rover of the family: in spite of his sentimental side a man's man, careless in his dress and, except for an occasional excursion into costume, clinging man-like to his old and shabby clothes. Donald's closest ties, apart from his brothers, are with his three nephews, an ebullient trio and a trial at times to their irritable uncle. Donald, too, is conservative in dress, wearing for preference his sailor suit. He has, however, assumed various disguises, even feminine ones. He likes gardening, cooking and the sea. When annoyed he taps with his toes, quacking under his breath. Goofy is the dandy of the family, appearing with patent delight in hunting pink or the correct swimming or ski-ing dress. He is never annoyed. Critics have observed that he is also never successful. The progress of the Disney Three has thus been from the aggressive triumphs of the early Mickey, through the exasperated defeats of the middle period Donald, to the joyful frustration of the late Goofy. The temper of the public has changed. Chaplin was once a tough and became a sensitive; crude conquest is no longer in fashion. The Disney Trio too have moved from victory to an uneasy truce with fortune. But to the world they are still champs. [1943]

The outstanding film critic of our time, Dilys Powell, was the wife of Leonard Russell, and contributed to THE SATURDAY BOOK *not merely film and theatre criticism but also short stories and sketches. She and Leonard used to lodge at weekends with a farmer in Kent, and she wrote delightfully about life on the farm in No. 10. She also wrote about Downland in No. 9 and about the Evenlode river, in No. 8. She and Leonard also engaged James Agate in a sparkling conversational exercise in No. 7.*

Palladium Nights

J. W. LAMBERT

TRUGGLING to keep my feet on the ground, I was swept upstairs, round corners, downstairs and out of the theatre. Ejected from the swirling crowd like a bead of mercury from a burst thermometer I slipped off the curb, bumped into a seedy character dangling woolly dogs on pieces of elastic, rebounded into the wing of a crawling taxi and at last reached a quiet pavement. I had been assisting at what was to all intents and purposes a religious ceremony; dazed by noise and light and the hysteria of the celebrants, I stood puffing, my forehead pressed for coolness against a shop window. Ever at my back I heard the grumbling thunder of the crowd, a little more orderly now, for the nightly battle was over between those who had just seen the first of the evening's two performances and those who were about to see the second, the latter, all agog, being sucked rapidly into the theatre like eager dust into the jaws of some monstrous vacuum cleaner. The little street in which the Palladium stands was clearing; the shop windows once again disclosed their goods—sweets and cigarettes, antiques and advertising lay-outs, wash-basins, water-closets, and the deserted alcove of the invisible mender. The moon, shining upon the cool shoulders of the South Downs, upon the peaks of Snowdon and Ben Nevis and upon the reed-fringed Broads, shone here too. Its beams threw a strange top-heavy radiance over the buxom statues on the Palladium's roof—statues which implacable floodlighting, so easily putting the moon in its place, had been cleverly adjusted to ignore. In a knife-edged glare pillars topped by frothy Corinthian capitals loomed above the stained-glass lozenges of the portico.

Beneath that portico the last of the new audience disappears. In a moment the curtain will swing up before nearly three thousand devotees, a mass of hot, relaxed humanity anxious to be amused, startled, and as a climax to the evening raised to a state of ecstasy. They have passed the unnaturally bright brasswork of the entrance, shuffled over the marble floor in the green and gold foyer, past the indoor window-boxes; they have accepted or rejected the good offices of the Ladies' Powder Room; they have eaten their ham, chicken or smoked salmon sandwiches in the Palm Court, where a floor of startling brilliance, patterned like a parody of Ben Nicholson, jeers at the misty lakeland scenes set in panels behind the bars. They are filtering through to their seats, and as they do so the band erupts into bright brassy life.

Aloft a nasal twittering floats out—it is as though all the starlings in Trafalgar Square had suddenly been afflicted with adenoids—from girls in very high heels and girls in slippers, girls with long hair swinging round their shoulders and girls with hair chopped into ragged snippets, girls in yearning pairs and girls escorted by possessive boys; boys with long hair undulating back from their temples to meet like the edges of a mussel-shell just above their grubby necks, boys with crew-cuts, or worse, which make their faces stand out bleakly and weakly beneath their hair-brush crowns, neat boys in ill-pressed suits, large-eyed boys with sullen expressions on sallow faces, wearing long loose coats, ties with knots two inches across and shoes with crepe soles an inch thick. Their voices bark and wail and whimper in a horrible agglomeration of cockney and second-hand American, and in them the old world meets the new on the lowest possible level of shoddiness.

The nearer the stage the higher the average age—and, of course, the price; the stalls present a bewildering array of quite unplaceable people. A quiet elderly couple sit placidly, hands folded in laps, for all the world as though they were awaiting the tea-time concert in a seaside Winter Garden; next to them a burly man leans stiffly forward, his thin hair plastered down, his ears protruding, his nose broken, his cheeks red and corrugated; his companion is a tiny, beautiful, elderly woman, her blue-tinted greying hair swept back in involuted, expensive waves which expose blazing diamond ear-rings; then a quite young couple, perhaps newly married and up from the country, both with thin, pointed faces, and both looking nervously around as though they expected to be attacked; then a very fat man, an assembly of uneasily interlacing curves, squashed into his seat, bulging like a melting candle over the sides, his small face quivering on its chins and cowering behind a very large cigar; and with him, rather oddly, a pleasant-looking little boy of eight or so, sitting on the edge of his seat and trying to unscrew an ashtray with his thumb-nail; and just behind the boy a pair of metropolitan grotesques—a fox-faced man with shoulders padded to curve upwards and a toothbrush moustache, who exposes a gold tooth when he turns to grin at his neighbour, a raw pink blonde, ageless and patched together with crude cosmetics, her mouth a sea-anemone and her eyes twin oysters, her demeanour at once predatory and terrified.

Row after motley row stretches back in the immense auditorium; the dark reddish-brown, the gilt and the dusty plush fade as the lemon-yellow house lights go down and the footlights come up. The band cracks out a brassy common chord, and at once another; as the framed numbers at the side of the stage change from 1 to 2 a row of chorus girls prances on, dressed perhaps as sailors or ballerinas or hussars or birds of some metallic paradise. Twenty legs swing up and down together, and innumerable eyes follow with longing or resignation the line of shin and thigh; with grim fixed smiles the girls circle, kick, bob, swirl and at last dance off, with one eye on the wings and the other on the audience as they jog towards oblivion. When the curtains part again we shall almost certainly see some gleaming chromium apparatus upon which two or three well-muscled acrobats will perform feats of strength and skill; they will dive from trapeze to trapeze, swing by their heels supporting a spinning partner by their teeth, or, balanced upon what looks like a hatstand, with a partner quivering yet higher upon one upraised foot, will desperately twirl large cardboard rings upon their wrists and even round their necks. The band will play waltz tunes *pianissimo* while they prepare, with many a flashing smile, their arduous feats, and each climax will be indicated by a roll on the drums. Alas! that such prompting should be necessary; but although the circus supplies the music-hall with so many of its acts, these are watched, it seems, with hardly more than respect; the agonized dwellers in discomfort must prolong each physical *tour de force* interminably to wring from the crowd a slow backwash of applause.

Only occasionally a team of acrobats appears whose evolutions, fast, elegant and sure, are delightful to the eye; and after the acrobats anything may happen. The footballing dogs, the bicycling chimpanzees, the bears that put out their tongues at their trainer do as they should without obvious distaste. Legions of impersonators persist in giving impressions of film stars not seen for ten years or more; American comedians of all shapes and sizes make jokes of which only a small proportion is intelligible on this side of the Atlantic; English comedians surfacing in the Metropolis from who knows where put on false moustaches, crack jokes about bookmakers, mothers-in-law and the National Health Service, and sometimes even today finish up with a sentimental recitation in the manner of the late Nosmo King. But, when it comes to the point, we must admit that all these—along with the jugglers and ventriloquists, the ballet dancer who year in year out does nothing but spin in ever-diminishing circles, the puppets, the occasional troupe of clowns, the tap dancers and jazz pianists, the gentlemen who perform extravagant antics in time with other people's gramophone records, who play several wind instruments at once or imitate brass ones—all these are incidentals, hors-d'oeuvres. Their thankless task it is to keep us reasonably happy until it is time to bring on the real attraction; for, with a half-climax just before the interval, the evening's entertainment is built up to burst into splendour, like a wave on a sunlit beach, around the godlike being who will hold the stage for almost the whole of the second half of the programme.

Whoever he (or, of course, but much less often, she) may be, his impending appearance in London will have been much publicized; his departure from the United States (he is almost certain to have come from that inexhaustible witch's cauldron) will have been noted, his arrival in this country will be amply reported. If his private life is in some disorder, so much the better. Gossip writers, admitted in a bevy a hundred strong to his hotel suite, will hurry away to write paragraphs suggesting long and confidential conversations. The sale of his gramophone records will mount rapidly;

and if he proves a success in this one grubby corner of London, his name will resound inescapably in cottage and palace alike. His is fame on a scale which would have dumbfounded the old originals of the music-halls, those rough and ready men who quelled, with jaunty ditties and powerful voices, the even rougher and readier patrons of what were once public-house annexes.

It would have astonished hardly less the Edwardian heroes of the music-hall's heyday; but the devotion, or at least enthusiasm, aroused by our modern entertainers is different in kind, and perhaps less desirable. Marie Lloyd and George Robey, Dan Leno and Albert Chevalier were human beings from the same world as their audiences, seeing it from a highly individual point of view, but a part of it and finding their material, however fantastic, in the mishaps, deprivations and daydreams of lower middle-class English life; even the coons made themselves up so that nobody could possibly mistake them for real Negroes. But the large-scale entertainer today must find material which is funny in New England and in England, in Florida and Ohio and California and British Columbia; and he must do so at a time when taste has largely turned away from silent clowning. So, he is compelled to seize upon some basic human weakness—Jack Benny is mean, Bob Hope is permanently vain and suspicious—and exploit it for all it is worth, if not more; as a variation, be rude about some well-known colleague or encourage some well-known colleague to be rude about him. A bunch of expert chefs in the shape of gag-writers get to work upon these simple recipes, and concoct from them a flow of machine-made wit. The result is an act which requires great skill in the performer; it is often extremely funny; but it does not seem to establish any enduring bond between player and audience. Several English comedians do, in fact, with homelier material establish this relationship; but they do not, unfortunately, carry very big guns; perhaps one cannot, in the long run, do both—and it is still an open question whether the prodigious Danny Kaye is the exception which proves this particular rule, if it is a rule.

One thing all our great variety players—except Maurice Chevalier—have in common; they are slaves to the microphone. These sinister objects rise like snakes from the boards of every stage; but the ancient order is reversed, for instead of the snake dancing for the charmer, the charmer must dance round the snake. Yet the coming of the microphone has not been all loss; as far as the comedians are concerned it has immensely widened the range of humour open to them, and enables relatively subtle jokes to be shared by many more people at the same time.

If that were all, all were well; but the music-hall is not the undisputed domain of the comedian, any more than the circus is that of the clown. It is still the *music*-hall, and the great majority of those who have come to top the bill at the Palladium have in fact been not comedians but singers.

Well, more or less. They certainly appeal to the stupid, or sensuous, side of us, and an inward unity in their part of the show certainly creates for us a mood. Even Gracie Fields, who ranges from the exuberant absurdity of 'The Biggest Aspidistra' to the revolting commercial religiosity of a setting of the Lord's Prayer, provides an immensely satisfying inner unity. But few of her fellow luminaries range as wide as she does; for the most part they are at pains to make all their songs sound the same. Some are relatively straight-forward, some exploit a particular foible—notoriously Johnnie Ray, a slim young man who not only weeps at the microphone himself but urges every-body else to do so too: 'Cry! It's no secret, you'll feel better if you cry.' Mr Ray has put it on record that his lachrymose bellowing is his conception of the words Faith and Hope. But Mr Ray is an extreme case; better by far the wicked, old-fashioned enchantment spread by the fabulous Sophie Tucker, proclaiming in pink satin and sequins that nobody loves a fat girl, or the dark artistry of Lena Horne, celebrating the fall of the walls of Jericho, rapt and trembling from head to foot, her eyes glittering and her pace relentless. These singers mostly come from America, but that means nothing; behind them lie a thousand years of living and suffering all over the world; and the songs we hear have been cooked up from the plaintive Celtic chants of the ceilidh, the long lamenting of the Jews and the Negroes' exile from Africa. And they have all boiled down to a series of lugubrious ditties about disappointed love—but disappointment with a difference.

The newcomer to the Palladium, returning to his seat after the interval—having, if he is wise, waited until the chorus girls have pattered through their routine—will probably find that the band has left the orchestra pit and set itself up at the back of the stage. After some unfortunate juggler or con-jurer has worked off his tricks to an impatient round of applause the band strikes up, a piano is wheeled in, and the conductor, beating time with one hand and holding a microphone in the other, announces the hero of the night.

The great man—let us once again assume that it is a man—either strides confidently on like a majority shareholder at an annual general meeting or rushes in as though there were a mad bull advancing on the wings; in which case he will bring himself up all standing at the piano's edge, beaming round the house in acknowledgment of a welcome equally compounded of normal applause and wails of joy. Not that his appearance is at all striking, for he is a thick-set man of medium height, wearing a very long double-breasted coat which makes his legs look even shorter than they are. He has a heavy jowl, eyes rather close together and very short, fuzzy hair. He then says what everybody says—that he is glad to be here, or to be back, as the case may be; and adds that he is feeling terribly nervous. Then he announces that next week his latest gramophone record will be on sale, and that he would like to sing us one of the numbers, which has been a great success back in the States.

And then, huddling up to the microphone, he sings. His voice, even as it comes through the loudspeakers, is no more than a light baritone; it is clear that he has no idea how to use it to the best advantage, and if one is sitting close enough one can see the tendons of his neck tying themselves in knots as he negotiates some awkward passage (to be quite fair, one can often see the same thing in an opera-house). His songs are, like everybody else's, nightmare dirges; he pounds away at the duplicity of women, expresses his anguished love in a strangulated crescendo, and brings every song to an end on the same high note (high for him), the same flick of the arm as he stands with his head back and his veins swelling.

Is his success, then, a haphazard thing due to some personal emanation which really sensitive natures automatically reject? By no means; this is a highly skilled performance. His words, such as they are, are perfectly clear. He keeps an unshakable rhythm going; and within that rhythm he so cunningly plays upon note-values, here slowing a little, there quickening a little, he so neatly times and grades his little sharp scoops upward, and his plunging husky scoops downward, that the effect is, if you are capable of responding at all, almost unbearably erotic; that squat and sweating gentleman on the stage can play upon the senses of the girls upstairs more surely than could any amorist at closer quarters.

Soon the cries for old favourites come down; he complies—pauses to present his accompanist—complies again, like the hero of *The Country Wife*. He sings on, at times through an almost continuous shuddering chatter of excitement, or excitation. Sometimes he stops and calms the girls down a little, or pretends to try to. As the troubadours once sang of courtly love to refresh the ladies who knew every move in the game, this modern minstrel sings of broken love, in pulses of ecstasy reproduced at twenty times life size, for baffled young people whose sensuous and stupid selves imagine a rapture they will be lucky ever to know.

[1954]

Jack Lambert, for many years Literary Editor of the SUNDAY TIMES, *might have become a dramatic critic in the grand tradition of A. B. Walkley and James Agate if he had not had the mischance to serve his paper at the same time as Sir Harold Hobson (another early S.B. contributor). As soon as the present Editor took over* THE SATURDAY BOOK *he realised that Lambert's critical sense and his fastidious use of language were ideal elements for our pages. He got him to write on Noel Coward, 'the Blithe Spirit of the Twenties', in No. 12, and for No. 19 he persuaded him to write on one of his chief recreations, singing.*

On Being an Actor

LAURENCE OLIVIER

ATH NOT A JEW HANDS, eyes, organs, dimensions the same as a Christian? Is he not fed with the same food, and hurt with the same weapons? If he is pricked, does he not bleed? And if he is tickled, does he not laugh? These are questions that every schoolboy knows. A Jew is a human being. So is an actor. The actor, who is a human being in all other respects, is also a human being in this: he works for his living. Acting, like, say, bricklaying, is a job.

It is an exhausting job, too, though few people realize it. Ask any ordinary man if he would like to be a coal miner, and he will admit that in a very short time the work would knock him physically to pieces. Yet he probably thinks that he could—physically—take acting in his stride. He might say that acting requires æsthetic appreciation, a certain kind of temperament, a strong memory, a capacity for working at the wrong times of day, and that for these reasons he wouldn't like it. But it is a hundred to one that, looked at purely from the point of view of the physical strain that it entails, he regards acting as a soft job.

Yet a year's acting would physically wreck an ordinary man—if he were not trained for it. In particular it would wreck his throat. Nothing on the stage is what it seems to be. That drawing-room, which at first sight looks exactly like a real drawing-room, has only three side walls. The food on the table is not real food. That jewel, which flashes like the morning star, is not worth three-and-sixpence. And the whisper which sounds like a whisper in the front row of stalls is—if a whisper at all—a very special kind of whisper. It can be heard three hundred feet away at the back of the gallery.

Most people talk from the backs of their throats. They articulate their words with their throat muscles. If they want to speak louder than usual, they force these throat muscles. Now this would ruin them on the stage. No throat would stand this treatment of being forced for long. It would become permanently hoarse. It would give out. The first thing an actor has to do, then, is to learn how to speak without straining his throat muscles.

I myself studied speaking under Miss Elsie Fogerty—that most admirable of teachers—at the Central School of Speech Training. Miss Fogerty put her pupils through a most rigorous course, all of it designed to make them place their voices anteriorly. Much of it consists of breathing exercises, for on proper breathing successful speaking depends. You have to breathe from the diaphragm, whereas the great temptation is to breathe from the chest. If you do, you quickly get out of breath, and your voice gets tired. But if you bring up from the diaphragm a clear stream of air, allowing it to pass through the throat without affecting the muscles of that organ, and do not begin to mould it into words and distinct sounds till it reaches the teeth and the tip of the tongue—why, then you can on the stage every night shake whole theatres with sound and fury, and keep on doing it for years without feeling any vocal strain at all.

These, of course, are merely the mechanics of speaking. They are in essence simple enough; but even so they cannot be mastered without concentrated work.

The voice is in fact almost the actor's main instrument, and it has to be guarded with care. It is an odd thing that actors find that their voice is never so good, so responsive, so moving as when they are on the verge of a cold. That great tenor Gigli would often go to his doctor and say, 'I'm in for trouble. My voice was magnificent last night.'

It is possible, if one speaks properly, to give quite a good performance even when the larynx is strained by a cold. In such circumstances, it could be done by talking through the throat. I once saw that fine player Frank Vosper give a superb performance of Henry VIII in Clifford Bax's *The Rose without a Thorn* when he had a bad attack of laryngitis. If I have a cold before a performance I take a teaspoonful of brandy—no more. At other times I never in any circumstances drink anything intoxicating before a show.

When you are qualified to speak your part, you have then to learn it. Some people find this difficult to do. It is said that Sir Herbert Tree was always liable to disconcerting lapses of memory; that he used to hide prompters in all parts of the stage—behind sofas and under tables. So I consider myself lucky in having the sort of memory that learns lines easily, and then forgets them as soon as the run of the particular play in which they occur is over. It takes me about a fortnight to forget completely a really big part. The other evening I was talking to a friend who remarked that he remembered *The Rats of Norway* as a play full of an odd tortured beauty. It was obvious from the way he spoke that he expected me to remember it. But I couldn't. Keith Winter's very moving drama of the young schoolmaster who began his career full of ideals, and then saw them broken down into cynicism and despair, had completely passed from my mind. Not for some time did I recall that it provided me with one of my most effective earlier parts in London.

I do not wish to appear to pose as an authority on the history of the theatre. I have never pretended to be a man of theory. All my efforts have been directed towards getting some small grasp of the practical side of acting. But here I should like to make a suggestion. It is, I believe, a more or less generally recognized fact that somewhere about a hundred years ago a great change came over if not the character, at least the behaviour, of Englishmen. People like Oliver Cromwell or Horatio Nelson would think nothing of breaking down into tears in public. They showed their emotions in the most unashamed manner. They knew nothing of that stiff upper lip which Dr Arnold standardized at Rugby to the admiration and imitation of other public schools. Until the middle of the last century Englishmen, like the people of the Continent, seem to have behaved instinctively much more than they do now. They acted upon impulse rather than upon thought.

It is my impression that this holds true of the theatre as it does of other walks of life. Till about 1840 the theatre was a Bohemian, uninhibited, lighthearted, reckless, rather scandalous sort of place. It did not attract thoughtful people. And it is difficult to believe that the men and women who found their living in it did much in the way of serious study. They relied on temperament to carry them through.

But a century ago there arose an actor of a different kind. William Charles Macready is the forerunner of the modern type of actor: the man who finds that acting is something more than a way of merely instinctively expressing his personality. Macready was as studious as a university don. His days were spent in devoted contemplation and inner argument. 'Without study,' he said, 'I can do nothing . . . Inspiration is all very well, but the painstaking labour of a man with a conscience is better.' You have to think about each scene in your performance carefully before starting—such was his experience; otherwise you do not get evenness in the various big moments.

This rule was neglected even by so great an actor as Edmund Kean, with the result that his performances were never of level quality throughout. Some of his scenes were as soul-shaking as anything known in theatrical history: others were flat and poor. To see him, said Coleridge, was like reading Shakespeare by flashes of lightning. There was the blinding inspiration, and then the gulf of darkness.

The modern player follows the example of Macready and not of Kean. That is why, on the whole, contemporary actors, when they are good are good all through a play, and do not die of drink before they are fifty. The value of study—serious, painstaking study, such as a man might undertake who is reading for a university degree—is well known; for example, to my friend John Gielgud.

When Gielgud is contemplating the production of a Shakespearean or other Elizabethan drama, he does not hesitate to consult the best literary authorities. For his *Midsummer Night's Dream* and *Duchess of Malfi* he availed himself of the assistance of Neville Coghill, who is a don at Oxford, and of George Rylands, of Cambridge. Every ambitious actor has something of the Gielgud attitude in this respect.

If, for example, I am preparing a Shakespeare part, I look into the Variorum edition to get the different readings and interpretations. I read Granville-Barker's invaluable prefaces, which are full of brilliant practical suggestions; and I read Hazlitt. True, there is nothing very practical in Hazlitt. But he fires the mind. He sets it alight. Consider a passage like this—on Kean's Richard III.

> Mr Kean did equal justice to the beautiful description of the camps the night before the battle, though, in consequence of his hoarseness, he was obliged to repeat the whole passage in an underkey. His manner of bidding his friends good night, and his pausing with the point of his sword drawn slowly backward and forward on the ground, before he retires to his tent, received shouts of applause. He gave to all the busy scenes of the play the greatest animation and effect. He filled every part of the stage. The concluding scene, in which he is killed by Richmond, was the most brilliant. He fought like one drunk with wounds; and the attitude in which he stands with his hands stretched out, after his sword is taken from him, had a preternatural and terrific grandeur, as if his will could not be disarmed, and the very phantoms of his despair had a withering power.

To read a passage like that sets the mind of the actor aglow. It shows what tremendous heights fine acting can reach—even though Kean *was* hoarse, which he wouldn't have been if Miss Fogerty had shown him how to manage his voice properly. But Kean belonged to the instinctive school of actors who knew not the methods of Macready.

Having got myself into the proper mood of enthusiasm, I then try to find out what I can about the actions that past actors have invented to accompany the speeches of the character I am studying. Little pieces of 'business' are often most illuminating. My friend Roger Livesey suggested that slight nervous cough with which my film performance of Henry V begins, whilst I am still supposed to be a player acting the part for the first time, and I thought it rather a clever touch.

In 1833, by the way, while Macready was delivering the St Crispin speech, his truncheon broke—one of those mishaps to which actors are periodically liable. They do not cause as much distress as the public might imagine. One afternoon when I was playing *Macbeth* at the Old Vic, my crown fell off as I jumped on to the table in the banquet scene; but I am told that it did not much interfere with the effect of the performance.

[1945]

Dilys Powell contributed a biographical and critical study of Laurence Olivier, with many photographic illustrations, to No. 6.

Salvador Dali's portrait of Laurence Olivier in the part of Henry V was one
of the illustrations to Ivor Brown's survey of 'The Golden Age of Acting'—
by which he meant the 'sixties and 'seventies—in No. 20.

ASPECTS OF ART

The Return
of Art Nouveau

The illustrations shown here are
from Barbara Morris's scholarly
reassessment of the Art Nouveau
movement which she was asked
to contribute in 1962, when Art
Nouveau was right out of fashion.
The book-binding opposite is
Beardsley's design for his *Morte
d'Arthur*, 1893. The copper
plaque above was made by
Margaret Macdonald and her
sister in Glasgow in 1896. On the
right is a vase of Gallé glass.

Howard Spring on L. S. Lowry

In 1957 only a few art critics with their ears to the ground had heard of L. S. Lowry, although he was then seventy and had been painting and exhibiting in Manchester for some forty years. Howard Spring was one of the few who had been aware of Lowry's work since he was a reporter on the staff of the *Manchester Guardian* after the First World War. In his first novel, published in 1934, Howard Spring wrote about a mythical artist living in Manchester who said there were only two artists worth looking at in the town—himself and Lowry. In his later novel, *Fame is the Spur* (1940), he made the chief character, Hamer Shawcross, a collector of Lowry's work. Having admired an early Lowry in Spring's house in 1957 we asked him to write an appreciation for *The Saturday Book*.

The painting above is 'The Fever Van', 1935, and is in the Walker Art Gallery, Liverpool. The street scene opposite, 1956, came from the collection of Mrs John Mann.

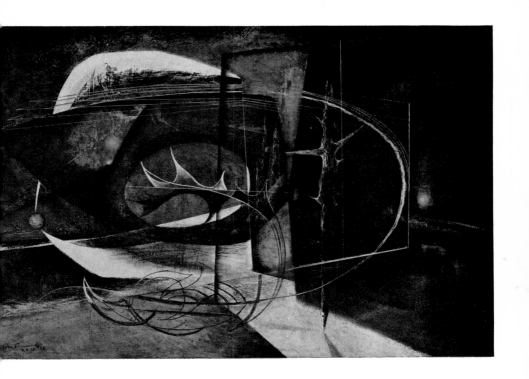

Sir Herbert Read on John Tunnard

As often happens when an artist is an individualist and is ahead of his time, his work tends to be ignored as he grows older, and this is what happened to one of the first of the English surrealists, John Tunnard, who had a style that might be regarded as geometrical, based on shapes and forms with little representational meaning, but in fact closely related to animal and plant life and marine objects.

Feeling that his work was undervalued, even when he had become an Academician, we asked Sir Herbert Read to evaluate it for our No. 25. His essay was an extraordinarily perceptive one, and the illustrations (one of which was specially commissioned as a frontispiece to *The Saturday Book*) were charged with an unearthly but compulsive beauty. They needed colour of course, which has to be dispensed with in the two subjects reproduced here. The one opposite is called 'New Day', dated 1959, and is from the collection of Paul Stobart. Above is 'Release', 1960, by courtesy of the McRoberts & Tunnard Gallery.

Felix Kelly's Romantic America

Felix Kelly combines a precise and scholarly knowledge of architecture with a controlled romantic imagination. Writing about him in No. 29, Robert Harling said: 'He is a rare master of the art of evoking the *mood* of a house . . . the misty grandeur which attends a Stately Home set remotely and preposterously on some moorland eminence; the gaiety of an old rectory newly inhabited by the carefree children of pagan parents; the melancholy of a great Palladian mansion set in the misty keys of the Deep South'. *The Saturday Book* reproduced eight such examples of 'Romantic America': in Alabama, New Orleans, on the Mississippi, at Martha's Vineyard, and on the Connecticut shores. All give a kind of mythical dimension to old houses, tramcars, riverboats and sailing ships, vintage cars and ancient locomotives. Treasure trove for nostalgiacs!

136

Priestley as Painter

Britain's senior Man of Letters is also a competent actor (who once played the chief part in *When We are Married* when the star fell sick), a knowledgeable musician, and a by no means negligible painter. For No. 29 we invited him to write on what he modestly described as a holiday pastime. He has travelled in many parts of the world, and wherever he has gone he has returned with the equivalent of tourists' snapshots, painted in gouache, often on tinted paper, and representing his own view of what he saw. The example shown above is his view of the fantastic rocks of Meteora in Thessaly. Other landscapes illustrated in *The Saturday Book* were in Guatemala, Georgia, California, Kerry, Wales and—of course—Yorkshire. His account of his aims and methods, his problems and pleasures, must have given encouragement (and good advice) to thousands who share his recreation.

137

'Perspective' (Madame de Récamier), 1950. *Private Collection, U.S.A.*

'La Révélation du Présent', 1936. *Coll. Marc Hendrick, Brussels*

The World of René Magritte

In 1958 there was an exhibition of the Urwater Collection of surrealist paintings at the Tate Gallery in London and the present editor became aware for the first time of the distinctive vision of the Belgian surrealist, René Magritte. Magritte had, in fact, participated in the surrealist exhibition in London in the 'thirties, and that enterprising collector Edward James had commissioned work from him. But interest in the early surrealists had been smothered by the towering talents of Picasso, Braque and the Cubists. The delicate realism of Magritte, bringing purely representational images into "impossible" relationship, was in total contrast to the work of the fashionable masters. For No. 19 we asked an old friend of Magritte, E. L. T. Mesens, to sum up his work; and the very impressive *Saturday Book* feature undoubtedly sparked off intense interest in this modest, bowler-hatted, bourgeois Belgian artist, whose fame is now international and whose paintings now command vast prices. The Editor cherishes the illuminating correspondence he had with this extraordinary genius whilst the feature was in preparation.

139

Above: 'La Magie Noire', I, 1934. *Coll. Mme. Happé-Lorge, Brussels*
Opposite: 'La Durée Poignardée', 1939. *Art Institute of Chicago*.

The Discovery of
Art Déco

IN THE THIRTY-SECOND ISSUE of *The Saturday Book* we devoted a large part of the book to a retrospect over fifty years to the fashions, social life, arts and entertainments of 1923. We asked the painter and art historian Martin Battersby to write about the fashionable arts of that year, and he summarized them under the general title of Art Déco.

Martin Battersby traced the origins of the Art Déco movement back to Art Nouveau, through the artists of the Russian ballet and the designs of Bakst and Erté, to the furniture of Ruhlmann and Groult, the clothes designed by Paul Poiret, and the glass of Lalique.

In the following year we invited Philippe Garner, of Sothebys Belgravia, to write about the Art Déco sculpture in bronze and ivory produced in the 'twenties. Demetre Chiparus, one of whose figures is reproduced overleaf, was perhaps the most distinctive artist of the movement, combining Egyptian themes (deriving from the opening of Tutankhamen's tomb in 1922/3) with stage fantasy—depicting dancers with full, heavy, dipping-hem skirts, standing on marble and onyx bases. Frederick Preiss was an Austrian who specialized in more realistic figures, such as the 'Blessing Girl' opposite, and the cabaret girl on the right (Collection of Bryan Catley).

These figures were once regarded as *kitsch*, and the Editor confesses that this was his view when he bought a Preiss tennis-girl in 1973 for seventy pounds in a country sale and quickly sold it to a dealer for £200. An extra nought could now be added to the value of that piece!

Aubrey Beardsley

W. G. GOOD

UBREY BEARDSLEY gave his name to a period in English art and letters, but in the decades after his death he did not command widespread attention. In recent years, however, the 'Beardsley period' has been, in common with *Art Nouveau*, the subject of renewed interest. The great changes which have come about since the turn of the century result in the period being far more distant from us in spirit than a normal life span, and the time has come when it can be seen with fresh eyes.

Beardsley was born at Brighton in August, 1872, and died in March, 1898. For one with so short a working life the quantity of his output was remarkable, and the speed and range of his development astonishing. Signs of the tuberculosis which killed him were evident from childhood, and, as may be seen from his letters, behind the alternate hopes and despairs occasioned by his rallies and relapses there was the grim presage, most courageously sustained, that his life would be short. He worked with feverish energy, passing from childish drawings to the highest technical mastery in a decade. It is profitless to speculate concerning the advances he might have made had he lived longer, but it is probable that he had already given of the most which was in him; that the world lost many a lovely drawing is certain, but it is unlikely that the quality of the best which we have could have been much exceeded.

Beardsley was intelligent, but his mind was not of the commanding order of genius whose work induces a sense of awe by its intellectual force. Content, to the extent that his malady and the modest rewards of his work allowed, to enjoy the good things of life, he had no message for the world, no philosophy to propound. Elements of caricature, of eroticism, and of pure lyrical loveliness are seen in his work, but when he sat down to draw his dominant intention was no more than to 'make a picture'. Thus it is that although many of his designs are striking in content, their main appeal lies in his skill in employment of pen and ink and particularly in the immense clarity, strength and sureness of his line. Beardsley in modern issues of his work has often been ill served, the printing blocks having been made from reproductions, with consequent loss of definition. In preparing the illustrations for the present article pains have been taken to work wherever possible from the drawings themselves, and the artist's limpid brilliance is seen at only one stage removed.

Opposite: Art Déco figure by Demetre Chiparus. *Collection: Bryan Catley.*

Commissioned to illustrate an edition of *Le Morte Darthur* which was issued in parts, the first in June, 1893, Beardsley made approximately 350 chapter headings. No great evidence of his future mastery appears, but the work imposed a discipline which brought its reward. Before this task was complete he was engaged in illustrating Wilde's *Salome*, from which 'The Stomach Dance' is here reproduced. In this is seen his skill in the handling

of black and white masses and in the portrayal of the human figure, the forward thrust of the dancer's body being most vividly conveyed.

It is said that the publisher, John Lane, aware of the impish delight which Beardsley took in introducing improper detail into his drawings, scrutinised the Salome set with special care. Two drawings, indeed, were bowdlerised for publication, but Lane's perception evidently failed him when he examined the demoniac musician in the present design.

The Salome drawings, sometimes irrelevant (Salome performed the dance of the seven veils), impudent (two designs contain caricatures of Wilde) and erotic, show in their swirling, sinuous lines the influence of the Japanese colour print and of *Art Nouveau*. They were successful and have always deservedly attracted more attention than the play. The book was published in February, 1894, at about which time Lane planned *The Yellow Book*, 'An Illustrated Quarterly', appointing Beardsley as art editor. Above appears his strong cover design for Volume I, issued in April. The simple treatment of the face shows the vein of caricature so often present in his work.

Beardsley's four other designs for the first number were made conspicuous by their bold use of black and white masses and suggestive insouciance of style. The issue was a popular success and London 'turned yellow overnight'. Censorious voices, of course, were heard: *The Times*, referring particularly to the cover design, spoke of 'repulsiveness and insolence . . . a combination of English rowdyism with French lubricity'. But Beardsley's brief hour of general acclaim had come.

THE SCANDAL of the Wilde trials in the spring of 1895 induced Lane, unjustly, for the artist's appetites were entirely normal, to dismiss Beardsley, and thereafter his work was published by Leonard Smithers. In January, 1896, *The Savoy* was launched. Two numbers in pink boards were followed by six in blue paper, all with cover designs by the artist, that for No. 1 appearing here. *The Yellow Book* in the foreground, for which the manikin is showing his contempt, was removed from the published design.

The idyllic scene above was used for the prospectus for Volume V of *The Yellow Book*, although in the volume itself all Beardsley's contributions were suppressed. The design was later adapted for the covers of two of Smithers' Catalogues of Rare Books.

AB.

IN 1896 appeared an edition of Pope's *The Rape of the Lock* 'embroidered' by Beardsley. His designs are triumphal, both in reflecting the mood of the poem and in artistic skill. Particularly noteworthy are the drawing of the folds of the sleeve and the foreshortening of the figure in 'The New Star', above, and the rendering of material surfaces in 'The Battle of the Beaux and the Belles'. His 'dotted line' demanded the greatest control of hand and pen.

151

THE flowing freedom of design and the firm, supple outline of the figure make 'Apollo pursuing Daphne' particularly successful. The drawing is unfinished and in the original the left foot is pencilled in.

In the summer of 1896 Beardsley made a set of eight full-page illustrations for the *Lysistrata* of Aristophanes. A limited privately printed edition was issued by Smithers but the drawings were not published in England for many years in their unexpurgated form. On the right is the frontispiece.

The spirit of the play has been caught with true insight by the artist. Ribald and bawdily impudent, the illustrations have none of the prurience to be found in some earlier works; there is about them an air of maturity. Technically, they are superb, showing all Beardsley's mastery of his medium; he described them as 'in a way the best things I have ever done'.

LYSISTRATA.

Acknowledgements are made for permission to reproduce from Aubrey Beardsley's original drawings to R. A. Harari, Esq., the Brighton Art Gallery, the Fogg Museum of Art, Harvard University, and the Tate Gallery. [1965]

Canal Boat Baroque

WOODCUTS BY JOHN O'CONNOR

ANAL BOAT decoration is more severe and generally smaller in scale and form than that of the gypsy caravan. The shape of the boat itself, built for narrow bridges, tunnels, and wharves, denies excesses and frills. Canal boats in the 1960s still used a formal pattern of décor, in the style of road transport vehicles, and the rose and castle of the water bucket now have a strangely insecure position on the shelves of some departmental stores, although a few are still to be seen on the canals.

In brilliant green, scarlet, yellow, and pale blue, the landscape and flower pictures are painted in a tradition as rigid as a Gothic screen. Black is used as a foil to white cord in ship-shape order. These decorations are as incongruous in the setting of an English landscape, hedgerow, weed, and dark water, as a flowered teapot at a picnic. Cheap fairing pieces of china in the 1880s may be the direct source of inspiration for these designs, recalling as they do the crowded mantelpieces of a Victorian midland cottage.

154

157

Thoughts on Fish

ROBERT GIBBINGS

With wood-engravings by the author

N THE 28th February, 1832, Charles Darwin, writing of his first impressions of a tropical forest, noted in his diary: 'The delight one experiences in such times bewilders the mind; if the eye attempts to follow the flight of a gaudy butterfly, it is arrested by some strange tree or fruit; if watching an insect one forgets it in the stranger flower it is crawling over; if turning to admire the splendour of the scenery, the individual character of the foreground fixes the attention. The mind is a chaos of delight.' On the next day he noted that 'delight is a weak term for such transports of pleasure,' and after the third successive day in such surroundings he wrote: 'I can only add raptures to the former raptures.'

If Darwin had had the opportunities that I have had of wandering in tropical *submarine* forests of coral, he could only have repeated his expressions of delight with even greater emphasis, for though I have visited tropical forests ashore I have never felt such exaltation of spirit as when alone some twenty feet below the surface of the water on the coral reefs of Bermuda or the Red Sea. Unfortunately, when Darwin visited Tahiti and the neighbouring coral islands he had no such devices as shallow water diving helmets or aqualungs to enable him to move about at leisure below the surface. Like myself, when I first visited Tahiti almost a century later, he could at best only wade into the lagoons or float in a canoe and look down from above, seeing as little of the inhabitants in their grottoes as an aviator from his plane sees of human beings in their homes. He confessed to disappointment on the reefs and considered that earlier descriptions of their beauty had been in 'rather exuberant language.'

It was a French artist by name Chevelange who, living in Tahiti when I first visited the island, fired my enthusiasm for undersea drawing. It was his habit to put a clothes' peg on his nose, goggles over his eyes, and with one end of a long rubber tube in his mouth walk into the lagoon and submerge. The other end of the tube was fastened to a floating log and by this means he could obtain enough air to keep him below the surface for ten minutes or more at a time. Paper or canvas were, of course, impracticable, so he worked on copper.

When eventually I reached Bermuda, and some months afterwards the Red Sea, I had at each place the use of a diving helmet which rested on my shoulders and into which air was pumped from a launch overhead. At the time it seemed luxury: today, of course, the youngsters have aqualungs and webbed feet and are in no way restricted in their movements. But I didn't mind restrictions, I was happy wherever my feet chanced to meet the bottom —I nearly said dropped onto it but that would have been incorrect, for with the air in the helmet and the natural buoyancy of my body I reached the sea floor as light as a leaf. Everywhere around me was coral and everywhere in the coral were fish—coral that was ever-varying in growth, fish that were multitudinous in species, each one surpassing the last in colour or eccentricity of form. Truly, as Darwin said, 'the delight bewildered the mind': in foreground or distance, in near objects or in their background, there were for me transports of pleasure. Never had I seen such profusion of subjects for drawing, and having brought with me sheets of white xylonite, a substance unaffected by water which, when roughened with sandpaper takes pencil as well as any paper, I presently fell to work. The engravings on these pages were made from such drawings.

Fish! Most people think of them either as something to be enticed on to a hook or to be served on a plate. In fact, many of them are amongst the loveliest things in creation, as brilliant in colour and exquisite in form as any bird or butterfly, and with a power of changing colour unequalled by any other living creature, not excepting the chameleon. Fear, anger, hunger, love, change of light or background, may cause a fish to change colour as quickly as a maiden may blush and with infinitely greater variety of hue. Some species have as many as seven distinct phases, ranging from silver white to almost black, through many coloured patterns of stripes and spots. I have seen a blue fish come to rest beside a piece of brown weed and, almost before I had time to register in my brain the contrast in colour, that fish had become brown, hardly distinguishable from the weed. I have seen a passing shoal of golden fish, with horizontal turquoise stripes from nose to tail, come to a momentary halt. Even while they paused their bodies became suffused with dark vertical bands as on an English perch: when they moved the gold shone forth again, bright as lemons in sunshine. One day I caught several small silver fish and put them into a bucket; in a moment they were grey, almost invisible against their background. Fish can show temperament, too, by their colouring. A large bright yellow sea-bass when put into the Bermudian aquarium changed to a dark brown and remained so for several months; only when a golden fish of another species was put into the same tank did the first occupant flash forth into its normal colouring and so remain.

Not only do fish excel in colour but in movement, their effortless evolutions and gyrations as entrancing to watch as their power of coming to a sudden halt is surprising. Close acquaintance brings more surprises: there is a species in Bermuda known as the Four Eye, so called because on either side of the base of its tail is a large circular black-and-white spot which from a short distance has all the appearance of and is much more conspicuous than a real eye. So conspicuous is this ocellus that its owner when attacked relies

upon it for defence, and pretending that it is his true eye swims backwards
for a yard or two. Then while its aggressor is mystified it surprises again by
going ahead in the normal direction.

An individual that I met many times in the Red Sea was a small bronze fish
with vertical white bands which made its home among the high-powered
stinging tentacles of a giant anemone. To any other fish of the same size a

touch of the tentacles would mean instant paralysis and death; but in some strange way this particular creature has obtained immunity from the poison and so lives at ease and in safety where others dare not follow it. But as if to repay such hospitality and protection, it sometimes sallies forth from its cover and drives other small fish within reach of the tentacles. Biding its time until the anemone has finished its meal, it then picks up all it wants of the fragments that remain.

It would not be difficult to multiply instances of such seemingly intelligent yet instinctive behaviour; nor would it be difficult to prove that fish can distinguish between certain colours and in some cases remember them; but for the artist it is essentially the sight of these clouds of marine glory that enchants. As he wanders on the white coral sand among the reefs they come about him in their myriads, glinting like specks of dust in sunlight, glowing in kaleidoscopic radiance. The less he moves the closer they will come about him, even peering through the window of his helmet to inquire what manner of new inhabitant has joined them. Sad it is when he must return to upper air and feel again the weight of limbs. How heavy a leg can be as it is lifted over a gunwale! It often seemed to me that a flying fish has achieved the best of both worlds. Beautiful as a mackerel, it can spring from its natural element and glide as a bird among curling wave crests. Did not the Rev. Dr. Robinson in the reign of the first Elizabeth, being unexpectedly raised to the Bishopric of Carlisle, take to himself for armorial distinction a flying fish, symbolic of his sudden transfer from a lower to a higher medium?

And to return to home waters, whatever lowly place the majority of human beings assign to the piscine race, there are at any rate some among them of noble and ancient ancestry who have not only assumed the names of the fish of our own shores and rivers but have proudly borne their semblance on shield and helm. Families such as Tench, Breame, Chubb, Salmon, Roche, Herring, Whiting, Sprat, Haddock, Pike, Turbutt, Eales and Sturgeon have all thus honoured their namesakes. I would like to speak of that most beautiful of all marine residents, the mermaid, and of the many humans, from peers to admirals, who have hugged her to their shields, but that might lead me into deep waters. Here's long life, and may they never thirst, to all who love fish!

[1956]

Robert Gibbings entered our pages in No. 12, with some sketches of life on the Seine. To No. 14 he contributed some thoughts on well heads in Venice; to No. 17 a piece on the craft of which he was a master, wood-engraving. In his skill, his versatility, and his enjoyment of life he was a born SATURDAY BOOK *contributor.*

Even the creatures that have their being beneath the sea are not immune from the effects of the internal combustion engine. Here corals sway and fish are thrown about in the backwash from a passing steamer.

THE SCARBOROUGH LILY
Vallota purpurea

Cottage Window Plants

DRAWN AND DESCRIBED BY JOHN NASH

N THE LAST few years there has been an influx of a certain type of plant considered suitable for 'contemporary' house decoration. It is exemplified in the pages of the smarter journals that deal with the home. The chief virtue of these invaders lies in their decorative foliage. Their floral attributes are almost non-existent. Fashion (if we follow her) condemns us to have our plant companions dressed in a sober and severely cut garb, in keeping with air-conditioned rooms, streamlined bookcases, and tubular steel furniture. I cannot deny that in a place like the Festival Hall *Fatshedera Lizei* looks well enough. There, too, *Ficus elastica*, the India Rubber Plant, might be considered a decorative asset. But I should not care to rub shoulders with it in the home.

Plants grown in less sophisticated interiors, particularly cottage room and window plants, have as much variety as their smarter relatives, and more independence as they stand massed on the window still, contemplating life outside, with perhaps only an occasional backward glance at the room's occupants.

Then consider the names of cottage window plants. Titles such as Scarborough Lily, Creeping Sailor and Bridal Wreath have a rich suggestion of human association. By contrast, our smart 'modern' plants must, with a few exceptions, endure the coldness of botanical nomenclature. They have not attained the comfort of nickname.

The Scarborough Lily or *Vallota purpurea* is one of the most handsome of window plants. I have always thought there must be something exotic about our North-east-coast Spa (which I have never visited), and I am willing to think every other window there ablaze with the flowers of this plant. But I expect the reason for its name is more prosaic, and may denote a similar town in South Africa from which the plant was introduced in 1774. *Vallota* commemorates the name of Pierre Valot, a seventeenth-century French botanist. The plant has a sturdy stem, crowned with crimson red Amaryllis-like flowers, and shining strap-like leaves. It may be hardy in the open or against a wall.

Another South African plant, with the charming name of the Partridge-breasted Aloe—derived from the leaf markings—is an old favourite. *Aloe variegata* was introduced to England in 1790, and, like many succulent plants, provides the bulk of its own moisture in its thick, fleshy leaves. It should not be over-watered. Its tubular, soft orange-pink flowers make no attempt to distract from the handsome leaves.

China provides us with *Saxifraga sarmentosa*, a trailing member of that vast genus which puts out long runners, with young plants at intervals, like a strawberry. This habit of growth has earned it a wealth of nicknames— Mother of Thousands, Wandering Jew, Creeping Sailor, Aaron's Beard, etc. It has also relegated it to a life of suspension in pots and baskets, and in this way it provides a floral curtain. There is a form with leaves variegated in cream and red on the green ground.

Another plant of a trailing disposition is *Campanula isophylla*, which has an unusual distribution, being confined, in the wild state, to a few hundred yards of cliff on the Capo di Noli in North Italy. From this fastidious position it has been introduced to Great Britain and propagated extensively. It is now as common in greenhouse and window as it is rare on the precipitous rocks overlooking the Mediterranean. The open saucer-shaped bells, in white or violet blue, cover the plant in an almost solid cascade of bloom. I was once admiring a particularly fine specimen in a cottage window with my friend Clarence Elliott, and speculating about the chances of a deal with its owner, when, our noses pressed against the glass in our enthusiasm, we became aware of a duplicate cascade behind that of the plant, and encountered the stony glare of a bearded cottager.

The Pot Geraniums, or Zonal Pelargoniums, and the Show or Royal Pelargoniums, are some of the main standbys of window gardening, together with many species and varieties with scented leaves. How willingly and often they bloom! And what window is complete without the great scarlet heads of the old favourite Paul Crampel? To save space I would grow the miniature 'zonal,' Petit Henri, with its little cherry-pink blooms—almost a doll's house plant—and Black Vesuvius, so aptly named, with its dusty-purple leaves and flame coloured flowers. Of the Royal Pelargoniums, Black Prince is an old variety, with maroon purple flowers having a black centre. I like the well-shaped single varieties in all colours; modern doubles do not seem to have the perfect regular design of the double plants one sees depicted in old horticultural plates, and tend to be loose and untidy.

It is difficult to say why the Bridal Wreath, *Francoa ramosa*, a Chilean plant of the Saxifrage order, came to be a once popular member of the cottage window club, or so named. The genus which commemorates F. Franco, a Spanish promoter of botanical research in the sixteenth century, seems to have no particular connection with bridal occasions. The plant has lyrate leaves, like a turnip, and terminal heads of white flowers. It used to be trained and tied up to hooped sticks in its pot, but it is now more remembered by its name than seen.

Most succulent plants loosely referred to as 'cactus' can be grown in the window if watered judiciously before and at their flowering time, and kept dry in winter. Though a great number of species and varieties are available

CAMPANULA ISOPHYLLA

there would seem to be a few special favourites that can be seen in cottage windows. Those preferred are mostly varieties of *Phyllocactus* and *Cereus*, and perhaps *Epiphyllum* and *Crassula*. I have seen a small cottage window almost filled with a large scarlet-flowered *Phyllocactus* eagerly catching the sun's ray through the small panes of glass, with the black cottage cat curled up, snug and warm, among the tropical blooms.

The Rat's-tail Cactus, *Cereus flagelliformis*, was a favourite because it could be mounted on another, inverted, pot so that its prickly whip-like stems, studded with pink flowers, hung down all round and made a centrepiece to the window display. This old plant was introduced from Peru in 1690. *Epiphyllum truncatum* also has a graceful pendant or arching habit, and was sometimes grafted like a standard rose to give height. The soft, satin-textured flowers, in pink, crimson or purple, hang down from the ends of the flattened leaves, which look as if they had been bitten off at the extremities. Several colours used to be grafted on to one stem, and they must have presented a handsome appearance. *Epiphyllum* came from Brazil in 1818.

And what of the Aspidistra? We are told that its flowers, which appear at ground level, are fertilized by the movements of slugs. Maybe it thereby acquired a sense of inferiority which could only be lived down by a retired life indoors, where at least this shameful act could not be perpetrated. Here, safe from the attentions of revolting garden pests, it can lead a dignified existence, in some pot of fearful design and colour, thinking wistfully of its far-away home among the damp rocks of China or Japan, and asking only for an occasional leaf-sponging by the mistress of the house. Nicholson, in his *Dictionary of Gardening*, says that the Aspidistra is hardy. If that is so, should there not be a mass movement for the general release of countless Aspidistras from countless boarding houses, and a great enlightened planting out of them in dells and grottoes? But stay, we have forgotten the slugs!

The word Aspidistra is derived from the Greek *aspidiseon*, meaning a little round shield, in reference to the form of the flowers, which are about as big as a small cherry, cup-shaped, pendulous at ground level, with pointed petals of a fleshy chocolate hue and a mushroom-shaped stigma.

We must leave this fascinating subject and consider a few more plants likely to be met in cottage windows. The cultivated form of the popular *Cyclamen persicum* is certainly one of them. The parent of all these mass-produced varieties, introduced in 1731, is a native of Greece, Palestine and parts of Syria, and is quite one of the handsomest wild species. The pure form of its flowers, with their twisted propeller-like petals, has been pre-served in some of the cultivated forms, despite an increase in stature; in others it has been spoilt by over-emphasized twirls and frills. The best kinds I have in mind carry the flowers well above the mound of kidney-shaped leaves.

The Sultan of Zanzibar's Balsam, *Impatiens Sultani*, is quite a favourite in some windows. One hardly connects its flat blooms and bushy stature with those of other members of the family, such as *Impatiens glandulifera*, that towering annual which by means of its explosive seed dispersal has invaded our river banks and has most complicated flowers in which bags, wings, spurs and lips are wonderfully co-ordinated. *Begonia semperflorens*, a neat little plant when divorced from its usual role of carpet bedding—so beloved by park superintendents—has a charm of its own. And there are other Begonias with fine decorative leaves that can be used to grace the window-sill.

The Cobweb Houseleek, *Sempervivum arachnoidum*, figures in our list, grown, one presumes, for companionship and close observation, since it is perfectly hardy out of doors. And there is that other little cushiony subject, that ubiquitous sponge of greenery, *Selaginella Kraussiana*, which used to be employed as a foil to bright flowered plants in conservatories, since it loved damp and shade and grew happily under the greenhouse staging.

I cannot show any enthusiasm for that nasty plant, *Solanum capsicastrum*, the Winter Cherry, grown for its most uncherry-like berries, whose attach-

ZONAL PELARGONIUM

EPIPHYLLUM TRUNCATUM

ment to its stems can be only too easily imitated by artificial means.

But I must not spoil the pleasures of window gardening by carping tones. Here is enough to show the variety and interest to be had in this horticultural microcosm. Experiments might be made with other plants, so far unthought of, that might take kindly to window conditions. In that valuable book of reference, Nicholson's *Dictionary of Gardening* (1895) which, as regards its illustrations, has certainly not been equalled by any modern edition, there is a delightful woodcut depicting *Convolvulus arvensis*, the Lesser Bindweed, growing out of a hanging rustic basket such as only the Victorians could conceive, and very pretty it looks. In the garden the malignant growth of the plant precludes any enjoyment of its real beauties; but the jaded gardener might derive a sadistic pleasure from seeing it suspended and confined in at least one situation where it is both harmless and decorative. To the window with it! [1957]

The Sailing Barge

JOHN LEWIS

With wood-engravings by Zelma Blakely

AILING BARGES were in their day the most humble, least considered of commercial sailing craft. They were to be found, in their different types, in most of the shallow estuaries of Europe from the Tagus to the Thames. They carried every kind of bulk cargo on coastal passages and up rivers and creeks. They even carried haystacks on their decks. When London had tens of thousands of cab-horses and cart-horses there was a constant procession up the Thames of these 'stackies' as they were called. Their deck cargo stretched almost from one end of the vessel to the other. The mainsail had to be brailed up and a jib set on the bowsprit. The skipper would sit on the top of the stack shouting orders to the mate at the wheel. These stackies came from East Anglian and Kentish ports and often picked up their cargo from farm landings far up some tidal river. Though they were such a lowly form of water-borne transport they provided an inspiration for a whole spectrum of landscape painters. Constable painted them; Whistler etched them; Doré drew them; even Arnold Bennett sketched them.

The Thames sailing barge developed during the nineteenth century from a swim-headed lighter, that carried a bit of sail to help push it along, into a highly sophisticated sailing machine. Even though at a first impression the basic shape of a barge may be a bit like a shoe box, further investigation shows considerable subtlety in the lines. The flat bottom, which is so convenient both for cargo stowage and for sitting on the mud, does not make for a weatherly hull. A sailing ship, if it is to do more than just blow downhill before the wind, needs some grip of the water. This is usually provided by a keel. In the case of the Thames barge, two lee-boards, one on each side somewhat forward of midships, which can be lowered or raised, give this very necessary windward quality. Flat-bottomed Dutch craft have used such lee-boards for centures.

The average-sized river barge will carry 140 tons of cargo and is over 80 ft long and 18 ft beam and draws about 7 ft when fully loaded. Her main and top masts tower some 70 ft above the deck. A vast Oregon pine sprit 56 ft long pivots from the foot of the mast just above deck level. This massive pole provides the answer to the question how these really quite large vessels are handled and sailed by a man and a boy—some man and some boy! The sprit provides the support for the peak of the mainsail, which never has to be lowered to the deck but is brailed up like a theatre curtain. The topsail likewise remains aloft but can be set or furled from the deck.

Though the East Coast was the main trading ground of the sailing barge, the larger coasting class went further afield. Some of these barges were of a considerable size. The largest barges ever built belonged to F. T. Everard and Sons, Ltd., of Greenhithe in Kent. These were the *Alf Everard, Ethel Everard, Fred Everard* and *Will Everard*. They were all built of steel and were 97·6 ft long, 23·1 ft beam and drew 9·6 ft. They carried a cargo of 300 tons and were driven by 5,600 sq ft of sail. The truck of their topmasts was over 100 ft above the decks. They were mule rigged with standing gaffs on their tall mizzen masts. These Everard barges were all employed in the coasting trade, but one or two barges travelled a lot further. In the 1920's the *Norvic* and the *Cymric* belonging to Goldsmith sailed out to the Amazon in South America. They were boom-rigged for the voyage, their sprits being considered too dangerous for ocean voyaging. A year or so later three other barges sailed to British Guiana, where they traded for many years.

I remember one limpid summer evening, standing on Mistley Quay on the River Stour in Essex. Several hundred swans were gathered in the channel. From down river a barge was running up before a following wind. As she came level with the Baltic Wharf the crew brailed up her mainsail and dropped her foresail and mizzen. Then, under topsail alone, she came sailing towards the swans and the quay. Mistley Quay is in the form of a hollow curve. The barge still appeared to be travelling fast, but the tide was ebbing against her. As she came alongside, the mate, with a stern line in his hand, jumped ashore and took a turn round a bollard. He was back on board in an instant, picked up a bow line, jumped ashore again and made his line fast. The barge's way was checked and she edged up to the quay, touching it as gently as if she had been one of the swans. The crew consisted of a boy of seventeen and his young brother who could not have been more than twelve or thirteen.

I congratulated them on their performance. 'Nothing in it,' the elder one answered, 'that is, if you been born to it.' That about summed it up, though Bob Roberts, skipper of *Cambria*, the last coasting barge to trade under sail, once said: 'Crews of coasting barges need to be either bloody fools or horses.'

I first became interested in sailing barges when I was an art student living in Deptford High Street. I spent a lot of time down in the docks drawing these handsome red-sailed work boats. Later, I made closer acquaintance with them when I had my own little sailing boat, which I kept alongside a barge-repair yard at the entrance to Faversham Creek. I never ceased to wonder at the manner in which these barges would turn up the narrowest of creeks. The bargemen used to say, if they were travelling light, that they would float if it had been raining. This ability is reflected in the often re-peated, probably apocryphal story of the barge skipper taking his barge up to Landermere at the head of Hamford Water.

BARGES AT PIN MILL

'Joe!' he shouted to his mate who was up forward, 'is that sea-gull swimming or walking?'

'Walking,' answered the mate.

'Time to come about then, Lee-oh!'

Sailing out of the river Swale, we used to be passed by barges sailing two knots to our one. A pair of Cremer's barges, close-hauled, racing into Faversham Creek, barely heeling over, their spars and sails silhouetted against a piled-up cumulus sky, is a sight I shall never forget.

After the 1939–45 war I went to work in Ipswich, and within the first week of arriving there I saw eight barges turning up the Orwell together on a flood tide. Little did I realise that I would never see such a sight again. Ipswich was the most important East Coast port for barges. More than once we saw over two dozen sailing barges lying in Ipswich docks, and not one of them had an auxiliary engine. This was up to 1950. By 1970 only one sailing barge was still trading. This was the *Cambria*, a former Everard barge, that was kept going by her indomitable skipper, Bob Roberts. Today there is not one sailing barge still trading. Those barges that are still trading have been stripped of their sails and spars and are now power driven.

In 1947 I moved to Manningtree on the Stour. Manningtree and Mistley are to all intents and purposes one place, and Mistley has the pride of claiming to be the home of probably the greatest of the barge-owning families—the Horlocks. They were certainly the greatest of the racing-barge owners.

Races for trading barges on the river Thames were started by William Henry Dodd in 1863. Dodd, a muck-contractor and refuse collector, had made a fortune in this unsalubrious trade, and earned the nickname of the 'Golden Dustman'. He must assuredly have been the model for Mr Boffin, the 'Golden Dustman' in Dickens's *Our Mutual Friend*, published the year after the first barge race was sailed.

Dodd's aim was not only to provide a sporting event, but also to improve the design, build and equipment of the barges as well as the status of the men who sailed them. The races proved a triumphant success, and soon it was noted that the appearance of the barges had greatly improved, as had the gear. By the third year patched sails had disappeared and the barges were undergoing the kind of preparation usually reserved for racing yachts.

Bargemen do not like being passed when under way. Dodd knew what he was about. This competitive spirit was given plenty of opportunity in these sailing barge races, which continued for exactly a hundred years. There was a gap in the races from the beginning of the Great War in 1914 until 1927. In 1928, however, thirty-three barges took part in the coaster class alone. It was a blustery day, blowing half a gale from the south-west. The course was from Gravesend down to the Mouse Light Vessel and back, a distance of fifty-six miles. Starting at high water, the barges had wind and tide with them

on the outward leg, but once they had rounded the Mouse they had to beat over the tide against strong head winds. In spite of this the race was won at an average speed of nearly ten knots by the Mistley barge *Vigilant*, captained by the most famous of all racing skippers, Alfred Horlock, with his nephew Chubb Horlock as mate. They were an invincible pair. *Remercie* was second and *Alf Everard* third. *Vigilant* took five first prizes in this race. In *Vigilant* and later in the barge *Phoenician*, of which he owned a half-share, Alf Horlock won both the Thames and Medway championships nineteen times out of twenty-one starts.

When the series of sailing barge races started by the Golden Dustman ended in 1963 there were few barges still trading under sail. However, there were still a dozen or so barges which were being sailed as yachts. The owners of these barges arranged a new series of races, four in each year, to be held at Southend, and in the Medway and the Blackwater, and at Pin Mill on the Orwell. These races continue to this day. Amongst the most successful barges in these later races have been the *May*, the *Edith May* and the *Spin-away C*. The *May*, which was built at Harwich in 1891, is owned by a subsidiary of the sugar firm Tate and Lyle and is used by them as a sail training ship. On occasions she still carries a cargo of sugar. The *Edith May*, built at Harwich fifteen years after the *May*, skippered by seventy-nine-year-old Jack Spitty, won the 1971 Blackwater sailing barge race. The *Spinaway C* was built by W. H. Orvis in Ipswich in 1899 and was owned from 1912 by the millers Cranfield Bros. She won the 1966 Pin Mill race. The *Spinaway C* is a very pretty barge with some hollow to her bow and a beautiful sheer.

A number of barges have been converted into yachts, but a few, including most of the ones that race, have been restored to their original condition. To re-spar, re-rig and fit out a barge with a new suit of sails is a costly operation. It is still possible, and there are still one or two barge sailmakers in business. The fact that it is possible to sail even a coasting barge with a man and a boy does not apply to the average yachtsman. Most of the privately owned barges still make use of the professional skills of men who had once skippered their own barges, particularly in the annual sailing barge races.

Though we shall not see them in their hundreds again, we shall at least— thanks to the few enthusiasts who organised the new series of sailing barge races in 1963 and also to the East Coast Sail Trust and others—see the rich red sails of a few Thames sailing barges for some years to come.   [1972]

John Lewis is not merely an author of books on sailing, but a typographer and art historian. He contributed a feature on 'Popular Printing', with enchanting examples of old billheads, broadsheets and theatrical posters, to No. 31, and to No. 34 a study of the strange Edwardian illustrator, Sidney Sime. His wife, Griselda, contributed features on Staffordshire pottery to Nos. 17 and 27.

Sitting in the Garden

MILES HADFIELD

With drawings by Michael Felmingham

TUDENTS of the history of gardening are fortunate in that they are able to start a lap ahead, as it were, of those who pursue other subjects—in the Book of Genesis. No sooner have we reached the second chapter than we are made aware of an important but often unrecognized fact: that of the multitude who take pleasure in sitting in gardens the gardener himself can never be one. Adam was put into the Garden of Eden 'to dress it and to keep it'; not (as every subsequent gardener knows) to rest in it. The most the gardener can find time to do (in the words of an eighty-year-old of my acquaintance) is momentarily to 'rear up on his spade.'

Nonetheless, for those who are more concerned with green thoughts than green fingers, sitting in the garden has always been a favoured recreation. When the habit of sitting in the garden first became taken so seriously as to warrant the erection of buildings specially for its purpose is a matter for speculation. In ancient time sylvan groves were the sheltering places of scholars, wits, statesmen, politicians, and young people who 'made love in their cooler shades.' As gardens were developed, far away from woods, then arbours and bowers (in their old sense) were constructed to give the shade and shelter so necessary to overcome man's strange agoraphobic fear of sitting in the middle of a field. The deeply rooted desire of man for some degree of shade and shelter, away from his house, where he may reflect, or be merry, or make love, is a phenomenon which, I think, was never denied until the twentieth century discovered the questionable delights of sunbathing.

In medieval times, whether or not on account of some Roman or, rather, Italian tradition, the favourite sitting-out-place seems certainly to have been by water—sparkling wells or fantastic fountains—rather than in arbours. This is seen in that guide book to the early medieval (though clearly not quite English) garden, *The Romaunt of the Rose*. The charming Flemish fifteenth-century illustration of this poem is sometimes reproduced to serve as an example of the British medieval garden—no artist of our own, apparently, having ever recorded the subject. In the largest of the carefully enclosed court-like spaces the ladies are seen being entertained musically by their knight as they loll near the fountains, while other pairs dally amorously in the pathways.

The absence of substantial garden structures is noticeable in the collection of medieval garden pictures made by Sir Frank Crisp. Turning the pages of his two monumental volumes, we realize that there was really not much need for garden houses in which to sit, so small and cosy were the gardens themselves. They seem to have been but little enclosures fenced in by wattle hurdles or trim hedges. Within, fountains played, a few shaped trees grew, and a turfed bank was raised as a seat in the midst of a minute and flowery meadow. Perhaps, outside its confines, a tent-like pavilion might be erected for shelter; do we not all remember the scene called *A mon seul désir* in the glorious tapestries of *La Dame à la Licorne*? It was not, I think, until Tudor times that the fabric of such pavilions became solidified into warm red brick or golden stone, to form an integral part of the design of gardens and court-yards.

Bacon does not refer to them in his famous essay. To set against this, we certainly have the evidence of those lovely pavilions that still stand around the garden at Montacute. The Phelips family must have watched the placing of the stone finials on the points of their tent-like roofs when Bacon was well

A MEDIEVAL GARDEN

PAVILION IN THE STYLE OF THOMAS ARCHER

on the way to power. And these are not exceptions, for other Jacobean garden houses still exist. From this period onwards, as gardens increased in size and grandeur, so did the building of structures in which to sit.

Before we pursue their history further, we should, perhaps break off for a moment to discuss the most unsophisticated form of sitting out, under no roof, near no fountain—simply beneath trees. There is a prodigious number of trees under which notabilities—Queen Elizabeth I, Shakespeare, Milton, Hogarth and Dr Johnson are names that come to mind—have sat in gardens. And should we not include in this category Widow Wadman—for the arbour from which she directed her defence of the siege laid to her by Uncle Toby was, we are told, of thorn trees set in a boundary hedge.

Then there is, too, the matter of sitting *in* trees. Charles Stuart up the oak at Boscobel scarcely qualifies, but in the neighbouring county of Shropshire there is still one of the most charming and Peter Pan-like houses to be seen anywhere. On what was presumably the 'mount' of the old garden at Pitchford Hall remains a prodigious and ancient lime tree. High among its now lumbering and spreading branches stands a garden house, reached by steps. Today, externally, it is in the early Gothic revival style, but its wooden framework seems undoubtedly to go back to the seventeenth century or earlier.

By the time of Charles I garden houses had, under Italian influence, developed ambitiously: the famed pavilions at Stoke Bruerne, in Northamptonshire, among the few works actually designed by Inigo Jones himself, have happily been reprieved from ruination and survive for all to see their perfection.

As the formal garden developed, so, it seems, did the art of sitting within its firmly determined confines. John Rea writes of the necessity for 'a handsome octangular summer-house roofed every way,' and other writers describe 'verdant halls' and summer-houses made of arbour-work. The old engraved plans show seats abounding—often placed to command views of the canals and works composed of 'sheets, buffets, masks, bubblings, mushrooms, sheafs, spouts, surges, candlesticks, grills, tapers, crosses and vaulted arches of water.'

How pleasant to sit comfortably in a pavilion designed, say, by Nicholas Hawksmoor, or the amateur Thomas Archer—even the great Vanbrugh himself—and contemplate on an April day the passage of light and shade over such a baroque, stage-like scene!

This style of gardening was soon to end. One of the exponents of the new manner was Addison; though his own garden at Bilton, near Rugby, remained old-fashioned, and his *Inscription in a Summer House* related to a neat Queen Anne building, and not to one in the style of the 'modern movement' which he led.

Secluded from the world, oh, let me dwell
With contemplation in this lonely cell;
By mortal eye unseen, I will explore
The various works of nature's bounteous store. . . .

When formality as the informing spirit in garden design was dethroned, and Nature was crowned in its place, the great era of garden houses began. Vistas prevailed, and a vista must have a point from which to be viewed, and an 'eye-catcher' at its terminal point. So we have classic temples in abundance, sham Gothic ruins in variety, pagodas from China—every imaginable sort of building which would, in addition to its aesthetic purposes, serve as a sitting place where one could ponder upon the sublime and beautiful.

One of the most extraordinary of these buildings is of special interest today since it stood in what is now Kew Gardens—where surely more people now sit than in any garden elsewhere. It was called Merlin's Cave, and was built for Queen Caroline. The several roofs looked precisely like old straw bee skeps, and its keeper had the odd name of the Rev. Stephen Duck. He had started life as a farm labourer, but his verses had gained for him this post of royal patronage. His only poem remembered today begins with the surprising lines—

> Dear madam, did you never gaze,
> Through optic glass on rotten cheese?

It seems that this tangle of incongruities was too much for him, for he terminated his own life by drowning. Have any good ladies sitting in Kew Gardens ever reported a ghostly vision of this odd building and its strange custodian?

We may gain an idea of the importance that the eighteenth century attached to our subject by following the published itinerary of a walk round William Shenstone's garden in Worcestershire. We have scarcely entered when an inscribed tablet invites to sit

> Here in cool grot and mossy cell

though wisely concluding with the admonitory lines:

> And tread with awe these favour'd bowers,
> Nor wound the shrubs, nor bruise the flowers;
> So may your couch with rest be crown'd!
> But harm betide the wayward swain,
> Who dares our hallow'd haunts profane!

By the time the tour ended, sitting upon a slab of stone within a grotto, the sightseer would (if my count is correct) have been urged by appropriate mottoes to rest upon thirty-nine seats, ranging from 'rough, common benches' to refinements such as assignation seats, a lofty Gothic seat, a seat in a temple of Pan, an octagonal seat . . . indeed, one cannot conceive many more variations on our theme.

At this stage a reference must be made to the gazebo, a period feature which, I suspect, we have come to misunderstand. The word is held by some to be of obscure oriental origin, by others to be a jocular Latinized version of the verb 'gaze,' comparable with *videbo*, 'I shall see.' It seems to have been applied correctly only to towers and look-outs; the Hon. John Byng in the record of his travels refers not infrequently to 'gaze-abouts,' which may have been the same thing, and were invariably viewpoints on high spots, such as the tower on Broadway Hill. Whether we can claim them as garden seats, I doubt.

As the nineteenth century came in, the fashion for stone or brick-built garden houses seems to have waned. In the age of the romantic and the picturesque, outlandish wooden buildings became popular; or was it that they were less expensive? Connoisseurs such as Beckford would build substantial, high gabled huts in the Norwegian or Polish manner, though it is a little difficult to identify these nationalities in the resultant buildings. The more normal householder would have either a root house or a moss house. One still comes upon an occasional relic of the former. They were

JOHN PAPWORTH'S UMBRELLA SEAT

pillared with the gnarled and rooty boles of ancient trees, and walled with patterned rustic work. The roof was usually of thatch. Moss houses were a strange mingling of the romantic and the botanic. They were entered through a portico of rustic work, arranged in the Gothic style, and were lit by Gothic windows filled with coloured glass. The interior of the walls was covered with slats into which was inserted moss. This process resembled the lining of the walls of Georgian grottoes, but, instead of sparkling minerals, the different colours and textures of perhaps twenty or thirty different species of moss (whose names would be known to the constructor) were so placed as to give 'an appearance not unlike that of a Turkey carpet.'

But the less fashionable and smaller houses would be content with a simple arbour. In the year 1827 (famous in Pickwickian history) we read of such a place. 'There was a bower at the further end of the garden, with honeysuckle, jessamine, and creeping plants—one of those sweet retreats, which humane men erect for the accommodation of spiders.' Such was the setting of the dramatic episode between Mr Tracy Tupman and Miss Rachael Wardle, which was so indiscreetly observed by the fat boy of Dingley Dell.

Cast iron, too, became 'modern.' A fantastical cast garden seat in the form of acanthus drew from J. C. Loudon what must be one of the first homilies on functionalism and fitness for purpose. And there was the superb umbrella-like garden shelter designed by John Papworth—fine flight of fancy. Did it, one wonders, ever materialize? Does a specimen still exist, rusting away in some neglected suburban garden?

As Victoria's reign lengthened into the present century, so our subject entered a period of decline. People sat more and more in gardens, no doubt, but on metal chairs and benches of great discomfort, and often of a high degree of ingenious if unreliable collapsibility. The languid hammock arrived; the treacherous deck-chair was introduced, and still exists in even newer and more dangerous forms. But with a few Lutyenesque exceptions, the garden sitter was no longer honoured by the shelter of a gracious building.

[1957]

The writer of this piece, who happens to be the present Editor's brother, is the author of many books on gardens and trees, including the standard HISTORY OF BRITISH GARDENING. *He contributed essays on 'Gardens of the Great' to No. 12, on 'Eccentrics in the Garden' to No. 26, on 'Chinoiserie in the Garden' to No. 27, 'On Fountains' to No. 29, and on 'The Victorian Garden' to No. 30. He also wrote about Dragons in No. 13 and the Glastonbury Thorn in No. 15.*

The Art of Smoking

J. B. PRIESTLEY

T IS NOW OVER SIXTY YEARS since I first began smoking a pipe. I smoke when I am working, smoke when I am thinking or pretend to myself I am thinking, and rather too often smoke when I am talking. (The point here being that a pipe and a rumbling lazy voice sometimes make me inaudible. But are my hearers missing much? Probably not.) As any good dictionary of quotations will testify, different generations of sensitive and sensible men have regarded tobacco as their friend. But now, in our age of pollution, an enormous attack is being mounted against 'smoking'.

Now I am not blaming doctors, asked to cure lung cancer or chronic bronchitis, for denouncing 'smoking'. But when they tell me that they themselves have long ago 'stopped smoking' I feel inclined to retort that in fact they never really started smoking. Putting a quick succession of lighted fuses into the mouth and then drawing their fumes deep into the lungs—this is not smoking as I understand and practise it. The enjoyment of tobacco hardly comes into the picture. Most cigarette addicts would continue even if their paper tubes were filled with dried camel dung.

Moreover, while I do not blame the crusading doctors, I must reveal a certain suspicion that troubles me. Some of the more fanatical enemies of tobacco seem to me to be puritans popping up again. They hate it because it gives pleasure. Your genuine puritan always combines with his hatred of pleasure a deep respect for power, business, making money. I remember how a group of New York medical men, when reporting on 'leading executives', denounced their smoking, drinking, hearty dining, but passed over in silence their daily commuting among diesel fumes, the eight telephones on their desks, all the idiotic fuss and worry of intensely competitive commerce.

Three other points are worth making. No doubt I might be healthier without tobacco, but, though health is important, I do not feel I exist in order to be healthy: I try to be a fully creative, hard-working, friendly, tolerant human being. Again, we are angrily denounced for spending so much money on tobacco, when in fact what we are chiefly doing is making a huge contribution to state revenue. If everybody stopped smoking this year, non-smokers would soon be horrified by the new increase in taxation. Finally, we are told that using tobacco is a dirty habit. Well, of course, stupid slovenly people can make anything dirty. But there is nothing particularly dirty about enjoying good tobacco in a clean cool pipe. If we are going to be so wonderfully fastidious, then life itself is a dirty habit—all that eating, drinking, sweating, defecating and urinating and procreating—what a messy business! Clearly we ought to exist in sterilised glass cases, waited upon by computers.

Now I must explain why the proper enjoyment of a pipe is quite different from the 'smoking' that is now being attacked and savagely condemned. (And there is such a cry for banning tobacco that I may find myself enjoying my final pipes only in the lavatory.) First, no pipesmoker in his right mind ever inhales. He is not filling his lungs with smoke, hardly filling his mouth. He is gently and rather slowly puffing away. Secondly—and this follows straight on—if he really knows how to enjoy a pipe he is producing no great heat but keeps the tobacco merely smouldering. No burning paper is involved. Tobacco itself does not burn easily, soon going out if not attended to; so I suspect that it is highly combustible paper that makes constant cigarette-smoking a risk.

Certainly I have known a good many pipesmokers who behaved as if they were in charge of a furnace. Often their pipe bowls would be burnt and charred out of shape. This is idiotic smoking, making the worst of the job. Equally idiotic is the man who smokes hard but carries only one pipe with him so that he is for ever puffing away at a hot pipe and destroying the flavour and fragrance of his tobacco. It is these fellows who give us a bad name. For my part I always carry three pipes, and keep about a dozen on my desk, so I never fill and light a hot pipe. I think I can safely add that even a pipe I had just finished smoking would not be really hot, because I smoke slowly and am not in the furnace business. Good tobacco tastes best and smells best when it is simply smouldering. Here begins the art of smoking.

Almost all the men I have known who tried a pipe but then declared they could not 'get on with it' have made the same two mistakes. They began with pipes that had bowls that were not big enough and were not thick enough. They also began with the wrong kind of tobacco, probably a Light Virginia, finely cut, rather like cigarette tobacco. Puffing away at this bad combination of pipe and tobacco, they would soon find themselves with a very hot smoke indeed, would react by producing a great deal of saliva, would then decide they were 'wet smokers' and have no more to do with a pipe. Whereas if they had tried a bigger and thicker pipe and what they imagined to be a 'stronger tobacco', simply because it looked much darker, then all would soon have been well.

Now a few brief notes on pipes themselves. I have experimented with all kinds, but what we call the Briar* is by far the best. Pipes with patent gadgets in them and pipes made of synthetic substances never seem to me to taste right, so should be avoided. Good pipes are very expensive these

*Actually the very hard root of a species of *Erica Arborea*, grown in the drier Mediterranean regions.

days; but, even so, it is false economy to buy cheap pipes. If a pipe is kept clean and occasionally rested, then if it is any use at all it ought to offer friendly service for years. Bear in mind, though, that while bowls should be cleaned out not all the carbon inside should be removed, because it keeps the pipe cool.

Tobacco next. I have no statistics but I fancy that twenty-nine out of thirty pipemen smoke the same tobacco year in and year out. This puzzles me. Do they want the same dish for dinner every night? I suspect them of having no interest whatever in tobacco itself. Years ago they discovered 'a good smoke' and ever since have been buying a tin or two of it every week. This is not my style at all, and never was. I like different tobaccos for different times and occasions. And I enjoy experimenting. There can hardly be anything fit to be smoked at all that I haven't tried at some time or other. But here—alas—I must give a warning to young pipesmokers who want to settle down with Dad's favourite old brand. The sad truth is that many of these favourite old brands have fallen off lamentably during the last ten or fifteen years. It is not that my palate now demands too much; too many popular flakes and mixtures are nothing like as good as they used to be: the flavour and guts have gone out of them.

Having announced this mournful news, I will at least offer the young pipesmoker a useful tip. (But possibly the old pipe-smoker, if he has never thought seriously about tobacco, might find my advice even more useful.) If you find the popular old brand, the one your dad used to enjoy, lacking character, tang or bite, then you should proceed to give it some extra flavour yourself. This is done by adding—and mixing in thoroughly—small proportions of what are often called 'seasoning tobaccos', of which the most successful, to my taste, are Latakia, Perique, and a strong black Cavendish. They might be described as the onions, curry powders and peppers of the tobacco cuisine. Latakia and Perique are expensive (I have used for some years a fairly cheap and effective Cavendish), but then you need only add small quantities of them, especially Perique, which is strong and pungent—the black pepper in the dish.

Perique comes from Louisiana, and is a natural dark leaf, which has an unusual curing process and is very finely cut. (Anybody who wants to understand the various curing processes, which give tobacco leaves their particular character and flavour, should consult Mr Alfred Dunhill's book, *The Gentle Art of Smoking*.) Cavendish starts its life as a bright Virginian leaf that is steamed and then pressed into cakes. Latakia, the darling of them all because of its wonderful aroma, comes mostly from Asia Minor and Macedonia, with some inferior contributions from Africa nowadays. It owes its special character to the way in which it is slowly cured by the fumes of smouldering oaks. Because its flavour and fragrance are so rich Latakia was popularly supposed to contain too much nicotine, and I well remember, in the 'thirties, the old man who kept the Greek tobacco shop in Jermyn Street (there no longer) denouncing this legend, telling me he had customers who had smoked nothing else but pure Latakia for years. I have tried this myself, but it is too rich, rather like having Christmas pudding at all meals.

I may be wrong, being no expert, but I am under the impression that Virginian tobacco, apparently so bland and guileless compared with those dark Levantine products, actually has the largest nicotine content. Indeed, I remember a Greek telling me, years ago, that when Greece offered to settle a debt to Britain in tobacco, the cigarette manufacturers here refused the offer: they said Greek tobacco, as opposed to Virginian, was not sufficiently 'habit-forming'. This may or may not be true, but what is certain is that British firms base their trade on Virginian tobaccos. If the British suddenly stopped smoking there would be a financial crisis in the American South. Many of these tobaccos, maybe, have never seen Virginia. But what is called 'Old Belt', the aristocrat of Virginian tobaccos, a reddish leaf with plenty of flavour, still arrives from plantations in the neighbourhood of Richmond. 'Middle Belt' and the various 'bright' or 'golden' Virginians are grown and cured in other Southern states or in Africa. They are all good for blending but always seem to me rather boring, even the best of them, when smoked alone. One of these, unpressed and very finely shredded, is 'Shag', almost forgotten now by pipesmokers. I seem to remember it was Sherlock Holmes's choice; it was certainly never mine.

To my mind Virginian tobaccos are discovered at their best after they have been subjected to various processes that involve enormous hydraulic pressures, blending their several juices, and are then, by subsequent processes, turned into *cakes, flakes, Navy Cuts, rolls* and *twists*. I can still see, with my inner eye, the navvies of my youth carefully cutting and rolling between their palms their *Thick Black Twist*—at 3½d. an ounce. It was a bit too powerful for my taste—though in those days I often smoked *Cut Black Cavendish*, also at 3½d. an ounce—but of its sort it was a fine honest tobacco. Possibly I am now too accustomed to rich mixtures, but I cannot escape the impression that all these Virginian tobaccos on the less-expensive popular level have lost much of their character during these last years, and so are much improved by judicious 'seasoning'. But if you can afford them, the best importers and manufacturers, people like Dunhill, McConnell, or Rattray in Scotland, can still offer you fine examples of Virginian turned into *cakes, flakes* and *cuts*.

I do not know what is happening to pipe tobacco in Russia now, because I prefer to stay away while so many writers are being persecuted there. But when I used to visit the Soviet Union I found its pipe tobacco very unsatisfactory indeed. It was excellent tobacco in itself but it had not been properly cured. If what I heard was true, then there is some sharp irony here. There was, I gathered, a little nation—or at least a considerable group of people—in the far south, where the tobacco was grown, who were expert at curing it fit for the pipe. But they were among those unfortunates who were removed from their homes and scattered into exile by the ruthless Stalin. Now Stalin (I am sorry to say) was a pipesmoker, and because he had banished and scattered all these expert tobacco curers, there was no longer any good pipe tobacco in the Soviet Union. Its dictator was reduced to stuffing his pipes with cigarette tobacco, a wretched substitute that could not possibly be smoked slowly. And may I repeat what is almost the *leit-motif* of this piece—that pipes must be smoked slowly and not be allowed to generate much heat? The pipesmoker, above all, must 'keep his cool'.

While so uncertain about so many things, we British can still be sure of one thing—that to the knowledgeable pipemen of the world our island is the Mecca. Though I have bought a few serviceable briars in France, our British pipes are supreme. So is our tobacco. American pipe tobacco, which I have been compelled to buy when travelling in the United States for weeks on end, is almost always too sweet and sticky, as if were meant to be eaten, not smoked. Most of the Dutch tobacco, now making headway in Britain, is artificially scented, belonging to the perfumery department. South African was not bad years ago, though always too dry, but some presented to me by a friend quite recently seemed to me impossible, as if the sour spirit of Apartheid had ruined it. On the other hand, I cannot praise the tobacco we do not import and blend here but actually grow and attempt to cure on the spot: the only sort I ever tried was horrible.

On my desk, as I write this, is a wide range of tobaccos for blending, many of which I bought some weeks ago at Dunhill's. (The rest I already had.) There they are—from the brightest Light Virginia and Turkey leaf to the mysterious black 'seasoners', Latakia, Perique, and the rest. I am already deciding—to fill one of the four pouches I keep going—on a new mixture, on the dark side—omitting Light Virginia, Turkey, Cigar Leaf (never really successful), using a darker Virginia as base, very little Cavendish, only a pinch or two of Perique, but including rather more Latakia. Hurray! But, however this turns out, I am still left with one nagging thought. These fine mixtures, like everybody else's, tend to be rather dry, and so a pipeful of them does not last long enough. What is needed is the type of rich mixture that has a broader cut, to make it last. Does anybody remember now the Craven *Double-Broad*, the creation of a vanished age? I don't ask for its return; I fancy it would seem too mild now; but if this informal piece should catch the eye of any tobacco blender—and it will be a shame if it doesn't— might I suggest he should have a shot at a splendid rich broad-cut? I warn him now, however, that even if he succeeds I may start trying to improve his mixture, gilding his gold, painting his lily.

One last point. It may be that the great brains of our time, like the late Sir Gerald Nabarro, are right when they fanatically oppose all use of tobacco. Possibly we old pipesmokers already look like a rickety, coughing, choking, pathetic gang of red-eyed addicts. Perhaps if we had to start all over again we would never put a match to a pipe. But I must say I have enjoyed my sixty years of ruining myself, and if, as it is, I have been too often restless, impatient, and perhaps arrogant, without a pipe I would have been ten times worse. Moreover, it happens that the wisest men I have known have been pipesmokers. Of course, there are silly pipesmokers. But they might have been even sillier, more unreasonable, bigger nuisances, more fanatical bashers of other men's little weaknesses, if their pipes had not steadied them down. Oddly enough, most of the notable non-smokers I have known, from Bernard Shaw downwards, could resist the fatal weed but could not resist publicity, pulling faces for press cameras while the rest of us—the weak, the fallen—were simply enjoying a quiet smoke.

[1971]

J. B. Priestley came into our pages in No. 28 when, in a feature called 'In the Days of My Youth', he cast his mind back over 'light music' of his youth, recalled by old gramophone records. We have already referred to his fascinating piece on 'Holiday Painting' in No. 29. Mrs Priestley (Jacquetta Hawkes) contributed an illuminating study of Martinware, and its eccentric brotherhood of potters, to No. 32.

L. T. C. Rolt, one of whose contributions starts on the next page, was one of the cornerstones of THE SATURDAY BOOK *from the time the present Editor assumed office. Each of his contributions may be said to have given impulse to a growing public interest. In No. 13 he wrote about vintage cars; in No. 14 about tunnels and disused mines; in No. 15 about steam engines; in No. 17 on 'Engineering as an Art'; in No. 20 on the Talyllyn Railway, which he did so much to revive. Although so many of the subjects he wrote about have come to be taken up almost as hobbies, he was in fact one of the originators of serious industrial archaeology.*

Down on the Farm

L. T. C. ROLT

With drawings by Leslie Thompson

FIFTEEN YEARS ago I wrote for THE SATURDAY BOOK a lament on the passing of steam from the farm which ended with a question: 'Is it too much to hope that we may soon see a parade of traction engines, restored to their former glory, snorting proudly round the show ring?' Such is the perennial fascination of steam that what was then only a pious hope has now become a reality. Farm traction and portable engines are now highly prized collectors' items. Barns and farm-yards in Britain have been so thoroughly combed for them that there cannot now be many surviving examples left that have not been hauled out of rusting retirement and lovingly restored to their former glory by a prodigious expenditure of time and money. As carefully groomed as shire horses by their proud owners, they now show their paces before large and appreciative audiences at agricultural shows and traction engine rallies all over the country. One of the happiest features of this movement is that so many of its devotees are farmers. Some have restored their own old engines and given them an occasional useful job to do in addition to taking them to local rallies or shows.

Moving with slow and majestic deliberation, sucking up water from pond or ditch through the long proboscis of its armoured hose, the farm steam engine was an endearing monster. But, like the monsters of pre-history, it was doomed to extinction by its sheer bulk and weight. In some countries where the land was light and the rainfall low, direct haulage of agricultural implements by steam might be practicable, but in England, for most of the year, such a thing was quite out of the question. Here, the steam traction engine had to be restricted to the headlands, hauling plough or cultivator to and fro across the field by steel cables. Even so, when the land was particularly wet and heavy it was difficult to get such a cable ploughing engine on to the field at all. Even the humble farm 'portable' engine, used to provide power for chaff-cutters and other barn machinery, needed a team of horses to move it from place to place. So it was that when the smaller, lighter and more nimble internal combustion engine appeared on the agricultural scene steam rapidly disappeared from the farm. The law of the survival of the fittest operates far more swiftly and ruthlessly in the mechanical than in the natural world.

Nearly forty years ago I worked successively for two small firms of agricultural engineers in Berkshire and Wiltshire. The sale and repair of farm tractors of makes now rarely seen, such as Rushton, International, Massey-Harris, Case, and, of course the early model Fordson, formed a substantial part of their business. Your farmer has ever been a shrewd and hard bargainer, and the sale of a new tractor could only be clinched by offering him a generous allowance for his old one. This was often a weird and wonderful contraption that looked like a steam traction engine minus its boiler. I once had the job of collecting one of these primitive machines from a remote farm high on the Wiltshire Downs. To start it up and drive it home would have been a far too uncertain and tedious operation, so we decided to tow it away behind a rubber-tyred tractor. I had the job of steering the veteran, and I shall remember that ride as long as I live. It was just as well that there was much less traffic on those Wiltshire byways then than there is today. For the old tractor had steering of traction engine type, with chains controlling a swivelling front axle, and the most frenzied and incessant wheel-winding on my part could not prevent it weaving drunkenly from side to side of the road. My seat was hard, the tractor unsprung, the wheels were shod with steel strakes, and the road was rough. This combination produced a vibration so intense and appalling that I was reduced to a quivering jelly while the machine shed intimate bits of itself as it went along. Because my towing driver could not hear my urgent calls to stop, some of these parts were never retrieved. For all I know they may be lurking in roadside ditches to this day, to be discovered and puzzled over by future industrial archaeologists.

An American 'primitive': a 1913 Avery 40-80, with flat opposed engine, which slid backwards and forwards to change gear.

I had thought that this was the last primitive tractor of this kind I should ever see; but a few years ago I discovered I was wrong.

Forty years ago, mains electricity had not penetrated far into rural England and the farmer relied on many small engines, not only to drive his barn machinery but to pump his water supplies and generate current. While some of these were diesel engines of fairly modern type, many more were very old and primitive, as I can testify, for, in response to urgent SOS calls from the farmers concerned, it used to be my job, when they broke down, to go out and coax them into reluctant life again. Many of them were of American origin and were called 'Three Mule Team', 'Five Mule Team' and so on according to their power, presumably for the benefit of farming pioneers in the Middle Western States. These were small horizontal engines, looking like small steam engines in that most of their vital parts were exposed to view—and, incidentally, to the dust, chaff and pig-meal which adhered readily to their oily surfaces. Like the farm tractors of those days, they started on petrol but, when they were hot, would accept with reluctance the cheaper paraffin. Their speed was crudely regulated by what was then referred to as a 'hit-and-miss' governor which operated on the principle of switching off the ignition whenever the engine threatened to run too fast. An engine so regulated emitted a characteristic coughing and wheezing noise; the heavier its burden the more frequent the coughs, and *vice versa*. For three decades this was a familiar sound on the farm, but now, like an old tune, it can be heard only in memory. Such engines were often cooled by an open tank or 'hopper' of rusty water directly above the cylinder. The recurrent paroxysms produced by the hit-and-miss mode of operation caused the water in this steaming cauldron to slop over, occasionally finding its way into places where water was never intended to be, such as the carburettor or the magneto.

Occasionally engines of this kind displayed spectacular foibles. I remember one such at a lonely house on the Wiltshire Downs. It was an unusually large engine and it drove an antique dynamo which would now be considered a prize piece by an industrial museum. It exhausted into a large underground expansion chamber outside the building. Inflammable vapour used gradually to build up in this chamber until there was a violent explosion followed by a miniature earthquake. This happened regularly. Every three months or so we would receive an agitated telephone call and, crying 'It's done it again!', pile into our old service van to repair the damage.

Having served my apprenticeship on steam traction engines and steam locomotives, I had steam in my veins and was inclined to be contemptuous of all 'stink machines', be they tractors or stationary engines. But that was the time of the great Depression when a young engineer was glad to get a job of any kind. Had I been told then that the steam traction engine would one day be lovingly preserved I should have been mildly surprised. But if anyone had assured me that the despised 'stink machines' which had usurped the place of steam would also, in their turn, become collectors' items I should have regarded such a possibility with frank incredulity. Yet this is precisely what has come about.

Collectors are apt to be curiously intolerant of each other. Thus the philatelist is apt to regard the philumenist with patronising amusement as a harmless crank, although to an unprejudiced outsider it appears as logical to collect matchbox tops as postage stamps. Similarly, your steam devotee should pause before he dismisses the collection of early farm tractors and farm machinery of equivalent date as an eccentric pastime. The primitive farm tractor may appear a crude, puny and altogether contemptible machine beside the massive steam traction engine. Yet this is a case of David and Goliath, for in the light of farming history the tractor is by far the more significant machine.

The effect of steam power on agriculture was limited. Too expensive for the small farmer to afford, the majority of owners of steam traction engines were steam ploughing and threshing contractors. It was in the large, flat fields of the great corn-growing districts of East Anglia that steam came into its own. In the hillier lands of the north and west steam power was employed to a much lesser extent, and in some areas it was almost non-existent. Steam brought about no significant decline in the population of farm horses. Indeed, it relied on horses to some extent. A set of steam ploughing tackle at work, for example, needed horses to draw its supplies of coal and water. The first primitive tractors, on the other hand, represented the spearhead of a farming revolution that has now eliminated the draught horse altogether.

Although the evolution of machines is a much more rapid process than the evolution of natural species, there is, none the less, the same 'inevitability of gradualness' about it. The first specimens of a new mechanical species always betray a close family resemblance to the species they are about to supersede. They lose these vestigial traces either by a slow process of adaptation or when some engineer of particular genius and foresight re-designs them from the ground up. So, just as the first motor-cars resembled horse carriages without the horse, the first farm tractors, when they were born in America, resembled steam traction engines without the boiler. They were even called 'Gasoline Traction Engines' and their design was simple and crude. A large single- or twin-cylinder horizontal engine, running at slow speed and with a heavy flywheel, was mounted in a simple frame in place of the traction engine's boiler. This engine drove the rear wheels through a cone clutch and large, exposed gear wheels. The first of these ungainly, coughing monsters (they were the very devil to start) was actually a converted steam traction engine, built in Chicago in 1889. Primitive though it was, it was lighter than the original traction engine and it needed no coal or water, which was quite a consideration in the Middle West of America. Its success was such that a number of different makes of 'Gasoline Traction Engines' were built in America over the next twenty years or so. Some of these, notably the 'Waterloo Boy', the 'Titan', and the 'Overtime', were exported to England, and it was on one of these that I made my ever-memorable journey in Wiltshire. Some early tractors of the same primitive type were built in England; but only one of these, the Saunderson, succeeded in competing seriously with the American machines.

The 'Waterloo Boy', 1917, model 'N', 12-25, made by the Waterloo Gasoline Engine Company, of Waterloo, Iowa.

It is a sad fact that the reason why Britain lost her proud position as the workshop of the world was not a lack of engineering initiative but a strange failure on the part of the commercial world to recognise engineering genius and give it adequate backing. The history of the farm tractor illustrates this point very well. For the first man to realise that the American type of tractor was merely an unwieldy compromise and that to take full advantage of the new power on the land he must forget the steam traction engine and design a completely new form of tractor was an Englishman, Daniel Albone. His tractor was called the Ivel, and it was first built at Bedford in 1903.

It is significant that although I had so much to do with farm machinery at one time I had not, until a few years ago, heard of Daniel Albone and his

Ivel tractor. I assumed, as I suppose most people do, that the prototype of our modern farm tractor was the American Fordson which was first imported into Britain in 1917 as part of the effort to counter the effect of the U-boat blockade. Then, a few years ago, I saw one of the three surviving Ivel tractors in the hands of a private collector and realised that in this small, neat and compact machine Albone had come up with the right answer fourteen years before Ford. This proves the value of collecting. No catalogue engraving, no faded photograph could have enabled me to appreciate the genius of Daniel Albone as did the sight of his actual creation.

The Ivel tractor was acclaimed by agricultural engineers on both sides of the Atlantic; but Albone died in 1906 and with his death British initiative failed and it was left to the Americans to follow where he had led. It is true that the Americans had the advantage of a very large home market which enabled them to produce their machines in great quantity. Nevertheless, it seems extraordinary, after such a brilliant start, that all attempts to make a good British farm tractor during the years between the wars failed miserably, with the result that our fields were almost entirely populated by American machines. One of the most ambitious of native efforts, the Rushton tractor, was almost a carbon copy of a Fordson, and failed only in those few features in which it departed from the American original. The engineer who was ultimately responsible for putting an end to this sorry state of affairs was Harry Ferguson of the Ferguson tractor, the originator of the tractor-mounted implement.

Today there are in Britain two main collections of 'post-steam' farm machinery, both on farms and made by enthusiastic farmer-collectors, one in Northumberland and the other near Ross in Herefordshire. I have not so far had the good fortune to visit the former, which specialises in early stationary engines, but it was on a visit to the latter that I saw the Ivel. It was a nostalgic day for me, for the Ivel was only one of many. There were not only examples of early 'Gasoline Traction Engines', looking as improbable as those fanciful machines dreamed up by Heath Robinson; there was an example of that dismal failure, the Rushton, miraculously surviving; and there were specimens of those American machines which had once lorded it in English fields, tractors with which I was once so familiar but never thought to see again. Agricultural machinery since the passing of steam is a neglected subject and such ardent collectors and restorers deserve the greatest credit. For their work enables us and future generations to understand what life was like down on the farm forty or fifty years ago.   [1970]

Acknowledgements are made to Charles L. Cawood, Esq., of Grimthorpe Manor, Pocklington, York, for supplying historical material and help with the illustrations.

IN SEARCH OF THE PICTURESQUE

The Emerald Isle

PATRICK CAMPBELL

'ACTUALLY,' said the nice young man, 'this couldn't be luckier. Both of you being Irish, I mean——'

'A very successful turn-up for the book,' Hogan agreed pleasantly, interrupting far too soon. 'It's the kind of chance,' he said to me, 'that makes everything seem worth while.'

It was a heavy party and we'd stayed beyond the point at which it was liable to provide any pleasure, but on the other hand the nice young man was scarcely up to Hogan's weight and in any case his wife was very pretty, in an elf-like, attenuated way.

'How do you mean—lucky?' I asked them. 'Perhaps you wanted some information——?'

'That's exactly it,' said the young man, obviously glad that things had taken a warmer turn. 'You see,' he went on, 'Sue and I are going over there for a few days—just a holiday, if you see what I mean. We thought we'd motor round and just sort of look at things—generally. We've hired a car in Dublin——'

'From the bold Dermot Ryan, no doubt,' said Hogan loudly. 'It's a pity you weren't over there for the radio-cab war. Until the bold Dermot appeared on the scene all Dublin taxis were mouldering American sedans, vintage 1936. Then Dermot shows up with a whole clatter of brand-new, radio-controlled cabs and holy murder breaks out. It was as much as your life was worth to hire one of Ryan's yokes. The other bunch were setting fire to them wholesale. D'you remember the Rolls-Royce?' he suddenly asked me. He turned back to the nice young couple. 'The flagship of the Ryan fleet,' he explained. 'It was like a sieve, with bullet-holes, after some eejit of an owner hired it to take him out to Leopardstown to watch his horse run around.'

There was a silence of some duration. The young couple didn't look at one another. 'I hope,' the young man ventured, 'that's all over now. I mean, we don't want to be involved in anything that might——'

'Of course it's all over,' said Hogan impatiently. 'Everything's all over in Ireland.' He helped himself to another drink. 'Ireland,' he said, 'is a dream, a legend. The only thing that's alive in Ireland is what happened yesterday.'

'And it gets added to a bit in the telling,' I explained. The young couple were looking genuinely worried. 'Not much goes on, you see,' I told them, 'so when something does happen we warm it up a bit to make it more interesting. It gives us the impression we're still alive.'

'A spot of the old Blarney, eh?' said the young man, trying to get into the swing of the thing.

'That's a legend,' said Hogan, 'that was invented by an Englishwoman, Lizzie the First. There was some fella she was besieging in Blarney Castle and he kept promising to yield it up to her, and then going back on his word. "I'll have no more of your Blarney," says she to him, and that's how it started. It's an expression used by the English,' Hogan announced. 'You'd never hear it at all in Ireland.'

'Oh,' said the young man, after a moment, 'I see.' He brightened. 'That's just the kind of thing we wanted to know,' he said. 'I mean, we don't want to go putting our foot in it. . . .' He hesitated. 'Are,' he said, 'are English people fairly popular over there. I mean, the Troubles and all that. . . .'

'God love you,' said Hogan enthusiastically, 'we can't do without you. After seven hundred years of oppression we throw out the English tyrant —and immediately ask him back, to open some boot, bicycle, and button factories, the way we won't all starve to death. . . .'

The pretty young wife was looking at Hogan with her mouth partly open. He was doing too well.

'In any case,' I said, 'the Irish and the English have practically switched countries. The Irish have come pouring over here in their thousands to draw down £14 a week for leaning on a shovel, while mobs of English are fighting to take up residence in Ireland, where income tax is lower and the licensing hours are longer, and if you can put up with her friends and relations singing in the kitchen you can still hire a skivvy to do some of the housework. You ought to go and live there yourself,' I told the pretty young wife. 'You'd flower.'

'That'd be the day,' said Hogan sombrely, and immediately regained her attention. 'Of all the countries ever invented,' he went on, 'including that island off the coast of Wales where there's nothing but monks, Ireland is the worst one for a woman. If Sophia Loren was to walk down Grafton Street stark naked half the fellas would turn to look into Switzer's window, telling their beads, and the other half——'

'Wouldn't even notice,' I said, 'They'd be too deeply preoccupied in talking to one another about horses, dogs, golf, fishing, shooting, poker, and the chance of getting a job in Birmingham——'

'They wouldn't even be doing that,' said Hogan crisply. 'They'd be running home hell for leather to their mothers, and when they got there they'd be in under the bed and they'd shoot the bolt on the door. The average Irishman,' said Hogan, rounding it off, 'gets married at the age of seventy-three, and only then if a couple of acres of land come with it.'

The silence this time was rather longer than it had been before. The young man struck out on a new line. 'The countryside itself, I believe,' he said carefully, 'is very beautiful. I mean, the lakes of Killarney, and that sort of thing.'

'You'll be lucky,' said Hogan instantly, 'if you get a dekko at *them*. The whole lot's been bought by an American tycoon and he's put an electrified fence around it and if you put your face near it you get it blew off. In any case,' he said, 'Killarney was never more than a few puddles of water and souvenir shops—if you could find them—selling models of bog-oak jaunting cars made in Japan——'

'He was done out of the concession,' I said. 'That's what has him so bitter. Killarney's all right, but give me Connemara every time. The only thing you'll ever see along the roads there is an Indian pedlar pushing a bicycle into a gale of wind and rain, with a fibre attaché case full of combs and toothbrushes on the handlebars. If you're looking for solitude and the undefiled splendours of nature, Connemara's the place to be. The picturesque peasants who used to grub a picturesque living out of its blue mountains, in between dancing jigs and singing heroic songs in the original Gaelic, are now all holding down good jobs on the Boston police-force, thanking God they got out in time.'

'There's a good few of them left, though,' said Hogan, seriously. 'I remember the time I pulled up outside a grand litttle thatched shebeen in those parts, licensed for the sale of beers, spirits, groceries, and paraffin oil, with tin signs, advertising Virol and cut-plug, nailed on the whitewashed walls. I went into the bar——'

'You were lucky,' I said, 'you were on your own.'

'I went into the bar,' Hogan said, 'and——'

'Hold on a minute,' I said, 'I want to explain something to this beautiful girl here. If you're a beautiful girl,' I said to the young wife, 'and you step into a country pub in Ireland, they won't let you near the drinking part. You'll be shoved into the best front parlour, where the lace curtains haven't been pulled in seventy-five years. Antimacassars on the chairs, lace doilies on the table, and over the mahogany mantelpiece a tinted photograph of the landlord's mother's brother dressed up in the uniform he went off in to the Boer War. There's great refinement in Irish country pubs. It wouldn't do for a young—even or a youngish—girl to see the men drinking in the bar, so they immure her in the parlour, which closely resembles Queen Victoria's spare sewing-den in Osborne House, on the Isle of Wight, minus of course the ornamental statuary——'

'I went into the bar,' said Hogan precisely, 'and it was then ten minutes to four on a Thursday afternoon. In Puritan England at this hour of day similar establishments would have been shut, with the manager asleep upstairs in his R.A.F. blazer and suède casuals, while his wife was at the flicks round the corner, watching a vegetable mass in full colour consuming Dracula's fathers leg—X certificate and the attendant will visit every part of the house with choc ices during the intermission——'

'The Irish film industry has come on enormously,' I said, 'since the days when I helped Frank Launder with two words of additional dialogue on *Captain Boycott*. On that one we dappled the horse with black boot polish——'

'At ten minutes to four, however,' said Hogan, 'on this Thursday afternoon, Hoolihan's Select Lounge and Bar was jumping with the distilled essence of Mardi Gras. That is, the overflow of stout on the floor had risen above the boot soles of the celebrants, the peaks of whose caps were poised with military precision over one eye, while they themselves bawled out— some perceptibly moved to tears—musical extracts from such popular transatlantic entertainments as *Kismet*, *Oklahoma*, and *The King and I*. Conceivably a preparation'—Hogan gave me a courteous nod—'for service with the Boston constabulary. Except,' he went on quickly, before I could help him, 'that the presence of a lorry outside containing two goats suggested that they were still devoted to the native craft of husbandry.'

He smiled brilliantly at the young wife, who had achieved a grip on her husband's hand. She backed away. 'Ever eager,' Hogan went on, 'to add my mite to the cornucopia of Gaelic culture, I obliged with two choruses of "Some Enchanted Evening", and was just about to follow up this success with a rendition of "My Heart Belongs to Daddy" when some mysterious migratory instinct warned the goat-traders that it was time to leave. Several of them fell down on facing the concussion of the outside air. They placed the one who wasn't able to walk at all behind the wheel of the lorry. Slowly, then, the whole gypsy equipage set out into the gathering darkness, on the wrong side of the road, with the horn blowing continuously, owing to the fact that the driver's forehead was resting on the button. I only hope,' said Hogan piously, 'they didn't meet any English tourists digesting the beauties of the countryside, and coming the other way.'

'I see,' said the young man, after the longest pause yet. 'Well, it's all been most interesting—really it has. Hasn't it, Sue?'

Words presented themselves to her for the first time. 'Well, yes,' she said. 'It has, really.' She gave Hogan a quick look. 'I can't believe, though,' she said, 'that Ireland's as bad as you make out. I mean, some friends of mine went over this summer for the Horse Show and they had a lovely time. They said the Irish people they met were awfully nice. There was no shooting or—or drinking, or anything like you've been telling us about——'

'Of course there wasn't, girl,' said Hogan. He shook his head slowly and sadly. 'I told you—everything's all over in Ireland. The only thing that's alive is what happened in the past. It's only the legends that keep us going.'

'Yes,' said the young man with resolution. 'Yes. Well, thank you very much. We've got to be going now.'

'Have a good trip,' said Hogan. 'You won't be able to tell the difference between Holy Ireland and Welwyn Garden City.'

We watched them to the door.

Hogan turned to me. We both felt spent, deflated, now that the audience had gone. 'Do you know what I'm going to tell you,' Hogan said bleakly. 'I don't know how it is with you, but I'd give a good few quid to be in Hoolihan's Select Lounge and Bar this very minute.'

'Stirring up a legend or two?'

'You're right,' said Hogan. He sighed heavily. 'Let's get out of this,' he said. 'I'm parched.'

We got morosely mouldy in a joint in Gerrard Street. It didn't help at all.

[1960]

Leonard Russell could claim to have been one of the first to recognize the comic genius of the Irish peer who became a national celebrity on television in 'Call my Bluff'. In 1947 Patrick Campbell was writing for a magazine called LILLIPUT. *Leonard Russell brought him into* THE SATURDAY BOOK, *No. 7, with an up-roarious piece called 'Let the English Alone—They Bite'. This was followed in No. 9 with 'A Short Trot with a Cultured Mind'. About this time the present Editor met and sat down to dinner with Paddy, and realised that ten minutes of his conversation was every bit as funny as ten pages in* LILLIPUT. *In the third number we edited, No. 14, we got him to write on 'How to Keep Goldfish'.*

On Waterways

WOOD-ENGRAVINGS BY GEORGE MACKLEY

Editors of THE SATURDAY BOOK *have quite a lot to be proud of, but the present Editor takes a particular pride in having introduced to a wide public the exquisite art of George Mackley, whose engravings might otherwise be known only to a few well-informed collectors. What follows—and the commentary below each engraving is written by the artist—is one of three series of engravings which appeared in our pages. 'Low Country Landscape', in No. 25, and 'Thoughts on Bridges', in No. 30, were the others.*

A SALUTE TO THE BOATMEN

BRIDGES which carry the towpath from one side of the canal to the other often possess a grace and elegance that could improperly be regarded as the expression of a conscious aesthetic purpose. They seem to be flung across the waterway with a flourish and a courtly gesture, a salute, perhaps, to the passing boatmen. Leaving the bank in a broadly sweeping bend, the path rises up and over the bridge, descends in an equally gracious movement and continues its course on the other side, thus completing a three-dimensional curve of absorbing pictorial interest. But the curves which give the bridges their elegance were governed less by the creative exuberance of the engineer than by the convenience of horses. Had the habits of horses been different, had they been able to negotiate rightangles without slowing down and allowing their boats to get ahead of them, we might have had less elegant bridges.

THE WATER STAIRCASE

RIVER MAN sees a boat breasting a hill-top or lying moored half-way up a mountain as guilty of gross impertinence and an offence against the laws of propriety governing navigation. The only decent course a boat can take follows the sinuous line marking the lowest part of a valley. Craft with effrontery enough to desert the valley and scale the hills mount a water staircase of locks which is a mighty feat of engineering skill. As so often happens when engineers are preoccupied with solving purely technical problems, the result of their endeavours acquires an adventitious beauty arising from the interrelationship of structural elements. From below, the locks are seen to rise up the hillside in a rhythmical interlacing pattern of gates and balance beams, culminating in a pair of beams silhouetted against the sky above and providing a spectacle which strains the credulity of a river man.

LOCKS AND LEVELS

O PERFORM the laborious task of taking their boats up to and down from the summit levels, the boatmen have, over the generations, worked out a procedure based on the utmost economy of movement and time. An uphill-travelling boat requiring to enter a lock left full by the preceding craft is stopped very close to the lower gate, perhaps with its bows gently nosing against the woodwork and sometimes with its propeller slowly turning. The boatman leaps ashore to draw the paddles and empty the lock. The levels having equalised and turbulence died down, the boat nudges the gate open for itself and enters the chamber. The lower gates and paddles are closed, the lock is filled, the upper gates are opened and the boat is away. The beat of the engine dies in the distance, the ripples cease to stir the rushes, the moorhens emerge from cover, and quiet returns to the waterway.

LOCK GATES

OME LOCKS, approached from below, appear to be guarded by two low, round bastions flanking the entrance, each with a flight of steps giving access to the top. Most things on the canal have a purpose and the purpose of these is clearly seen from above. To open a lock gate the boatman places his back against the balance beam and pushes against the ground with his feet. As the gate swings, he traces an arc of a circle and these brick structures are built to accommodate his track. A striking element in the scene, they are an essentially practical device. Canal engineering works, once no doubt raw and stark, have become mellowed by a beneficent patina. Woodwork has weathered and bollards are rope-scarred. They have domiciled themselves in the surroundings in which they once were a bizarre incongruity. They retain their strength of structural pattern, but time has enriched their texture.

THE LIVERY OF BOATS

UDGED by the usual criteria, canal boats cannot be declared beautiful. They have not the refinement of line of a clipper ship or a racing yacht. They are long boxes, with a point at the bows and a residential shed at the stern. They were designed for carrying the greatest possible bulk of cargo with the least possible sacrifice of space for living quarters. Their shape makes little or no concession to aesthetic considerations. Only in the extravaganza of ornate lettering and painted decoration could one see the vigorous if naive expression of an aesthetic sense. But exuberant lettering has given place to an austere livery, and the castles and roses, once so lovingly painted by craftsmen, are applied by transfers which are a crude travesty of the real thing. Yet, when drawing the boats, one discovers unsuspected subtleties of form which make them much more than mere pieces of mobile commercial equipment.

[1968]

Betjeman's Britain

An anthology of buildings

chosen and described by JOHN BETJEMAN

and photographed for The Saturday Book

by EDWIN SMITH

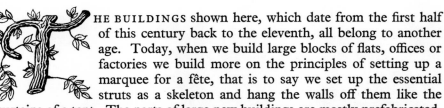HE BUILDINGS shown here, which date from the first half of this century back to the eleventh, all belong to another age. Today, when we build large blocks of flats, offices or factories we build more on the principles of setting up a marquee for a fête, that is to say we set up the essential struts as a skeleton and hang the walls off them like the curtains of a tent. The parts of large new buildings are mostly prefabricated, so that the chief job of an architect, when he is not filling in forms and complying with the regulations of local authorities, is assembling prefabricated parts in as pleasing patterns as he can devise from the standard patterns he finds in the catalogue. This is what modern architects call 'machine-made' architecture. I am not condemning it, though I think that at present far finer examples of it are to be found in America than in England. But I am not illustrating the style, because to put examples among the buildings shown here would be rather like introducing the latest types of motor car into an exhibition of post-chaises.

The buildings here represent 'hand-made' architecture, and are built from the ground up with their outside walls acting as their chief supports. They all imply a knowledge of masonry, of the carving of stone and wood, of the moulding of plaster and cast iron, and the knowledge, once common to all trained architects, of the Orders of Classical architecture (Composite, Corinthian, Ionic, Doric, etc.) and, in the case of Gothic architects, of mouldings and the centring of arches.

If one may make a rather dangerous generalization about the difference between Classic and Gothic architecture it is this. In Classical architecture you designed the outside first and fitted in the plan to conform with the façade. In Gothic architecture you made your plan first and that determined the appearance of the outside of the building. There are all sorts of exceptions to this generalization, just as there are exceptions to the current belief that all Gothic has pointed arches and all Classic has round ones. To take a literary parallel, Gothic architecture is rather like a poet using different metres to suit different moods, and Classic is rather like his trying to condense each mood into a sonnet.

The English buildings I have chosen are some of those I like, regardless of their date. Each is representative of a different phase of English 'hand-made' architecture. To those who object that there is an over-proportion of nine-teenth-century buildings I would say: 'Look about you next time you go out of your house.' Most of the 'hand-made' buildings you will see belong to the last hundred years, when our population suddenly and alarmingly increased.

I think that these are some of the chief things to ask yourself about a building, whatever its age and style:—On its outside, how does it fit in with the landscape or with its neighbours in a street? What is it built of, and do the materials suit the building itself and the district? If there is decoration on the building is it well proportioned to the whole? Are the windows too large or too small or just right in the wall space? Are the panes of the windows well proportioned to the window itself? Are the panels on doors in scale? Are the mouldings around the building itself of a satisfactory size? Is the roof at the right pitch or does it look like an ill-fitting hat? Do the chimney stacks look like afterthoughts or do they seem to rest securely on the roof? Has the designer considered the skyline? And when you go into the building, does it bring you to your knees if it is a church? Does it, if it is a house, lead you on to explore further and suggest grander rooms beyond? Does it lift you up if it is a public building? Or make you feel at home if it is a small house? Outside and in, is the building obviously what it was built to be? And when you walk round it, is it truly three-dimensional; that is to say, will it make a good sketch or Edwin Smith photograph inside or out from wherever you are standing?

As to why one building is better than another—why, for instance, the Port of London Authority building near the Tower of London is a heavy mass of piled-up sculptured masonry, while the little arcaded memorial to the Merchant Seamen by Sir Edwin Lutyens which stands in front of it is infinitely grander and more satisfying—I can give no answer. I suppose it is that Lutyens was a great artist, and the architect of the Port of London Authority building was less of an artist.

Looking at buildings is just like looking at pictures or reading poetry or listening to music. It is something which demands discrimination. Discrimination only comes, when looking at architecture, from constantly using your eyes, if you have been born with an intuitive interest in your surroundings. Date and style have little to do with appreciation of architecture, though we all have our favourite dates and styles, which change as we develop. Finally, I don't think you can judge buildings *in vacuo;* you have to consider them in terms of the purpose for which they were built and the social customs of their age. The gallery of our villages and streets is always open, free for all.

I hope you will like some of the following exhibits from a small and extremely personal selection. From the Ritz to the Norman barons I shall show you some of my favourite buildings. If some of *your* favourites are left out this is not because I do not like them, but because there was not room and I wanted to show some of the lesser-known buildings among the more famous.

[1958]

Opposite: ST MARY'S, WELLINGBOROUGH, 1904 onwards. *Architect and designer of all fittings, hangings and stained glass: Sir Ninian Comper.*

The latest and richest flowering of the Catholic Revival in The Church of England. Brown ironstone columns support white fan vaulting. The East End blazes with gold and red and blue. The idea of its builders was to bring beauty to the drab outskirts of a Midland manufacturing town.

The Ritz Hotel, London (Mewes and Davis)

Edwardian riches at their most elegant. A style which goes with
bridge, women and champagne and privilege. It has a hint of
Paris about it. The architects also designed the Royal Auto-
mobile Club in Pall Mall. What a contrast is this gilded international world of the south with the rugged high-mindedness

St Andrew's, Roker Park, Co. Durham, 1906 (E. S. Prior)

of the north of England. In this grand and solid church the lines of construction are severely shown. The woodwork and the stone tracery of the windows are solid and original. This church is born of the arts and crafts movement and is a Christian version of the aesthetic principles of William Morris.

Central Station, Newcastle-on-Tyne, 1850 (John Dobson)

The early Victorians, whether Gothic or Classic, had no fear of using cast iron, and civil engineers were still architects, and architects were not yet self-consciously artists who regarded engineers as 'practical' and insensitive. Dobson made the elegant roof of light cast iron blend happily with his severe and impressive main building of Newcastle Station.

So romantic, so convincingly old are the spires and towers of the Houses of Parliament that they are probably the most loved public buildings in the country, despite what goes on in them. The Victoria Tower seen opposite in contrast with the Buxton Memorial Fountain is my own favourite single part of this great group of buildings.

Left: The Victoria Tower, Palace of Westminster, 1847-60 (Sir Charles Barry)   213

Opposite: E. W. Bryan's Factory, Leicester, 1913 (S. Henry Langley). Above: Port Sunlight

Messrs. Bryan's factory is an example of the enlightened industrial style where the building was unashamedly a factory and the architect emphasized its vertical lines of construction by subtle devices. The style goes with the Dryad Handicrafts and the work of Ernest Gimson (a Leicester man) and non-conformist benevolence. A similar spirit pervades Port Sunlight, started by the Lever Brothers in 1888. Like Bournville built by the Cadburys outside Birmingham and the Garden Village built by the Reckitts outside Hull, Port Sunlight provided cottages of local materials in local styles to house workers in a garden setting, and the factories, too, were to be surrounded by greenery as suggested by William Morris.

Annesley Lodge, Hampstead, 1895
(C. F. A. Voysey)

Work of each for weal of all! Though the high-minded Liberal manufacturers hoped to make industrial England one leafy Bournville it was the middle classes who took more willingly to the idea. The small, detached house for artistic people of moderate income was first seen in the garden suburb of Bedford Park (1875), and by 1903 a whole city of such houses, each different, was invented by Ebenezer Howard for Letchworth. Architects in those days thought that they should also design fabrics and wallpapers and in the case of Mr Voysey everything for the house down to the very teaspoons and toast-racks. But the workers obstinately preferred the music hall to the folk music and good old fair-ground baroque to homespuns and un-stained oak. England's great contribution to Western architecture was, however, these small detached artistic houses, in local styles. Their designers were pupils of the church builders of the Tractarian Movement.

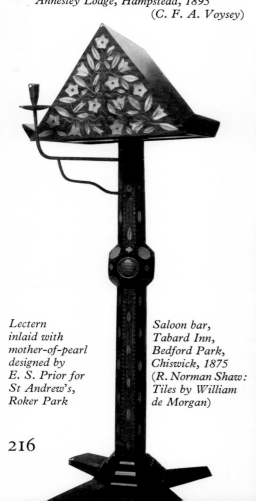

Lectern inlaid with mother-of-pearl designed by E. S. Prior for St Andrew's, Roker Park

Saloon bar, Tabard Inn, Bedford Park, Chiswick, 1875 (R. Norman Shaw: Tiles by William de Morgan)

Hampstead Garden City   *Below: Metropolitan Music Hall, Edgware Road, c. 1886*

St Bartholomew's, Brighton, 1874 (Edmund Scott)

If you had been a young architect in mid-Victorian times you would probably have been a high churchman and a voter for Mr Gladstone and your social conscience would have inspired you to build stately and original buildings in the slums so that the poor might have something in their neighbourhoods to uplift them. To this day the high church of a town is generally the one near the station. The great Victorian church builders did not copy medieval but went on, as they put it, where the Middle Ages left off, using modern materials and inventing styles of their own.

Right: St Augustine's, Kilburn, 1870-80 (J. L. Pearson)

Above: Town Hall, Manchester, 1868-77 (Alfred Waterhouse)

The new vigorous Gothic was not just for churches. George Edmund Street, who designed the Law Courts, taught himself to be a smith, a joiner and a stained glass maker because he thought that an architect should also be master of all the crafts. He inspired the arts and crafts movement; among his pupils were William Morris, Philip Webb and Norman Shaw.

Left: The Law Courts, 1868-82 (G. E. Street)

Above: Wharncliffe Viaduct, Hanwell, 1838 (I. K. Brunel)

The unconscious sense of scale shown by the builder of the mill on the opposite page (notice the larger windows on the ground floor and the relation of window to wall space above) is the survival of an innate sense of proportion which every builder seems to have possessed in the eighteenth century. Brunel, like all great civil engineers, was an artist. He favoured the Egyptian style in his youth, as at Clifton Suspension Bridge and in the Wharne-cliffe Viaduct where he gives it Georgian proportions. The flattish brick arches are his own.

Left: Early 19th-century Mill, Halifax

223

Monkwearmouth Station, Durham c. 1845 (John Dobson)

Splendour on top and squalor below in the industrial towns where the workers were as yet unprotected by the Factory Act. But what real splendour on top! Monkwearmouth station was the terminus of the line before it crossed the river. It was built when people were proud of railways and when, quite rightly, they thought they beautified the landscape. Dobson's design is on the early principle of railway stations, where the platforms were mere sheds and the waiting room was a huge public building where passengers sat until the train was announced.

The early Victorian terrace such as that at Pennsylvania Park, Exeter, was designed to show up sunlight and shadow by means of shallow grooves and light iron work and pale paint on the plaster. The people who lived in such terraces as these were probably as unaware of conditions in the growing industrial north as the characters in Jane Austen seem to have been unaware of the Napoleonic Wars.

> The day was fair, the cannon roar'd,
>   Cold blew the bracing north,
> And Preston's Mills, by thousands, pour'd
>   Their little captives forth.

Ebenezer Elliott might just as well have been writing of Halifax, instead of Preston.

On the right: Halifax, Yorks, with a well proportioned cast-iron lamp standard

Above: Pennsylvania Park, Exeter, c. 1840.

Above: The Mausoleum, Brocklesby Park, Lincs, 1787-94 (James Wyatt)
Opposite: Tombs of the Pelham family inside the Mausoleum, Brocklesby
Below: The Bridge, Tyringham, Bucks, 1793-c. 1800 (Sir John Soane)

Go back from the Industrial Age to the Classical one, to that brief period in our history, from Tudor to the nineteenth century, when most of the great country houses were built. Not only were the houses part of the landscape, but their adjuncts such as temples, bridges and lodges and clumps of trees were designed to turn the country into a moving classical landscape as the traveller by chaise went visiting. Man commemorated himself in the Age of Reason with the best sculpture: churches and mausolea generally contain works of art to the memory of local landowners.

227

The Manor House, Finstock, Oxon. Early seventeenth century

When it was no longer necessary to fortify your house, if you were a local lord, against your neighbours, when farmers and merchants began to prosper from the wool trade and when the great abbeys ceased to be the chief landlords, men displayed their wealth in their private houses. They built houses for their families instead of houses of God. All over England there are charming small manor houses in local materials, whether it be stone or timber, and the best are in the limestone villages, generally near the church and walled off from the cottages. The richest and most powerful Elizabethans delighted in huge glazed windows where their forebears had had to put up with the thick walls of castles. The festal light of candles shone on tapestry and fine Spanish chairs. English cherubs and carved fruit and capitals showed in wood, stone and plaster the Tudor and Elizabethan delight in the new-found knowledge, already firmly established on the Continent, of the ancient architecture of Rome and Italy.

The last phase of Medieval Gothic in England, known as Perpendicular, gave the stained glass artist his great chance, for the walls were almost of glass and the vaulted stone roofs were designed to have their weight carried by strong buttresses between the windows. Thus the grandest examples, clearly the work of architects and not merely local builders, were like enormous marquees whose supports were the buttresses and whose curtained walls

Hardwick Hall, Derbyshire, 1591–97   *Overleaf: New Building, Peterborough Cathedral*

were glass held in position by carved and traceried stone. These masterpieces had a pro-portion of their own, and were a unity of colour and sculpture and construction which, with the aid of music and a religious ceremony with vested priests, transported man from this world to the next.

Above: St Mary-at-Hill, 1670-1676 (Sir Christopher Wren)

Merchants in cities still had the tradition of the medieval guilds. The great Wren churches, sometimes Gothic and sometimes Renaissance (St Paul's Cathedral is a Renaissance building with a medieval plan), were the joint efforts of citizens. They sat in cedar-scented pews, summoned from their shops and halls by the tinkle of Anglican steeples.

Left: New Building, Peterborough Cathedral, 1438-96

Peterborough Cathedral, West Front, 1200–20. Porch, c. 1370.

In Medieval England the abbeys first created architectural styles. Here were the men of art, while the soldiers lived in castles. The West Front of the Benedictine abbey of Peterborough has long seemed to me one of the most daring creations of the Middle Ages—that detached west wall with its great hollow spaces and the narrow opening in the middle. A later generation of monastic architects had the courage to set down in the midst of this design that jewel-like porch in an utterly contrasting style.

Most village churches are buildings rather than architecture. But here and there are village churches which are all-of-a-piece. Patrington, which sails like a galley over the flat landscape of Holderness, is an example.

Opposite: Patrington Church, c. 1350

Gerti Deutsch's Japan

The illustration above has been chosen as a striking Oriental contrast to the temple of Bangkok opposite. But the sixteen pages of marvellous photographs of Japan which Gerti Deutsch contributed to No. 23 had abundant contrasts among themselves—contrasts not only of ancient and modern, but of town and country, age and youth, peasants and philosophers, traditional dancers and modern fashion models.

Stephen Harrison's Bangkok

Stephen Harrison's great interest is in the religious relics of the Orient. His photographs of the temples of Bangkok in No. 25, with accompanying commentary, revealed a strangely unfamiliar aspect of the country made famous in the west by the musical play, *The King and I*. These temples are havens of quiet, isolated from the noise and squalor of the rest of the city, and fantastic in their prodigality of ornament and statuary. He also contributed, to No. 26, a fine pictorial feature on the ruined cities of Ceylon.

John Guest's Sands of Time

The haunting face above is one of the superb photographs of the ruined Roman cities of Sabratha and Leptis Magna on the Libyan coast taken and described by John Guest for No. 26. The dolphins and sea-creatures tangled in the hair and the strange scallop marks on the cheeks suggest some ocean spirit breasting the waves. John Guest also wrote evocatively about the island of Ponza, west of Naples—said to be Circe's island—in No. 20.

236

Hammond Innes' Country of the Caves

Some eighteen thousand years older than John Guest's nereid are these deer, depicted swimming in a frieze on one of the walls of the Lascaux cave, which Hammond Innes was privileged to view in 1968, after atmospheric changes, causing the paintings to deteriorate, has compelled the authorities to close the caves to the general public. Readers of such books as *Levkas Man* will know that Mr Innes is as deeply interested in antiquity as he is in oil rigs and modern navigation. Besides the brilliant description of Lascaux and other prehistoric caves which he wrote (and illustrated with his own photographs) for No. 29, he had also contributed a hair-raising and compulsive description of Machu Picchu, the mountain fortress of the Inca Kingdom in Peru, to No. 28. He and his wife Dorothy had explored its fantastic grandeur when he was researching for his historical study of *The Conquistadors*, which many people consider an even finer piece of work than any of his novels.

237

John Maas's American Gothic

The illustration above, of a conservatory in San Francisco's Golden Gate Park, built under the influence of the Gothic Revival, makes a piquant contrast to the seventh-century Dome of the Rock in Jerusalem, opposite. Mr Maas's assembly of Gothic extravaganzas in the United States was an enchanting exercise in nostalgia, ranging from millionaires' mansions to Masonic Halls, from cast-iron galleries in New Orleans to 'parlour organs' and hatstands in New York. No. 22.

Alistair Duncan's Dome of the Rock

A hallowed place of worship for Islam, the Dome of the Rock stands on a rock where Abraham took Isaac to sacrifice him to God, and where later Mohammed is supposed to have landed on his winged horse. Its splendour was marvellously illustrated in Alistair Duncan's photographs (mostly in colour) in No. 27. This was one of the most beautiful pictorial features *The Saturday Book* ever presented.

Barbara Gompertz's Venice

Venice is so obvious and hackneyed a subject for photographers that we felt little excitement when Barbara Gompertz brought in her portfolio. But when she opened it we realised not only that the visual beauties of the city in the sea are inexhaustible, but that a photographer who combines a sense of form (as exemplified above) with a feeling for the humanity of the canals and the courtyards, can reveal entirely new aspects of the familiar. The series of photographs which Barbara Gompertz contributed to No. 19 called for no captions. Every picture told its own story, whether of historic grandeur or contemporary decay, of children playing in the *piazza* or old men wandering through the market, of women sweeping their medieval doorsteps, or nuns gazing up in awe at the bronze horses on the facade of St. Mark's. Other Italian features in *The Saturday Book* have included Olive Cook's 'A Street in Sicily' (No. 14), Richard Church's essay on Perugia (No. 16) and his poem on Ravenna (No. 19).

240

Philip Gough's Seaside Regency

We cannot claim to have 'discovered' Philip Gough. As an illustrator he had made his very individual mark before, in 1949, Leonard Russell asked him to design a jacket for *The Saturday Book*. Thereafter, alternating with Biro and William McLaren (who was responsible for the jacket designs based on famous paintings), Philip Gough produced as elegant a series of jackets as the twentieth century has seen. And he has contributed many illustrations over the years. In 1955 we discovered that one of his special interests was that elegant, classical, but distinctive architectural style which he calls 'Seaside Regency'. We persuaded him to let *Saturday Book* readers see some sketches from his note-books which are vivid reconstructions of Regency vistas as they must have appeared to Regency eyes. The view at the head of this page, for instance, reconstructed from an old print and from information gathered locally, shows Lyme Regis very much as Jane Austen must have seen it.

Worthing

Weymouth

Scarborough — The Museum

Hastings — Pelham Crescent

Laurence Scarfe's Morocco

Elsewhere we have paid tribute to the crucial part Laurence Scarfe played in the early days by designing *The Saturday Book* and illustrating many of the stories and poems that appeared in it. After the present editor took over the design of the book in 1952 Laurence was able to make a less practical but more personal contribution by providing drawings and commentaries on places that particularly interested him. Above is one of the drawings for a splendid series he contributed to No. 16 on Morocco. His bold and free draughtsmanship, allied to a natural sense of book design, made the pages of this feature a delight to the eye. To No. 21 he contributed a series of drawings of Italy, and to No. 24 a superb evocation of the sights, people and buildings of Malta. For the final issue of *The Saturday Book* he gave us a dramatic series of photographs of 'Salento Baroque', accompanied by a most perceptive summing up of the treasures of an area in the heel of Italy which is well off the beaten track.

Composers in Clerihew

who also wrote the verses

If Rossini
Was no libertine, he
Was certainly one for the girls
With his liquid eyes and his curls.
(Query:
His relations with *L'Italiana in Algieri*?)

Giuseppi Verdi
Admitted that a bird he
Once saw displaying her garter
Was the inspiration for *Traviata*.
It's only a rumour
That he cribbed the idea from Dumas.

It was a happy illusion of Brahms
That if he'd exerted his charms
On Jenny Lind
She might well have sinned.
Instead he taught Clara Schumann
That to err was human.

'Hi ya?'
Said Ravel to de Falla.
'Okay. You well?'
Said de Falla to Ravel:
Neither liked to confess
That he couldn't care less.

Handel
Thought it an absolute scandal
The way Bach
Cashed in on the *Passions* lark;
It was always a special yen of his
To compose a setting for *Genesis*.

Oh dear! What can the matter be?

ENGRAVINGS from THE ILLUSTRATED POLICE NEWS
set to verse by

CHARLES CAUSLEY

When her sister's stays she wore
Daisy fainted at the door.
It's a mercy Tim, so true,
Knew exactly what to do.

Henry Tomkins—such a swell—
    Used to shave beside the well,
Since his spouse, young Henry swore,
    Couldn't stand the sight of gore.

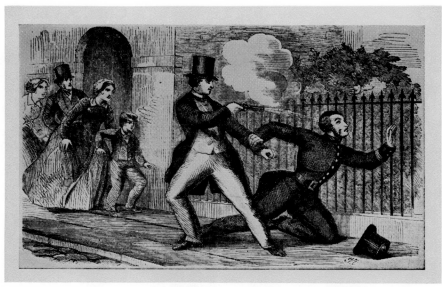

'Pray,' said Mamma, 'don't scream nor scoff.
Actors rehearse on-stage and off.
Their Method now is much more free—
And isn't one Sir Herbert Tree?'

His Lordship cried in accents strong,
  'The fish you caught was not *that* long.
Lie there, false heart, to weep and groan.
  I'm going to the Ball alone!'

'Unless,' the Sergeant said, 'you part
And think of Mr D'Oyly Carte
The dress rehearsal will be through
Of *Pirates of Penzance*, Act II.'

Mike Maginnes trimmed his mate
As he cleaned the kitchen grate.
Their mistress cried, 'It is a crime
To cut your hair in working time!'

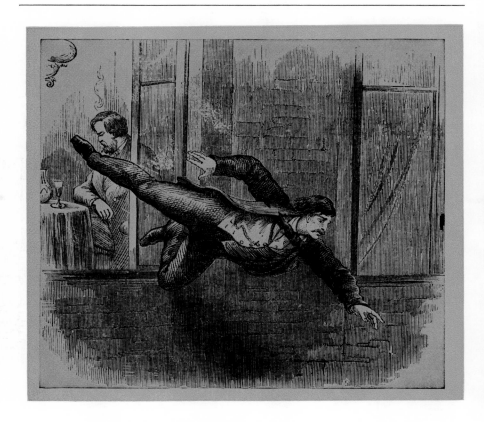

Mad Tregellar used to dive
  Fully clad from storey five
And his soul from sin restore
  In the swimming bath next door.

[1959]

There is no special novelty in allying irreverent modern verse to Victorian engravings which now seem slightly absurd, but we claim especial editorial merit for inviting Charles Causley to contribute appropriate verses for the foregoing engravings from THE ILLUSTRATED POLICE NEWS *of the 'eighties. Mr Causley contributed, in a very different vein, a Christmas poem to No. 18, entitled 'Innocent's Song', which is so moving, so genuinely terrifying, that it might be a little out of place in a light-hearted miscellany as this. We expect to find it in future editions of* THE OXFORD BOOK OF ENGLISH VERSE.

257

Extrovertigo

DENYS BLAKELOCK

With drawings by
RONALD
SEARLE

At Lady Barbiturate's ball
The fun was fast and furious,
They goggled in the servants' hall
At costumes rather curious.

Lord Neurosis danced the waltz
With motions past analysis;
Miss Id, whose love had played her false,
Sat supine with paralysis.

Miss Id had been a powerful force
In the world of fame and fashion,
Had swept men off their normal course
With gusts of stormy passion.

The Upper Ten their eyebrows raise
At loves that are erotic,
Miss Id had earned the stern dispraise
Of her Dowager Aunt Biotic.

Lord Oedipus had been her god
(A very complex fellow),
But soon she found him much too odd
And sadly streaked with yellow.

The escapade that followed this
Incurred some social odium;
She sought a temporary bliss
With Hildebrand, Lord Sodium.

At Amytal they lived in sin
And caused a County pother,
Until she fell for Aspirin,
His analgesic brother.

She flirted with Lord Fistula
And left a poisoned track,
Tormented Viscount Sistula
And kept him on the rack.

At last one day she met her fate—
A fiddler known as Chloral,
She loved him early, loved him late,
And sent him tributes floral.

He drew his bow across his gut,
He set her heart a-quaver,
Until the whole affair went phut—
He proved a bad behaver.

His passion soon outpaced Miss Id,
The fiddler false was he;
She saw him boldly make a bid
For the sisters M— and B—.

And now tonight with broken heart
She languished at the ball,
A woman static and apart,
A flower against the wall.

Lord Neurosis, too, had known
His share of tears and sorrow,
Had sought the sleep of Oblivon
As solace till tomorrow.

He saw Miss Id, and seized his chance
To be her lord and master,
He asked her if she'd care to dance
And be his soothing plaster.

And soon he found Miss Id was free
To entertain a new love;
He took his tablets, one, two, three,
And offered her his true love.

Ere long Miss Id and Lord Neurosis,
Who had known such stormy weather,
To wedding bells at St. Psychosis
Walked the aisle together.

A rake reformed, she soon retired
To Bumph, their country-seat;
And found at last what she required,
A sedative retreat.

So there, relax'd, m'lady lives,
And here my story closes,
For she forgets and she forgives
And tends three small Neuroses.

[1957]

IN RETROSPECT

Footnotes on Fifty Years

SIEGFRIED SASSOON

In 1946 the Editor invited Siegfried Sassoon, then in his sixtieth year, to look back to the 'nineties—the days of his youth that had been so vividly evoked in 'Memoirs of a Fox-hunting Man.'

REPRODUCE (from a fifty-year-old number of the *Illustrated London News*) the following sentences. 'For the first time in the history of warfare a typewriter is to be brought into play on the battlefield, the War Office having ordered a Remington for use in the Ashanti Expedition' . . . 'A prosecution under the Locomotives Act has made the public alive to the legal restrictions which at present hamper the experiments with horseless carriages. Parliament ought to take the matter up, for it is very probable that horseless vehicles will effect a revolution in locomotion.'

These extracts speak for themselves, and also speak volumes of commentary, not only on what has happened since 1896, but on the innocence which we are now able to observe when exploring the periodicals of that date. Not long ago I came across an 1896 copy of the *Daily Mail*, which had survived through being use as padding at the back of a framed engraving. How unsophisticated and old-fashioned it seemed—and was! I might almost have been reading a weekly provincial newspaper. Yet how comforting to find that even the *Daily Mail* had once been so unsensational!

As to the 'revolution in locomotion,' my pen (I have never used a Remington) is purposing to express and prove my personal antipathy to acceleration in all its manifestations. From which it may be inferred that I regard 1896 with affection and am not a whole-hearted admirer of 1946. Like others of my generation, I have seen two existences sink beyond the horizons of history. Of the interlude between wars I am not prepared to say much. It is beyond argument that those twenty years were something separate from the rest of one's life, but I find it easier to turn my thoughts to the pre-1914 world. I regret its vanished amplitudes and benevolences and its easy-going disbelief in any drastic alteration of the social structure. Of course, conditions weren't what they ought to have been; the working classes had even more to complain about than they have now, and the idle rich were reprehensibly privileged and prosperous. All sorts of things were crying out to be abolished or ameliorated, and most of the social reformers were regarded as cranks.

But the fact remains that it was a world of peace; and I found it a pleasant world to live in. For the village bells of my youth were Birket Foster bells. Their voices, across the summer evening fields, spoke security; unaware of wireless wave-lengths, they were insistently traditional in tone. It was an unprogressive population that they called to church, or, anyhow, a population ignorant of any impending acceleration of its way of living. There was nothing to indicate that the bells ought to be sounding a frenzied tocsin, warning us to make ready for a frenzied future. Changes were occurring, it was true; but they were temperate and uninterfering ones, and there was quite a chance that they would be absorbed into the social system without causing any noticeable difference. Everyday life would continue 'as safe as the Bank of England.' Socialism? Pooh! Only a few chaps in red ties. A European War? Unthinkable. Modern nations were too civilized for such a thing as that. Aeroplanes? Too dangerous for anyone except professional aeronauts. They would never amount to anything more than balloon ascents. Motor-cars alone appeared likely to increase the speed and mobility of ordinary citizens. They weren't breaking down nearly so often as they used to do before 1900.

'The modern consciousness,' as we are frequently reminded, is a subtle and complicated business. Since the Twentieth Century began, our mental approaches to all forms of phenomena have been altered and influenced by inventions, ideas, and the violence of public events. Human nature, though profoundly immutable, has been compelled to re-adapt itself to unprecedented conditions. There is the outlook of children, for instance—their attitude to religion and their emancipation from the notion of a relatively unchanging world.

Fifty years ago I was acutely conscious that God had got His eye on me. Vigilant and inescapable, He was there all the time. One might contrive to avoid being 'found out' by grown-ups; but it was no use trying to evade God, who had all the harps of Heaven and furnaces of Hell in His Archbishopric. Never doubting that God took a personal interest in everything I did, I grew up with a belief in my own inevitability similar to 'the divine right of Kings' which one learnt about in history books. It could not occur to me that earthly identity was a matter of biological fortuitousness. My antecedents and surroundings were accepted by me like the multiplication table and the Garden of Eden story. Nothing could possibly have been otherwise.

It must have been toward the end of my 'teens when I first experienced the queer sensation of my name being imposed on me by chance, thinking how funny it sounded, as though it belonged to someone else. In much the same way it never struck me that Victoria and Waterloo Stations were named after the Queen and the Battle. I hadn't an inquiring mind and the origins of things were seldom explained to me. I just vaguely appropriated life as it came along, supplying my own irrational interpretations. For example, while studying Sir Robert Ball's book *Starland*, I assumed the astonomer's name to be somehow connected with the fact that the earth was globular (like the man who remarked that 'pigs was rightly named'). I should have felt blank and lonely if someone had told me that everything hadn't been arranged for me by Providence and that Chance governs all. The suggestion that there might conceivably have been no such person as myself would have sounded positively blasphemous, like saying that Mr Gladstone or Dr W. G. Grace had only appeared on earth by accident.

It goes without saying that, for those of my age, the first World War is the barrier between them and the outlived social environment in which they spent their most impressionable years. But the barrier is more indefinite than its 1939 successor. Compared with that destructive cataclysm, the peaceful epoch died a natural death. One might almost say that it faded out, withdrew, and was superseded. In 1919 it was still possible to believe that we should preserve and resume something of the life which had been interrupted. People were not immediately aware of what had happened, any more than they realized that the civilized world was about to be run off its legs toward perdition. Everyone's attention was concentrated on recovering from the War. Few were awake to the fact that the pre-1914 period had unobtrusively expired and was only surviving in the minds and habits of its intransigent survivors.

I can claim to have been one of the earliest authors to demonstrate that it was good literary material, and that the remembering of its remoteness was enjoyable. When, in 1926, I began to write *Memoirs of a Foxhunting Man*, I surprised myself by discovering that 1896 felt as though it were much more than thirty years ago. This, though it can hardly be described as a spectacular achievement, afforded me much intimate felicity. 'Ten miles was a long way when I was a child,' I wrote, and the thought produced a delicious thrill of enchantment. For the 'nineties had acquired an idyllic flavour. Recreating them was almost like reading *Cranford* or the 'Barchester' novels. They were as far away as the boyhood of Richard Feveral. Stabilized and detached, the past had become a charmingly perspectived late-Victorian picture. How happily humdrum, how exquisitely unperturbed by innovations it all seemed when reflected in the mirror of memory. Time went as slowly as the carrier's van that brought the parcels from the station, and international events were comfortably epitomized in the weekly cartoons of *Punch*. France was a lady in a short skirt, Russia a bear, and the performances of the county cricket team more important than either of them.

Writing my retrospective book, I saw the orchards and meadows of the Weald of Kent in 'the light that never was on sea or land.' 'In this brightly visualized world of simplicities and misapprehensions everything was accepted without question. I find it difficult to believe that young people see the world in that way nowadays, though it is probable that many of them do. Looking back across the years I listen to the summer afternoon cooing of my aunt's white pigeons, and the soft clatter of their wings as they flutter upward from the lawn at the approach of one of the well-nourished cats. I remember too, the smell of strawberry jam being made; and Aunt Evelyn with a green bee-veil over her head. . . .'

For a man of forty to write like that about his early days was, I think, somewhat unusual. The past had become imbued with a peculiar intensity, simply because it was no longer possible for anyone to live in that candle-lit, telephoneless, and unmotorized Arcadia. To which it must be added that I am instinctively unhastening in temperament, and a deliberative experiencer of what comes my way.

Since 1926, the late-Victorian scene has been much exhibited for its oddness and obsolescence. Old photographs have shown how amusingly different things were in those days. Even the Edwardian decade has developed interest and attractiveness, and the hansom cab has come into its own as a clip-clop creator of 'period atmosphere.' With regard to rural conditions, however, I believe that this legend of a vanished world has been exaggerated. Superficial changes have not affected the elemental characteristics of country folk. An agricultural population is obdurate in its methods and addictions. Like the seasons of the year, it refuses to be interfered with. It is not easy to speed up a shepherd, a herdsman, or a woodman. They remain much the same as they were in Hardy's novels. Until sheep, cows, and trees are produced by atomic energy factories, the tempo of the farm labourer will continue to be moderate and traditional.

It can be said that the speeding up of modern life began about 1900. At that time the telephone came into general use. (During the previous twenty years of its career it had been little more than a 'stunt,' and most of the telephoners were go-ahead business people.) Undeniable though its advantages are, I consider this invention significant of restlessness and incontinent communication. In 1901 Dr Freud published the first of his psychopathological treatises—a landmark in the over-elaboration of our mental processes and the municipalization of 'the subconscious self.' The demise of Queen Victoria coincided with what I can only call the inauguration of an Era of Unreticence—an era in which Dr Freud was ultimately to become conspicuously influential.

Meanwhile the Fabians, and other persons of strong mental fibre, began to write and lecture a lot about the Future, following up the ideas of that great man and practical idealist, William Morris. And the inventive imagination of H. G. Wells, humane, prolific, humorous and adventurous, urged us to travel toward the Millennium as quickly as we possibly could.

The Future now became quite the intellectual fashion. We approached it with enthusiasm, though not as yet by air, thus exiling ourselves for ever from the comparative quiescence of the discarded Nineteenth Century and its optimistic belief in gradual evolution from (as Browning wrote) 'the developed brute to a God, though in the germ.'

By 1906, even to simpletons like myself, it was apparent that things were getting livelier; but I doubt whether many people were aware of what was really happening to the world. Twenty years later, G. M. Trevelyan summed it up as follows:

> Man's power over nature had far outstripped his moral and mental development . . . The application on a colossal scale of older processes of steam and electricity were perpetually transmuting the economic, social, and international fabric before it had time to solidify; linking up distant races too closely and too suddenly; and putting into the hands of personal and national ambition new weapons of conquest and self-aggrandisement which have proved the means of mutual destruction.

It is not for me to discuss the responsibility of Germany for the armament race, which was in full swing after 1904. I will confine myself to pointing out that one of the drawbacks of this armament race was a general ignorance of what its combative outcome would be like. Wiseacres confidently predicted that a European War would be all over in six weeks, basing their opinion on the assumption that no nation would be able to go on paying for it. The matter would therefore be settled by a few 'decisive battles of history.' As things turned out, the anticipations of military experts were progressively confuted. Lord Kitchener enlisted us for 'three years or the duration'; but otherwise he seems to have been rather unperspicuous as to how the details of the conflict would work out. Even for the British Navy and the German General Staff, things refused to behave according to plan. It was, in fact, a somewhat experimental version of Armageddon.

'In the debacle of 1914–18,' remarks a recent article in *The Times Literary Supplement*, 'the naked and evil genius of humanity had been laid bare.

And at the end of the period a ruined and disillusioned world was prepared to discard many of the accepted traditions and idealisms.' Which was what I was just going to say, though in less magisterial language. Yes, we were disillusioned; but we had also won the War. And there was always the future to be looked forward to, so the future was again very much to the fore. Hopeful intelligences referred to it as 'the New World.' It was to be made wonderful by wireless, by television, by disarmament treaties, and through the transcendental achievements of Science.

It was also necessary to believe that it would materialize successfully —faith, as a shrewd American writer has informed us, being 'an illogical belief in the occurrence of the improbable.' They are no laughing matter now—those Utopian anticipations which deluded so many of us in the early 'twenties. And why shouldn't we have felt hopeful, when the best minds in all civilized countries were agreed that Europe had learnt its lesson and that war was utterly discredited as an instrument of national policy?

I can remember talking to a poet of genius one evening about twenty-two years ago. He said (and I made a note of his words at the time) that he passionately desired to be a young man again so that he could belong to the new world which was beginning. We ourselves, he exclaimed, might live to see a world in which every child would be born to a life of security—a life in which riches would have ceased to possess any meaning, since lack of security is the only thing that fosters the acquisitive instinct in men. He went on to say (while I sat with mouth and eyes wide open) that the controlled release of the atom would be followed by the release of the human mind. 'It will be done by something akin to what we call prayer. The old religions have failed and Science must invent a new one.'

That sort of thing, over mid-nocturnal cups of tea, sounded splendid, and we all went away feeling, like Shelley's Titan, 'Good, great and joyous, beautiful and free.'

The sequel emerges grimly from a letter which the same poet has sent me from America quite lately. 'The Atomic Bomb—does anybody talk about anything else? The next *Tables of History*—if there is ever another published— might very well take as sub-title *or the Contentiousness of Nations*. The whole wretched story seems to spring from nothing else, unless it is from the ambitions of persons—and their peoples. Anyway, doom seems to lie ahead— and it is no good blinking at it.'

Thus—with the Atomic Bomb—ends the half-century which began with a Remington typewriter being bought by the War Office for use in the Ashanti Expedition. We are confronted by a climax which dumbfounds intellect, nullifies emotion, and annihilates all literary expression on the subject.

[1946]

MCMXIV

PHILIP LARKIN

Those long uneven lines
Standing as patiently
As if they were stretched outside
The Oval or Villa Park,
The crowns of hats, the sun
On moustached archaic faces
Grinning as if it were all
An August Bank Holiday lark;

And the shut shops, the bleached
Established names on the sunblinds,
The farthings and sovereigns,
And dark-clothed children at play
Called after kings and queens,
The tin advertisements
For cocoa and twist, and the pubs
Wide open all day;

And the countryside not caring:
The place-names all hazed over
With flowering grasses, and fields
Shadowing Domesday lines
Under wheat's restless silence;
The differently-dressed servants
With tiny rooms in huge houses,
The dust behind limousines;

Never such innocence,
Never before or since,
As changed itself to past
Without a word—the men
Leaving the gardens tidy,
The thousands of marriages
Lasting a little while longer:
Never such innocence again.

[1960]

The Revolver in the Corner Cupboard

GRAHAM GREENE

CAN REMEMBER very clearly the afternoon I found the revolver in the brown deal corner cupboard in the bedroom which I shared with my elder brother. It was the early autumn of 1922. I was seventeen and terribly bored and in love with my sister's governess—one of those miserable, hopeless, romantic loves of adolescence that set in many minds the idea that love and despair are inextricable and that successful love hardly deserves the name. At that age one may fall irrevocably in love with failure, and success of any kind loses half its savour before it is experienced. Such a love is surrendered once and for all to the singer at the pavement's edge, the bankrupt, the old school friend who wants to touch you for a dollar. Perhaps in many so conditioned it is the love for God that mainly survives, because in His eyes they can imagine themselves to remain always drab, seedy, unsuccessful, and therefore worthy of notice.

The revolver was a small genteel object with six chambers like a tiny egg stand, and there was a cardboard box of bullets. It has only recently occurred to me that they may have been blanks: I always assumed them to be live ammunition, and I never mentioned the discovery to my brother because I had realized the moment I saw the revolver the use I intended to make of it. (I don't to this day know why he possessed it: certainly he had no licence, and he was only three years older than myself. A large family is as departmental as a Ministry.)

My brother was away—probably climbing in the Lake District—and until he returned the revolver was to all intents mine. I knew what to do with it because I had been reading a book (the name Ossendowski comes to mind as the possible author) describing how the White Russian officers, condemned to inaction in South Russia at the tail-end of the counter-revolutionary war, used to invent hazards with which to escape boredom. One man would slip a charge into a revolver and turn the chambers at random, and his companion would put the revolver to his head and pull the trigger. The chance, of course, was six to one in favour of life.

How easily one forgets emotions. If I were dealing now with an imaginary character, I would feel it necessary for verisimilitude to make him hestitate, put the revolver back into the cupboard, return to it again after an interval, reluctantly and fearfully when the burden of boredom became too great. But in fact I think there was no hesitation at all, for the next I can remember is crossing Berkhamsted Common, gashed here and there between the gorse bushes with the stray trenches of the first Great War, towards the Ashridge beeches. Perhaps before I had made the discovery, boredom had already reached an intolerable depth.

I think the boredom was far deeper than the love. It had always been a feature of childhood: it would set in on the second day of the school holidays. The first day was all happiness, and, after the horrible confinement and publicity of school, seemed to consist of light, space and silence. But a prison conditions its inhabitants. I never wanted to return to it (and finally expressed my rebellion by the simple act of running away), but yet I was so conditioned that freedom bored me unutterably.

The psycho-analysis that followed my act of rebellion had fixed the boredom as hypo fixes the image on the negative. I emerged from those delightful months in London spent at my analyst's house—perhaps the happiest months of my life—correctly orientated, able to take a proper extrovert interest in my fellows (the jargon rises to the lips), but wrung dry. For years, it seems to me, I could take no æsthetic interest in any visual thing at all: staring at a sight that others assured me was beautiful, I would feel nothing. I was fixed in my boredom. (Writing this I come on a remark of Rilke: 'Psycho-analysis is too fundamental a help for me, it helps you once and for all, it clears you up, and to find myself finally cleared up one day might be even more helpless than this chaos.')

Now with the revolver in my pocket I was beginning to emerge. I had stumbled on the perfect cure. I was going to escape in one way or another, and because escape was inseparably connected with the Common in my mind, it was there that I went.

The wilderness of gorse, old trenches, abandoned butts was the unchanging backcloth of most of the adventures of childhood. It was to the Common I had decamped for my act of rebellion some years before, with the intention, expressed in a letter left after breakfast on the heavy black sideboard, that there I would stay, day and night, until either I had starved or my parents had given in; when I pictured war it was always in terms of this Common, and myself leading a guerilla campaign in the ragged waste, for no one, I was persuaded, knew its paths so intimately (how humiliating that in my own domestic campaign I was ambushed by my elder sister after a few hours).

Beyond the Common lay a wide grass ride known for some reason as Cold Harbour to which I would occasionally with some fear take a horse, and beyond this again stretched Ashridge Park, the smooth olive skin of beech trees and the thick last year's quagmire of leaves, dark like old pennies. Deliberately I chose my ground, I believe without any real fear—perhaps because I was uncertain myself whether I was play-acting; perhaps because so many acts which my elders would have regarded as neurotic, but which I still consider to have been under the circumstances highly reasonable, lay in the background of this more dangerous venture.

There had been, for example, perhaps five or six years before, the disappointing morning in the dark room by the linen cupboard on the eve of term when I had patiently drunk a quantity of hypo under the impression that it was poisonous: on another occasion the blue glass bottle of hay fever lotion, which as it contained a small quantity of cocaine had probably been good for my mood: the bunch of deadly nightshade that I had eaten with only a slight narcotic effect: the twenty aspirin I had taken before swimming in the empty out-of-term school baths (I can still remember the curious sensation of swimming through wool): these acts may have removed all sense of strangeness as I slipped a bullet into a chamber and, holding the revolver behind my back, spun the chambers round.

Had I romantic thoughts about the governess? Undoubtedly I must have had, but I think that at the most they simply eased the medicine down. Boredom, aridity, those were the main emotions. Unhappy love has, I suppose, sometimes driven boys to suicide, but this was not suicide, whatever a coroner's jury might have said of it: it was a gamble with six chances to one against an inquest. The romantic flavour—the autumn scene, the small heavy compact shape lying in the fingers—that perhaps was a tribute to adolescent love, but the discovery that it was possible to enjoy again the visible world by risking its total loss was one I was bound to make sooner or later.

I put the muzzle of the revolver in my right ear and pulled the trigger. There was a minute click, and looking down at the chamber I could see that the charge had moved into place. I was out by one. I remember an extraordinary sense of jubilation. It was as if a light had been turned on. My heart was knocking in its cage, and I felt that life contained an infinite number of possibilities. It was like a young man's first successful experience of sex—as if in that Ashridge glade one had passed a test of manhood. I went home and put the revolver back in the corner cupboard.

The odd thing about this experience was that it was repeated many times. At fairly long intervals I found myself craving for the drug. I took the revolver with me when I went up to Oxford and I would walk out from Headington towards Elsfield down what is now a wide arterial road, smooth and shiny like the walls of a public lavatory. Then it was a sodden unfrequented country lane. The revolver would be whipped behind my back, the chambers twisted, the muzzle quickly and surreptitiously inserted under the black and ugly winter tree, the trigger pulled.

Slowly the effect of the drug wore off—I lost the sense of jubilation, I began to gain from the experience only the crude kick of excitement. It was like the difference between love and lust. And as the quality of the experience deteriorated so my sense of responsibility grew and worried me. I wrote a very bad piece of free verse (free because it was easier in that way to express my meaning without literary equivocation) describing how, in order to give a fictitious sense of danger, I would 'press the trigger of a revolver I already know to be empty.' This piece of verse I would leave permanently on my desk, so that if I lost my gamble, there would be incontrovertible evidence of an accident, and my parents, I thought, would be less troubled than by an apparent suicide—or than by the rather bizarre truth.

But it was back at Berkhamsted that I paid a permanent farewell to the drug. As I took my fifth dose it occurred to me that I wasn't even excited: I was beginning to pull the trigger about as casually as I might take an aspirin tablet. I decided to give the revolver—which was six-chambered— a sixth and last chance. Twirling the chambers round, I put the muzzle to my ear for the last time and heard the familiar empty click as the chambers revolved. I don't think my heart beat any faster as I pressed the trigger. I was through with the drug, and walking back over the Common, down the new road by the ruined castle, past the private entrance to the gritty old railway station—reserved for the use of Lord Brownlow—my mind was already busy on other plans. One campaign was over, but the war against boredom had got to go on.

I put the revolver back in the corner cupboard, and going downstairs I lied gently and convincingly to my parents that a friend had invited me to join him in Paris.

[1946]

On Being a Boy's Writer

FRANK RICHARDS

With illustrations from 'The Magnet' and 'The Gem'

The author of this contribution was the inventor of one of the best-known characters in English fiction: Billy Bunter of Greyfriars School. It is not too much to say that the 'Owl of the Remove' is, like Mr Pickwick and Sherlock Holmes, a character known in most corners of the globe. For more than thirty years Charles Hamilton (for that was the author's real name) kept going three pen names, Frank Richards, Martin Clifford, Owen Conquest, and three schools, Greyfriars, St. Jim's, Rookwood. For the Magnet *and* Gem *he invented hundreds of characters, and the fame of Harry Wharton, Frank Nugent, Hurree Jamset Ram Singh, Tom Merry, Arthur Augustus D'Arcy and others is not a great distance behind that of Billy Bunter. During all this time Mr Hamilton was writing a million and a half words a year. This is an extract from a piece he wrote for the fifth* Saturday Book, *in his seventieth year.*

 S A VERY SMALL BOY, I secretly and surreptitiously taught myself the Greek alphabet, in the happy delusion that it would prove the Open Sesame to my father's mysterious books. But I wrote incessantly, my output being limited only by the quantity of writing paper on which I could lay hands. I wanted to be an author: also I wanted to be a great scholar: at the same time I wanted to go to sea, and also to become a famous cricketer. In my day-dreams I saw myself like Byron waking one morning to find myself famous: I saw myself translating the Iliad, ever so much more attractively than Pope or Chapman: I saw myself a 'ship's boy on the high and giddy mast': I saw myself knocking up centuries at Lord's and bringing off miraculous catches in the field, amid delirious cheers. All these things are possible in daydreams: but if I couldn't do them all, I could at least write about them, which was easier, and almost as good, if not quite as good. So I wrote and wrote, wasting reams of paper, putting what were really daydreams into words strangely real to me. It was a curious thing that when I wrote I seemed to see it all happening before my eyes, as if I were looking at a picture: I had a sense of writing down actual happenings. The phrase 'making up a story' would have had no meaning for me: so far as I was aware, a story unrolled of its own accord, with scarce an effort on the part of the writer, who was little more than a chronicler. I was very much older before I learned, with surprise, that all stories were not written in the same way, and that other imaginations were not so vivid.

At an early age an elderly relative pronounced me to be a 'clever fool.' I endorsed the adjective cordially: the noun seemed to me absurd. Only in much later years have I realised that he was right on both points: my doubt, later, being about the adjective, not the noun. Indeed it seems sometimes like a miracle that a daydreaming, unpractical fathead like Frank Richards ever got through seventy years at all. Anybody could diddle him—and many did. The truth must be that there is a sweet little cherub who sits up aloft and keeps a watchful eye on duffers who do not know their way about this wicked world.

Diffidence, a haunting distrust of one's own powers, is always a handicap: often most emphatically present in people who really can do things. They set their standards too high, and, failing to reach them, feel that they can do nothing worth while. Frank Richards knows, now, that he can write a good story: but only, I fear, because so very many people have told him so. In early days, though he wrote and wrote, and delighted in writing, it seemed a sheer impossibility that his writings should ever appear in print. Such glory was for far cleverer fellows than he! It was not of his own volition, but as usual on receiving a push from somebody else, that he made the desperate plunge. It was difficult for him to believe his eyes when the first story he had ever sent on its travels resulted in the first cheque he had ever received.

That cheque was the first of many thousands: and later in life one of Frank's bothers was to remember to send his cheques to the bank, and enter the amounts in his account-book for income and surtax purposes.

Frank wrote on many subjects: but he settled down at last to write chiefly the school story. He liked school: he liked schoolboys: he even, amazing as it may seem, liked schoolmasters! The subject was ever fresh to him: and time has not staled it. It is as fresh to him at seventy as it was at seventeen. Indeed, when he is writing a school story he utterly forgets that he is seventy at all, and is to all intents and purposes seventeen again. Never has he found it difficult to recapture the first fine careless rapture. This accounts for what was considered the astonishing output of a million and a half words a year.

Frank Richards's memory is his long suit. If an accident happened to a typescript, there was no difficulty in typing it over again. He never kept copies of his work, even when travelling in remote and outlandish places, and trusting his MSS to hands that were not always very trustworthy. If anything had happened, it would only have been a question of so much more typing to be done. In the *Magnet* there were hundreds of permanent characters, and more hundreds that came and went. It never occurred to him to forget any of them. He was asked once whether he did not 'mix' his characters sometimes, and make them say and do wrong things: a question that made him chuckle. Such a thing was unthinkable. Every character about whom Frank Richards, or Martin Clifford, or Owen Conquest has written remains as fresh in his mind as when it was first created, as far back as the 'nineties. No doubt this may be because they all seemed real to him: and indeed were real, being taken from life. Authors, like any other class of dealers in fiction, should have good memories: and Frank had a very good one.

It seems to me that everyone should train his memory and make the most of it. Good things should be committed to memory: once safely lodged, they

are always there if wanted, and one may be independent of books at times when books are not to be had. It has always been one of my pleasures to learn verses by heart. My own, whose name is Legion, may not perhaps be worth remembering: nathless they are all stored in the old nut, and I do not need to keep copies. Along with them are many selections of much more value. Often and often these have come in useful.

When I was about eleven or twelve, I was laid up for a time. It was a sore trial for an active kid, normally unwilling to keep still for five minutes, to have to do so for endless hours that seemed like centuries, weary day after weary day, with a bandaged leg resting on a cushion, and a sharp pang when that unfortunate leg stirred. I found a resource in learning Scott's *Lay of the Last Minstrel* and Macaulay's *Horatius* by heart: in those young and innocent days I believed these two sportsmen to be poets!

Later, in more mature years, I realised that I might have done better: they were hardly worth the trouble. Still, there they still are, if wanted. I have never been wrecked on a desert island, or sent to prison, or shut in at the bottom of a coal mine. But these things do happen: and in such circumstances how useful to have even a limited library at hand, stored in the memory.

Frank's present readers—that is, supposing, like Gilbert's sentry, that he's got any!—will notice that this article persists in dropping into the third person. They may put this down to Frank's shy modesty. He has, like Stendhal, an insuperable repugnance for the 'je's' and the 'moi's.' Indeed, he finds it far from easy to write about himself at all.

Facts, we are told, are stubborn things: they seem also to Frank lacking in interest. Real worlds are not so attractive as imaginary ones. Casanova's and Cellini's autobiographies are much more interesting than anything that actually happened to them. In dealing with facts we are bound like Ixion on his wheel: in fiction we mould the world nearer to the heart's desire. It is a singular thing how very much what is called an 'adventure' differs, in real life, from the same thing in fiction.

How did I invent my characters? I didn't. They just growed, like Topsy. I don't quite see how any character could be 'invented' for if it doesn't live already, how can anyone breathe into its nostrils the breath of life? Harry Wharton was mine own familiar friend. He is still sixteen in my mind's eye: for owing to circumstances which it would be interesting not to relate, I never saw him after that age: and I just cannot think of him as seventy-one. In my memory he remains exactly as I saw him last, and as he is depicted in the *Magnet*. Johnny Bull I did not meet till he was in his forties: but I had only to visualize what he must have been like at fifteen, and there he was. Every-one, I suppose, must have known a Bob Cherry: and Hurree Jamset Ram Singh derives chiefly from a dark gentleman whom I met for five minutes in the early 'nineties. Frank Nugent is, or was, no other than Frank Richards himself, so far as one could draw one's own portrait: quite a nice boy, I am persuaded, but booked always to go in with the tail. Tom Merry is just an average healthy schoolboy such as one may see every day. Arthur Augustus D'Arcy owes his existence to a suggestion from H. J. Garrish, then editor of the paper in which he first appeared: but later he was slowly but surely modelled on a sub-editor, a delightful young gentleman who really knew what clothes were, and how to wear them.

Billy Bunter—the one and only—derived from several sources. There was an occasion when Frank Richards was simply fascinated by an editorial gentleman at Carmelite House, who overflowed his chair to such an extent that it was a mystifying problem how he had got into it, and a still more intriguing mystery how he ever got out of it. From him Bunter borrowed his remarkable circumference. His celebrated postal-order, which he was always expecting, but which never came, was in fact a cheque of which a relative of my own lived in a perpetual state of expectation, seldom or never realized. His big spectacles belonged to another relative, who had quite an entertaining way of peering at one like an owl. In these latter days Frank Richards himself is in still worse case: but retains, fortunately, his sense of humour: and if he stoops in the garden to stroke a cabbage, taking it for the cat, he can laugh instead of swearing.   [1948]

A long and illuminating study of 'The World of Charles Hamilton'—that is to say, the stories in The Magnet *and* The Gem—*was contributed to No. 24 by Robert Kelly.*

Memoirs of a Batman

ANONYMOUS

Illustrated by Edward Ardizzone

In 1952 the Editor happened to be reading The Journal of the Royal Pioneer Corps *and in it came upon a contribution from an ex-Batman which seemed to speak the authentic language of the 'Old Sweat.' The following is an extract from what we included in Nos. 12 and 14, printed exactly as the author wrote it.*

N the beginning I was not a Pioneer but Royal Artillery, but I didn't get on very well in there and was always in trouble and on the peg, see, and after I done my last twenty-eight days in the glass-house the battery officer says to me, 'You are crummy and I am going to send you to a crummy mob,' so I come to a Pioneer company and the major was a old sweat like me what I liked and when I come to the orderly room the S.M. marches me in to the old man—which is the way we calls the Major—who is looking at my crime sheets and he says 'This is a b—— poor show, my lad, and being a old soldier you did ought to know better.' So I says, 'Yes, sir,' and he says to remember I am no longer in the Royal Artillery but back in the real army, and so help me God if I play any monkey tricks he will break my b—— heart so that I go to bed and cry myself to sleep at nights, but he will forget my old crime sheets if I don't remind him of them and I says 'Yes, sir' again and thinks to myself watch your step, Ed., becos this old b—— means what he is saying and this is the sort of officer like what you had in the first war and proper b——s they was, but real officers. So when I am outside I says to the S.M. 'What is the old man like, Sergeant Major?' and he says, 'Stand to attention when you speak to me, you gutter sweepins, and say "sir,"' so I stands to attention and says 'sir' like what he said, but I thinks they are a b—— hot crowd and I am not going to like it very much.

There were some other blokes what come from other regiments with bad records like me. This S.M. tells us all, 'Now, you men, let me tell you something,' and he looks at our papers what he has in his hand, 'You have come from the guards and the tanks and the gunners and some lousy infantry mobs and they could not handle you and they sends you to us and now by God you will start proper soldiering and if you put one foot wrong you will wish you had never been born,' and that's the way it was. The officers and noncoms was nearly all old sweats and knew all the tricks and you could not get away with things like other regiments, and some of the blokes try

to play the old soldier but it does not come off and some of the blokes desert and the S.M. laughs and says, 'I hope they come back so I can tear their hearts out,' but they do not come back and some of us stop in the company and I was one of them and I done very well in the Pioneers and after I done a year on drills and work I was put in the sergeants mess as an orderly and so they send us to North Africa and I got a job as batman and was promoted to officers mess.

When I was in an officers mess I met all the brigadiers and colonels and General Friend, too, and at the beginning I was windy of them but afterwards I was not windy any more, because when you have seen them with no uniform on and only in their little short shirt with their teeth in a cup you know they are not so big like they make out but are just ordinary men like us.

I will tell you about the Brigadier and the Colonel's goat. It's when I am in Italy and I am batman to a Group Commander what is a very nice man too. An Eyetie what he knowed give him a baby goat for to eat. It was still alive and has only just left its mother. It is a very pretty little thing what the officers do not like to eat. So they makes a pet of it and calls it Wilfred and the Colonel became very fond of Wilfred what always follows him about the house. So the colonel says to me, 'You will look after Wilfred and groom him proper like a horse so he do not stink too much. And don't let no ruddy Eyetie pinch him.' I do like I am told and soon he is quite at home all over Headquarters which is a big private house. He follows me and the colonel around just like he was a dog and everybody make a great fuss of him.

Well, things goes along like this for quite a time. Then when Wilfred has growed up a bit, something goes wrong with his temper and he is not so friendly with everyone like when he was small. Only with me and the Colonel is he still friendly, but with everybody else he is just as likely as not to put his head down and charge at them. No body dont go out without first looking to see is that goat anywhere near. But worst of all Wilfred began to smell, only we never knew in the beginning it was Wilfred. It never come on until the hot summer and everybody starts a sniffin and a turning of their noses up. Some says it was the drains and some say a German soldier has been killed and buried under the floor. Some says it is just the natural smell of Eyetie houses in the hot weather but in the end you couldn't make no mistake what it was because that smell hung all round Wilfred. It was just like he wore it. Very powerful it was and the other officers wants the Colonel to get rid of Wilfred because he upsets their stummicks. For a long time he will not but then in the end he says to me, 'That there Wilfred do stink horrid bad dont he, take him outside the house and never let him come in no more,' he says. But that is easier said than done because Wilfred has lived in the Mess since he was a few days old and now he cannot understand why he cant go in no more. And this is where my trouble starts because everybody act like it is my goat, which it is not. Every time Wilfred gets away from where he is tied up he comes straight back to the house and it is me what gets blamed for it. It don't matter what I do that blasted goat always escapes. If I locks him up in a shed some b.f. always opens the door and he gets out. So in the end I find a long chain what I tie him up with to a post at the end of the garden. And that is when the Brigadier comes.

When the Colonel hears that the Brig. is coming he gives orders for everything to be spit and span. He says to me, 'You will look after the Brigadier as well as me when he is here and he will sleep in my room. Keep on eye on that b—— goat and if the Brigadier so much as sets eyes on Wilfred I will send you back to a company so help me.'

Well the day the Brigadier comes I have so much work to do in the Mess that I do not have time to think about Wilfred until he starts bleeting loud enough to wake the dead. So I goes down to where he is tied up and he has got his self all wrapped around the post and has nearly strangled his self. Well I undoes the chain and quick as a wink that bleeding goat races away with about twenty foot of chain a rattling and a banging. I chases him all over the garden and just as he heads for the front of the house, I grabs hold of the chain but Wilfred gives a extra hard tug and I slips on the gravel. Down I comes tip over elbow. Blimey what a panic. There is me lying on the ground holding on to the chain and at the other end of the chain is Wilfred with his head down trying to reach the Brigadier what is inspecting a guard of honour of black Basutos. Every now and then Wilfred gives a jump at the Brigadier but because I am still holding the other end of the chain he cannot quite reach him. Every time Wilfred jump the Brigadier jump and every time I try to get up on my feet Wilfred gives another jump and I ends up on my kisser again. Well them black Basutos was standing proper to attention at first but then one laughs and then another one. In a minute they is all stamping and rolling about and slapping each other and double up with laughing. The colonel is yelling and the Sgt. of the guard is yelling. Wilfred is jumping to get at the Brigadier and every time the Brigadier, what is getting a bit pot-bellied, gives a little hop in the air them black Basutos hollers and cheers and laughs. The Brigadier is getting as mad as hell. 'What is the meaning of all this,' he says in the end, 'and who is this man,' looking at me, 'whats it all about?' So I picks up my titfer what I lost and rub some of the dirt and blood off my nose and chin and stands to attention.

The Colonel he dont know what to say so I says, 'It is a goat sir.' 'I can see it is a b—— goat,' says the Brigadier 'do you think I am b—— well blind. Who does it belong to?' he says. He turns to the Colonel, 'Is this a pet?' he asks. 'You know there is orders against keeping pets,' then he sniffs once or twice and says, 'O God, nobody wouldn't keep nothing what smells like that for a pet. Whose is it?' he says. 'It belongs to an Eyetalian,' I says, 'and is called Wilfred, the goat not the Eyetalian, and I see it in the garden and was driving it out' I says. 'Take the damn thing away' he says. Then he looks at the guard of black Basutos what is now standing proper at the present again and says, sharp like, 'take them away as well.'

Well the Colonel was raving mad and dident half give me a basinful but he quiets down after a bit. He dont say no more about it only to see Wilfred dont get loose no more.

The next day the Brigadier and the Colonel is away all day inspecting companies and things goes off very quiet. In the evening before they got back I lays the Colonel's best uniform out on his bed for to change before dinner. The same with the Brigadier, he having brought a spare uniform with him, also I have got some hot water on so they can have a bath when they comes back.

I pops down to the kitchen for a few minutes and when I goes upstairs again I can smell Wilfred has got loose again and is in the house. I rushes into the Brigs. room and what do you bleeding well think. There is Wilfred standing by the bed a chewing of the medal ribbons what he had pulled off the Brigadiers tunic. I did not know what to do so I give that blasted goat a kick up the backside what lifted it clean in the air. Wilfred lets out one bleet, drops the chewed up ribbon and went out of the house like the devil was after him.

Well them ribbons wasn't no good no more so I takes them to the Lt.-Quartermaster and tells him what has happened and asks him can he let me have some ribbons before the Brigadier gets back. Lucky the other officers has medal ribbons the same as the Brigadier. Also they got spare bits in their kit, and the cook, what was a tailor in civvy street, makes up a posh new set and sews them on the Brigadiers tunic.

He asks me about them after he has had his bath. I tells him as the other ones was looking a bit scruffy I made up a new set for him. He says good man but he could not think of letting me buy new ribbons for him and I must let pay what they cost. So I let him.

He was very pleasant for the rest of his stay and tells the Colonel at dinner on the last day that he has got a very good Headquarters staff. 'I wish I had your cook,' he says to the Colonel, 'this meal is very well cooked and served. What is it?' he says looking at me who is serving at the table. 'Just ordinary

rations,' I says. 'There is more flaver to it than anything I get in my mess,' says the Brigadier. Then I sees the Colonel is looking at me a bit strange and not eating so well as he did before. When they goes out to have coffee in the other room the Colonel drops back a bit and comes up to me. 'Was that ordinary ration meat?' he says. 'No sir,' I says, 'its a bit of special what I got.' He says, 'Was it?' and then dont finish what he was going to say. 'Yes sir.' I says, 'Wilfred,' I says. So he goes outside and pukes his heart up. A nice bloke that Colonel was. Pity he had a weak stummick.

In the early part of the war we has one Coy. in the Group what is a proper terror. All the blokes in it was dockers what got took away from the docks when the war broke out and was put in uniform and sent to France to work in the docks there. They is first class when it comes to working but aint no good on parade becos they aint done no drills and does not have no use for disipline. Well no body dont bother about them being scruffy so long as they loads up the ships all right but arfter we has done a scarpa out of Dunkirk and they come back to England some body says they got to start looking like soldiers when they is not working on ships. Only it dont work out that way becos these dockers is not intrested in looking like soldiers. The first two majors what they send to this coy. dont get on very good becos the men dont take no notis of them and the only time every body is on parade is on pay day so these majors dont last very long. And it is the same with the sgt. major what is suposed to be a hard case but he is not hard enuff to handle these blokes what only shouts back at him when he shouts at them. Only they shout louder than what he does. Arfter this sgt. major has been took to horspital becos a brick falls on his head one day the col. what is in charge of the Group dont know what to do and it is just then that a new major is sent to the Group. He is a big bloke this major over 6 foot and has got the first war medals up but he wears a eye glass in one eye and all the time has a culerd hankchief stuck up one sleeve of his tunic and what is generaly hanging out a few inches. So the col. sent him to this dockers coy.

Well when these dock blokes see this new major what has come to them with his eye glass and everything they laffs and winks at each other and gets all set for a proper caper. But this major dont take no notis and lets on like he dont see they is making fun of him and starts orf by saying he will have a full coy. parade. Us chaps in the other coys. is hanging about to see what will happen becos we do not think the dockers will turn out on parade and is very serprised when the whole blooming lot falls in. They lines up 3 deep but dont take up their dressing like proper soldiers so they is all over the place like a snake and is all standing any how sloppy like. So the major looks at them and shouts to them to stand to Attention and with that every man jack of them puts his hand down the neck of his tunic and pulls out his identity disc what is on a string round his neck and puts the identity disc in their eye like they was monokles. Then they fumbles round the sleeve of their tunic and pulls out the ends of their hankchifs what they has put up their sleeves before they come on parade. And arfter that they comes to Attention or the best they know how never having lerned the drill. I near died of laffing becos I have not seed any think so funny in all my life. There was them 300 men a standing with their identity discs stuck in their eye and their hanky sticking out of their sleeve and the major standing looking at them with his monokle in his eye and his hanky sticking out of his sleeve. Well that major never batted an eye lid, he didn't. For a minute he stands looking at them and then he starts a inspection just like they was not taking the micky out of him. Some times he stops in front of a man and tells him not to screw his mouth up becos he is holding his identity disc in his eye and not in his mouth. And other blokes what kept on a dropping their disc out of their eye he shows them how to hold it proper. Some times he tells a man he has got too much of his hanky showing or another bloke that he did ought to wash his hanky before he let other people see it. And all the time he is as solem as a judge. There is quite a crowd hanging about the parade ground by this and it is as quiet like as in a church. Well the major finishes his inspection and then stands in front of his coy. a looking at them with them standing a looking at him and I reckon they was feeling a bit silly like by this. Then he takes his eye glass string from round his neck and holds the glass between his fingers. It is one of them glasses in a gold frame what has a sort of verander round it and he throws it up in the air and catches it in his eye and says Now let me see you do that you dock rats. So help me they stood and cheered him like he has promised them all a free drink.

The place where us and them dockers was working is a big factory and as there is secret stuff in there every coy. has to take it in turn to have a armed guard on the gates. Us other coys. does the guard proper like with our rifles at the slope and the sentrys marching up and down like they was in barracks. But not them dockers. Some times they carry their rifles under their arm like they is going shooting rabbits but most times they leaves their rifles leaning against the wall and the two sentrys stands talking to each other with their hands in their pockets. Fred Karnos army dont have nothink on them dockers I can tell you. They dont bother about officers or any think like that and if a officer chokes them orf they is as like to tell him to go and jump in the river as not. Well they is on guard the week this new major come to them and they carrys on like they all ways done but he dont go orf the deep end at them like other officers would only he just raise his peak cap when he goes parst the sentrys and says to them Good day gentlemen. If that major went in and out of that there gate once that first day he went in and out a hundred times and all ways he lifts his hat and says Good morning gentlemen or Good arfternoon gentlemen as the case may be. At first they think it is very funny and grins at him and says Morning major or somethink like that but by the arfternoon they is proper browned orf becos they see he is taking the micky out of them. In the canteen they says to us other blokes That there major thinks we dont know how to salute proper but we will show the old basket that we can do as good as any body else. Then the blokes what is down for guard duty the next day says to us will we show them how the drill is done so we done that. All that evening they lerns Stand at Ease—Attention—Slope Arms—Butt Salute—Order Arms and back to Stand at Ease again until they is fair wore out and by this time they does not do it so bad seeing as how they has not done it before.

Well the next morning us what is working near the main gate hangs about with our eyes skinned waiting for this major to come along and see what happens. Soon we see him coming down the road and as he gets near the gate he is just a going to lift his titfer when them 2 sentrys what has been standing proper at ease comes up to attention and slopes arms and give him as snappy a butt salute as ever I see and this major chucks them a salute back like he was in front of a general. He dont say nothing. No Good morning Gents or any think like that but when he as gorn parst them I see he is grinning away to his self and arfter that they all ways give their own major a proper salute but they dont bother with other officers.

In the end this coy. was transferd to the R.E. as a Docks Coy. and I never see them again but before he was finish with them this major with a eye glass has them eating out of his hand. They never become proper soldiers when they was with us but I never see men try so hard to please a officer like they done and if any body else makes fun of this major and his eye glass them dockers gave them a proper bashing. And that is the end of this story.

[1952–4]

A Trifle from S.E.17

FRED BASON

S A GREAT TREAT to myself on my birthday, August 29, 1927, I bought a seat in the circle (instead of the gallery) and witnessed one of the finest acting performances I have seen in many years of playgoing. I saw Robert Loraine in *The Father* by Strindberg. After the show I went round to the stage door to obtain the autograph of Mr Loraine.

Mr Loraine had been a brave soldier in the First World War, besides being a pioneer aviator. He was also a kindly man, and he made no bones about giving me his autograph. As he was signing my album he said to me, 'I don't go very much for this autograph hobby but I've often wanted to possess the autograph of Strindberg; it would be nice to put it amongst my souvenirs.' Immediately I said to him: 'Well! That's *easy;* you just tell me where the bloke lives and I will get it for you. No one has ever yet refused my request, and when I tell Strindberg how much I've enjoyed *The Father* I am sure he'll oblige. I'll get it twice—once for you and once for me.'

Robert Loraine stared at me a moment, and then said he thought the dramatist lived in Barton Street, Westminster, when he was in Town. He thought the number was 7. So I thanked him politely, and said he'd have it in a day or so.

The next evening I made myself particularly tidy and walked from 152 Westmoreland Road, Walworth, S.E.17 (where I still live today) to 7 Barton Street, Westminster, S.W.1, to find Mr Strindberg. Number seven, unlike No. 152, had a distinguished Georgian façade. I knocked, and a maid came to the door. I explained my quest. She was sure Mr Strindberg did not reside there, but she said she would ask the mistress and would I wait a few moments. Eventually a handsome lady came and said she was so sorry I'd had a journey for nothing; Mr Strindberg has *moved*. Yes, she happened to know the address. It was in a block of flats off Tottenham Court Road. She put down the address on a slip of paper.

I'd got half-way up Charing Cross Road when I met a friend of mine named Mr Lupane, who at one time had been estate manager to Beatrice Lillie. I told him where I was going and he said he'd be delighted to accompany me, just for the walk. I was glad of his company for he was a nice old man. We were just at the top of Charing Cross Road when I met another pal of mine, Harry Saunders, who I knew to be a keen autograph collector, so I told him we were going to see Strindberg and maybe he'd like to come along.

Eventually we got to the block of flats. I was rather dismayed to find the number we sought was on the fourth floor and there was no lift! Up and up we trooped. Poor Mr Lupane had to stop twice, for he was winded. When we got to the fourth floor we sat on the stone steps to get our breath back. We planned a manner of approach. I would do the talking, and, when the dramatist was signing the card for Robert Loraine, Harry would put forward his own album and say, 'Please would you mind signing my album as well?' Then Stanley Lupane would put forward my album and ask, 'Would you mind signing this one—please?'

I knocked at the door. No answer. I knocked twice. To the door came an elderly man with snow-white hair. He looked just the sort of man to write *The Father*. He looked artistic, foreign and a dramatist (just as Paderewski always looked a pianist). I took off my cap and bowed (yes, I bowed). Then I said: 'Would you graciously honour us with your autograph, Mr Strindberg? It will be truly appreciated.'

He said that he was not Mr Strindberg, he was not famous at all. I thought this to be false modesty. I said: 'Oh! sir, you *are* famous, and all we want you to do is to write "August Strindberg" and the date in our albums. This post card is for Robert Loraine. After all, sir, he is the star of *your* play.'

He wavered for a moment, and then said that if it would really give us any pleasure, he would write 'August Strindberg' and the date, as we seemed bent on it. But he made the point that he would not sign in ink—only in pencil! First he autographed the card, then Harry's book, and finally the book that Stanley Lupane put forward on my behalf.

There is a great personal satisfaction in capturing a difficult autograph. In forty years I've collected 11,193 different signatures of the famous and infamous—and only had 14 refusals in all this time.

The signing done, Mr Lupane made his way downstairs, followed by Harry. I lingered in order to shake the master's hand, and to congratulate him, very sincerely, on *The Father*. Then I bowed, all polite-like, and turned to follow my friends downstairs. I was half-way down the first flight when I looked back and there was Mr Strindberg staring down, so I waved him a cheerful 'Good-bye.' I really was a happy collector at that moment.

Mr Strindberg suddenly called: 'Come back! Come back *at once*—call to your friends. All of you—come back—*please*!' I called downstairs to my pals, and eventually we were all together again on the landing outside Number 16. We hadn't the slightest idea what was going to happen. The nice old man asked us back into his flat. I hoped that he was going to show us the manuscript of *The Father* and give us each a glass of lemonade.

Mr Strindberg went over to the bookcase and took down from it a large octavo book bound in bright blue cloth, which he put upon the table. He then started to thumb through its pages. We stood waiting.

'Ah! Here it is,' he said. 'Please listen very *carefully* whilst I read to you. "Johan August Strindberg was born in the year 1849. He was the most outstanding and prolific writer in Swedish literature. He died"—*note that, gentlemen*—"he died in 1912 following a brain operation"—note that, gentlemen—"*brain* operation!" You are fifteen years too late.'

We looked at each other. The penny dropped. I wished the floor could swallow me up. I had been kidded all along the line. I felt proper daft.

Out loud I said slowly: 'He died following a brain operation. Blimey! I reckon I best go and have me own head examined right away. To have been taken in like this!'

I turned to Mr Lupane and said: 'Didn't *you* know the old cock was dead?' No, he hadn't the slightest idea. Quite out of his line of country. 'Besides,' he said, 'when you tell me you are going to meet Mr Strindberg, naturally I assume the man hasn't been dead fifteen years!' He had a point there.

Then Harry got annoyed and said to the old man: 'So you've messed up a page in my album with a forged signature!' The old man got a piece of indiarubber from a brass inkstand and said: 'That can easily be remedied. Rub it out! That's why I insisted on using a pencil.'

Harry rubbed it out. 'It has been a good joke,' said the old man, 'but it's gone far enough. You, my boy [he said to me] were so polite that I simply could not allow you to become a laughing-stock. Let's all have a sherry and forget the whole thing!'

But I had to ask him how he came into the picture. He pointed to the telephone and said his friend in Barton Street had rung him up and explained that a young chap would come round asking for an autograph of Strindberg, and he was to pass him on to another of his friends not *too* far away—say Hampstead—and then ring his Hampstead friend and tell him of the plot and pass him on to someone somewhere else. Mr Robert Loraine was fond of practical jokes.

We drank our glass of sherry and parted the best of friends. I never saw Harry again, but Mr Lupane remained friendly for another twenty years.

I got on a bus, rode down to the Strand, and walked to the Savoy Theatre. I had to wait about forty minutes for the play to end. I told the stage door manager I had a gift for Mr Loraine. Eventually I was again in his dressing-room. 'There you are, Strindberg's autograph, all genuine, and dated 1927. I've been to HEAVEN to get the bleeding thing for you! And I walked blooming miles. All the way from Walworth to Westminster and then right up to Tottenham Court Road, and then up four blooming flights of stairs! I'm tired out!'

He got up from his dressing-table. He must have been well over six feet, and thirteen stone of solid frame. I was just over five feet four, and not a pound over seven stone. I felt like giving him a bomp on his stately nose.

He said: 'So you're tired out. Exactly! You've had some exercise. Exactly! You looked to me last night in need of exercise. I have given you a little exercise! You were also so cocksure that Mr Strindberg would oblige *you*.'

At that I pointed out that I had jumped at the opportunity to oblige *him*. Whereupon he asked me to shake hands with him and forget the whole thing. I shook hands—and then asked him for an autographed photograph by way of compensation. From a drawer in his dressing-table he got out a photo and signed it. (I still have it thirty-one years later.) He then got his dresser to take my book (and myself to go with him to see they were all alive) and we captured the signature of Dorothy Dix, Laurence Hanray, Milton Rosmer and Haidee Wright. A very satisfactory half-hour!

The next evening I went back to Barton Street to see the handsome lady who had sent me on the wild goose chase, stage two.

The maid opened the door. 'Oh! Good evening. I have a nice gift for your mistress who was so kind to me.' Would I go in and wait? She'd see if Madam would be able to see me. As I waited I wrote in ink above the forged Strindberg autograph: 'With compliments to a handsome lady. Your slave for ever!'

When Madam arrived I did a little bow and handed over the autograph without a word. She looked at it, and then at me, and seemed quite lost for words. 'As you'd been so very kind last night to misdirect me to August Strindberg I felt I had to bring back a souvenir of the meeting with him.' Then—I laughed. And she laughed—she had a lovely laugh. We both laughed. The tears came into our eyes.

She asked if I would care to stay to dinner. She had two friends with her but I was not to mind them. She'd be most happy if I would stay. She felt I deserved something for taking it all in such a nice way. I pointed out that my clothes were shabby and I wasn't really fit to dine with posh people. 'Oh! That's nonsense,' she said, 'you just come in and make yourself at home.'

So I put my cap on a hallstand and followed her into a magnificent room, where there were two men, both around 50 years old, with steel grey hair, and well groomed. One was a Colonel and the other was a Doctor, but I didn't grasp the names.

The two men got into some sort of conversation and I stood looking at a big oil painting as Madam went out of the room. Then one of the men asked what I did for my living. I told them that I was what is called in my trade a 'book-runner.' They wanted to know what a book-runner was and I had to explain that I bought books in one part of London, repaired them, and then *ran* with them to where they were wanted.

One of the men then asked what sort of books I mainly sold. I was just going to answer him when Madam came back with a long bottle and some glasses. 'Oh!' she said, 'so you are a bookseller by day and an autograph collector by night?' 'Yes, madam—and no regrets.' 'Well! What *do* you sell?' I told them that I mostly sold novels that were out of print to public libraries. One of the men then asked me who were my most wanted authors, or most wanted novels. I told them that my three best sellers, the books I could at that time sell easier than any others, were *King Solomon's Mines* by Rider Haggard, *Of Human Bondage* by Somerset Maugham, and *The Blue Lagoon* by H. de Vere Stacpoole.

They looked at each other as if I had said something astounding. But I had merely made a statement of fact.

The lady looked at one of the men—and so did the other man. Since they both looked at him, I looked as well—but he was an entire stranger to me. One thing I did know: he wasn't Strindberg.

Then the lady said: 'Didn't you hear this gentleman's name when I introduced you?' 'No, mam, I can't say I did. It sounded foreign-like.' 'But, my dear boy, this gentleman *is* H. de Vere Stacpoole.'

'Are you really and honestly the author of *The Blue Lagoon*?' I asked.

The man took from his pocket a used envelope, and there was the name on the envelope. Out came my autograph album, and Mr Stacpoole signed his name in it. He told me that I had paid him the nicest compliment of his writing life, and if I'd give him my address he would send me one of his novels autographed especially for me.

He sent *The City Under the Sea*, with a long inscription in it. The blitz destroyed it at my home in 1941. Mr Stacpoole has been dead for some years now. In the past thirty years I have never come upon another autograph collector with this author's signature.

And in the past thirty years I've only once had as good a dinner as I had that night.

Fred Bason first appeared in THE SATURDAY BOOK *in No. 5 (1945) with a candid and unusual sketch of Somerset Maugham, of whose books he had produced a bibliography. From then until his death in 1972 he was a regular contributor of personal anecdote, comments on the South London scene which he never deserted, and odd bits of information about the autographs, the cigarette cards and the second-hand books out of which he made a living. Unmarried, but enjoying for many years the loving care of a devoted housekeeper, he had a vast circle of acquaintances, and when he published the various volumes of his Diary he succeeded in getting them "edited" by such distinguished people as Nicolas Bentley, Michael Sadleir, L. A. G. Strong and Noël Coward. In the course of time he became the quintessential cloth-capped Cockney "character", and thousands of* SATURDAY BOOK *readers will recall his contributions with affectionate amusement.*

AN ALPHABET OF

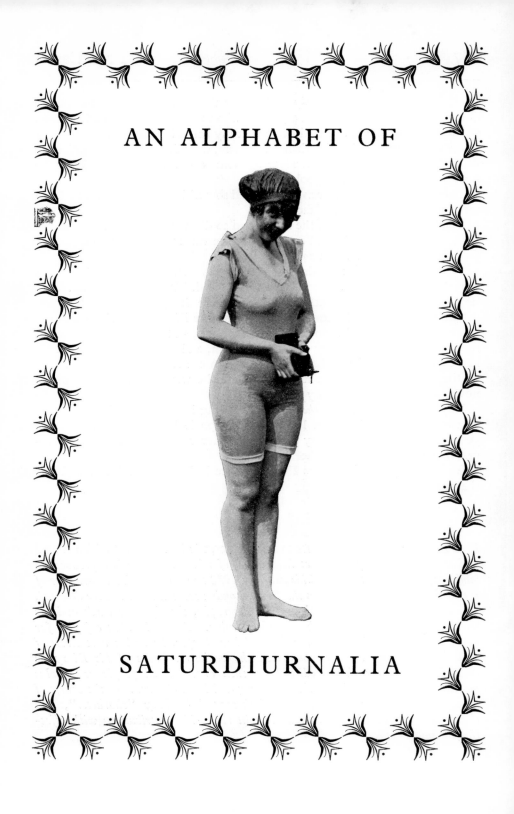

SATURDIURNALIA

RCIMBOLDO, who died in 1593 at the age of sixty-six, can claim to have been the first of the surrealists. Son of one of the masons of the Duomo of Milan, he became court painter to Rudolph II, the Hapsburg Emperor, who had a passion for the abnormal, which Arcimboldo served by painting fantastic portraits composed of vegetables, fish, books, fruit and other natural objects. Bernard Denvir wrote about him in No. 24. The painting above is 'Autumn', from 'The Four Seasons'.

VOCETS provided an example of the meticulously accurate, beautifully composed bird studies by Raymond Watson, whom *The Saturday Book* had the privilege of introducing to the public in 1967, the year after his first one-man show. The Editor was one of the first to invest—and how shrewd he was!—in this successor to Archibald Thorburn.

BATHING BEAUTIES were among the various feminine phenomena studied in our pages by that lively and learned zoologist, Charles Gibbs-Smith. The aquatic example shown here, who appeared with other birds of the seashore (including Gloria Swanson) in our No. 27, is the exquisite Alice Maison, "a perfect specimen of her time: handsome face, superb limbs and figure, but exhibiting a somewhat alarming contrast in costume. She is clearly about to act as shark-bait, sharks being said to adore being tickled by furry animals before they get to the meat inside".

Charles Gibbs-Smith, a fantastic combination of scholarship and ebullience, who was for many years, in effect, 'the voice of the V. & A.', contributed a series of pictorial comments on the female sex, with apt or inapt quotations, to six of our issues, starting with 'Ladies in Distress' in No. 20, and continuing with 'Ladies in the Air' in No. 22, 'Ladies in Love' in No. 24, 'Ladies at Sea' in No. 25 and 'Ladies at War' in No. 26. Throughout this period we had regarded him as a dyed-in-the-wool bachelor. Having delivered his final contribution, on 'Ladies on the Scaffold' for No. 31, he got married.

ALLOONS have always vied with women in Charles Gibbs-Smith's recreational studies. His two hobby interests came together in the piece on 'The Aerial Adventurers' which he contributed to No. 15. The painting by J. F. Rigaud shows the great Vincent Lunardi's well-advertised ascent in the company of his friend Mrs Sage in May 1785.

CHAHUT is perhaps not as familiar a word as 'Can-Can', but Le Chahut was a variant of the more famous dance routine which was a feature of performances at the Moulin Rouge and the Moulin de la Galette. Tudor Evans contributed a vivid essay on 'Paris in the Nineties' to No. 28, and the illustration above is one of several lithographs by Louis Legrand, in *Gil Blas* for May 1891, demonstrating the technique of the Chahut. They show how to obtain poise and balance while raising one leg almost completely upright or making a "split". The teacher above is exercising the dancer's legs so that she can achieve what was called the *brisement*. Grille-d'Egout, the most popular exponent of the Chahut, said that the ideal dress for the dance consisted of "white underclothes, a long petticoat enriched with beautiful lace, the drawers very full . . . the stockings should be of black silk". *Gil Blas* exhorted its feminine readers to "shock the hordes of men gathered round you . . . excite the old, distract the young".

ABBIES have many talents, but we doubt if any have the photographic skill and "eye" of Max Green, who gave the Editor a lift from Liverpool Street to Hutchinson's office one day and was promptly commissioned to contribute a highly amusing feature, 'A Cabby with a Camera', to No. 25. Above, he captures those famous buskers, 'The Road Stars'; below, an idyllic moment in the park, tactfully ignored by passers-by.

RINKING GLASSES of the eighteenth century were the subject of an illustrated study of her own collection by Anna Hadfield in No. 30. Those shown above are balustroid glasses made in Newcastle about 1745. They were used for toasting the Jacobite cause and are engraved with the Jacobite emblem—a seven-petalled rose and one bud. The rose denotes secrecy, as well as being a Stuart emblem. The single bud represents the Young Pretender. Sometimes an oak leaf was added.

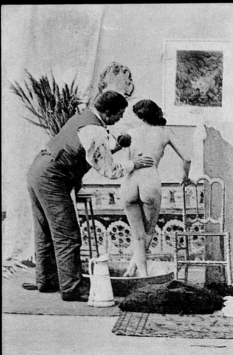

 DWARDIAN POSTCARDS (opposite) are a special collecting interest of Ronnie Barker, one of the Two of that Ilk, who possesses no less than twenty thousand cards neatly classified and filed. He contributed a characteristic piece entitled 'I Collect Everything' to No. 33. He assured us that the Coalman illustrated was, not surprisingly, French.

 ASHION PLATES have often enlivened the pages of *The Saturday Book*. The plate reproduced above, by Heloise Leloir, dates from the eighteen-sixties, and is one of a series for which accompanying verses were written by that enchanting writer who was best known for her children's books, Eleanor Farjeon. They appeared in No. 24.

ALCONS AND HAWKS were the subject of one of the contributions by one of our favourite contributors, Kenneth Allsop, who also wrote for us several brilliant essays on the history of jazz, a strange range of interests characteristic of the man. Having kept and trained a kestrel in childhood he remained a hawk-fancier all his life. This Iceland falcon from No. 19 was reproduced from Gould's *Birds of Great Britain*, 1873.

AUDI was the creator of that fantastic building which towers above Barcelona, La Sagrada Familia. Less well-known are the secular buildings which he built in and around Barcelona, on which Sir Sacheverell Sitwell contributed a commentary to No. 25. The illustrations to this feature were provided by that brilliant fashion and Royal Family photographer, Norman Parkinson. The spectral figure above is a chimney cowl at the Casa Milá.

OGARTH may well be regarded as an over-familiar subject for treatment in *The Saturday Book*. But there seemed to us no reason why Old Masters should not be given new treatment, and that is why in No. 12 we invited that percipient student of the eighteenth-century scene, Peter Quennell, to comment on a series of colour reproductions of the six original paintings for 'Marriage-à-la-Mode', in the Tate Gallery.

In 1964 the Fitzwilliam Museum, Cambridge, was presented with a pair of small oil-paintings by Hogarth, measuring only $14\frac{1}{2} \times 17\frac{1}{2}$ inches, which were unfamiliar to the public at large, as they had been for many years in private ownership, and only reproduced once or twice, and never in colour.

NDISCRETION I and INDISCRETION II are the polite names now given to this pair of paintings. In the eighteenth century they had been known as 'Before' and 'After', but they should not be confused with a pair of engravings by Hogarth with the same titles, which depict the seducer and his victim in a bedroom. The pair of *al fresco* paintings which came to the Fitzwilliam Museum are believed to date from 1730 or 1731. By courtesy of the Syndics of the Fitzwilliam Museum *The Saturday Book* was able to reproduce the pair in colour for the first time, as a tailpiece to a witty essay on 'The Art of Seduction' by one of our most valued contributors, James Laver, author of that very relevant little classic of erotic verse, *A Stitch in Time*.

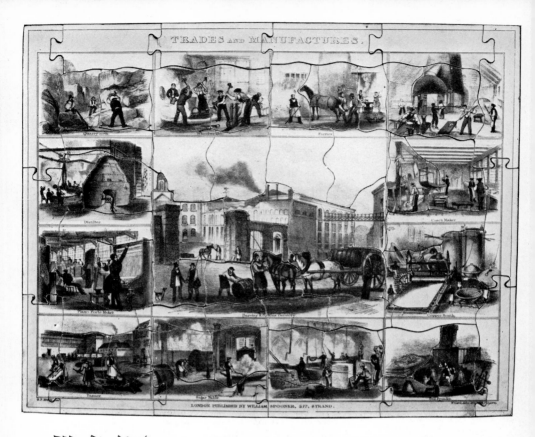

JIGSAW PUZZLES are a subject which unites *Saturday Book* readers of all ages. But our approach to them is that of the collector and historian rather than the competitor, and when we wanted to give them the *Saturday Book* treatment for No. 29, we went to the chief authority on their historical development, Linda Hannas, an antiquarian bookseller who has a unique collection. She was able to trace their history back to the 1760s, when they were invented as aids to the study of geography. Visually her examples were delightful. The one reproduced above, depicting Trades and Manufactures, was published by William Spooner about 1843.

KLEMPERER, opposite, was one of thirteen notable conductors, from Beecham and Boult to Britten and Colin Davis, whose personalities and methods were discussed by Charles Reid and photographed by Erich Auerbach in No. 29. We now choose Klemperer as an example, not merely for his commanding visual image but also for his personal heroism, triumphing over political persecution, a brain-tumour, paralysis and a broken leg, to resume his career triumphantly in his eighties.

 OWESTOFT porcelain was the subject of an illustrated appreciation by Noel Turner, an East Anglian collector, in No. 18. The two bell-shaped mugs in the top row are dated 1767 and 1768; the early dragon bowl and the barrel-shaped teapot 1770. The miniature teapot is c 1767; next to it is a mug inscribed with the name of a sailing ship.

INIATURES by
Nicholas Hilliard are beyond the reach of most *Saturday* pockets. This superb
example in the National Maritime Museum shows the 3rd Earl of Cumberland
flinging down his gauntlet to challenge all comers as Queen's Champion in
1590—an illustration to 'Dressed to Kill' by James Laver in No. 30.

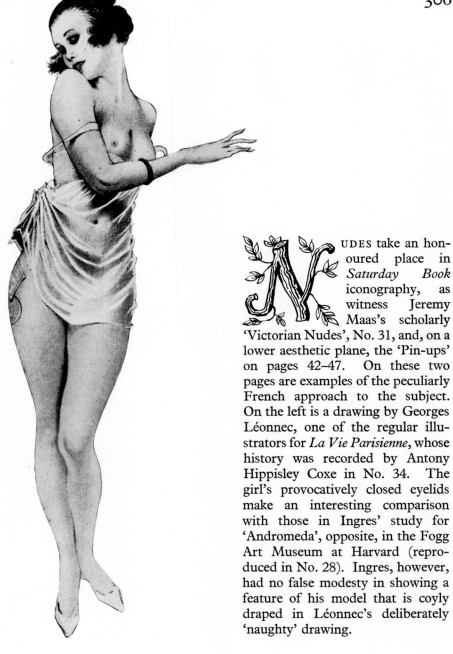

NUDES take an honoured place in *Saturday Book* iconography, as witness Jeremy Maas's scholarly 'Victorian Nudes', No. 31, and, on a lower aesthetic plane, the 'Pin-ups' on pages 42–47. On these two pages are examples of the peculiarly French approach to the subject. On the left is a drawing by Georges Léonnec, one of the regular illustrators for *La Vie Parisienne*, whose history was recorded by Antony Hippisley Coxe in No. 34. The girl's provocatively closed eyelids make an interesting comparison with those in Ingres' study for 'Andromeda', opposite, in the Fogg Art Museum at Harvard (reproduced in No. 28). Ingres, however, had no false modesty in showing a feature of his model that is coyly draped in Léonnec's deliberately 'naughty' drawing.

 RCHARDSON—Sir William Quiller Orchardson, R.A.—was once an eminent exhibitor at Burlington House; then he fell into some disrepute as a typical Victorian 'story painter'; but now he is coming into his own again as he had a very accomplished and indeed 'modern' technique. William Hardie wrote most perceptively about him in No. 34. What endears Orchardson to us particularly today is the subject-matter and titles of his paintings: such as 'Rejected', 'Her First Dance', 'Her Mother's Voice'. The painting on the opposite page is called, evocatively, 'Trouble'.

ETHER is not a very distinguished name in the history of British art, though there were three of them: Abraham the father, and two sons, Sebastian and Henry. But a painting by any of them is easily distinguishable, as it will almost always show a landscape by moonlight, often featuring a ruined castle or abbey beside a river. All are products of the Romantic Movement of the early nineteenth century. The painting above, unsigned but probably by Henry Pether, is in the collection of George Rainbird. It was illustrated and discussed in No. 34.

UEEN VICTORIA may be said to have been the monarch who presided spiritually over the early issues of *The Saturday Book*. They can claim a large share in putting Victoriana on the map of fashionable taste. But most of us still think of Victoria as that dumpy, black-bonnetted figure immortalised in Sir William Nicholson's famous lithograph. Do we recognise that dignified old frump in the charming portrait by Richard Westell on the opposite page (in the Royal Collection at Windsor), depicting Victoria at the age of eleven—one of the illustrations to David Piper's essay in No. 16, 'The Child is Father of the Man?'

EGAL ECCENTRICITIES have been of many kinds, but it is doubtful if any have given so much pleasure to the populace as the Royal Pavilion at Brighton, of which a superb series of photographs by the American, Clarence John Laughlin, were learnedly commented upon by Clifford Musgrave in No. 27. It is an enchanting monument to the originality and taste of the Prince Regent. Nash's North Gate is shown above.

TREWWELPETER has probably terrified more generations of children than any fairy-tale villain. But what do we know of his inventor, Dr Heinrich Hoffman, whose original drawing, done in 1844, is reproduced above? In No. 23 Donald MacAndrew traced his career and analysed the compulsive attraction of the best-selling shocker produced by this eminent German alienist, whose other works included textbooks on the Pituitary Gland and, more significantly, *The Physiology of Hallucination*.

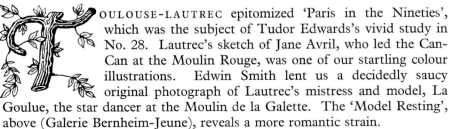

OULOUSE-LAUTREC epitomized 'Paris in the Nineties', which was the subject of Tudor Edwards's vivid study in No. 28. Lautrec's sketch of Jane Avril, who led the Can-Can at the Moulin Rouge, was one of our startling colour illustrations. Edwin Smith lent us a decidedly saucy original photograph of Lautrec's mistress and model, La Goulue, the star dancer at the Moulin de la Galette. The 'Model Resting', above (Galerie Bernheim-Jeune), reveals a more romantic strain.

NDERGROUND movements were considered glamorous during the Second World War but have got a bad name recently since terrorists adopted the term. To *Saturday Book* readers the word 'underground' denotes either the early tin, lead and gold mines in Cornwall and Wales explored by L. T. C. Rolt in No. 14, or the Lascaux caves opened up for Hammond Innes's readers in No. 29, or the 'Secret Passages' through which Jeremy Errand escorted us in No. 33. That shown on the opposite page is one dug into a cliff-face at Careg Cennen in Carmarthen, which is vaulted in stone and penetrates fifty yards into the hillside.

ALENTINO, seen above, was, as everyone knows, the Great Lover of the Silent Film. Here he is seen in *The Sheik* (1924), carrying Agnes Ayres into his tent in the desert before flinging her down on the divan with a view to 'having his will of her', a scene which always brought down the house. To No. 29 that accomplished playwright Rodney Ackland contributed a delightfully evocative study of Silent Lovers, with the title 'Love without Words'. What titles those films had!—the Gish sisters in *Hearts of the World*, Zazu Pitts in *Greed*, Pola Negri in *Forbidden Paradise*, and *The Sign on the Door* (in which 'the elegantly gloved hand of Norma Talmadge fired the revolver with which she put a peremptory end to the well-laid plans of Lew Cody to seduce her teenage daughter'.)

ATCHES AS JEWELS was the title of a marvellously illustrated feature by Anna Motson in No. 31, in which she
described some of the exquisitely wrought watches made
by Andrew Grima, the Jermyn Street jeweller, for Omega.
Above is a watch in a perfect rock crystal surrounded by diamonds. The fine lines in the stone are known as 'venus hair'.

ERXES, opposite, is depicted twice life-size, fighting a lion
in the eastern doorway of the Palace of the Hundred
Columns at Persopolis. Darius began the construction of
Persepolis in 518 B.C. Xerxes, the invader of Greece,
went on with it, and so did his successors. Yet, when
Alexander the Great looted and burnt it in 330 B.C. it had
never been regularly lived in, for the kings were not satisfied that it was
really finished. The photograph is by Lady Kelly who contributed a study
of this master-work of Achaemenian art to No. 17.

EWS are of great antiquity in the English scene and lend themselves more than any other trees to sculptural treatment at man's hands. The remarkable gathering of them on the opposite page, illustrating an essay on 'The Curious Art of Topiary' by Olive Cook in No. 29, is in the garden of Levens Hall, in what used to be called Westmorland. It probably dates from the mid-seventeenth century. An outstanding curiosity.

OETROPE was the name given to one of the precursors of the cinematograph. Inside its slot-pierced drum a long frieze was placed, and as it revolved the slots revealed little figures leaping to life, a negro jumping through a hoop, or a dolphin undulating through the waves. Above are illustrated some discs for the Zoetrope, photographed by Edwin Smith for No. 15, in the collection of John and William Barnes at Mousehole. This was one of the illustrations to a fascinating piece by Olive Cook on 'Moving Pictures before the Cinematograph'—vintage *Saturday Book* stuff!

Afterword

RONNIE BARKER

'M SURE you will agree that this book has been (or *will* be, if like me, you always look at illustrated books backwards, starting from the end, and working forwards to the foreword) a treasure house of charm, a repository of wit and elegance, a country attic crammed with curious contents. This present distillation from the original thirty-four *Saturday Books* contains several items I haven't seen before, because, although I collect *Saturday Books*, there are many I haven't yet managed to obtain; which is why this splendid volume is doubly welcome to my groaning shelves (and incidentally, my groaning wife, who loves books, but insists that we all need somewhere to sit).

So many collectables beckon from its pages; and, whilst I have decided that the results of my mania for collecting should be confined to some seventeen categories*; nevertheless I am sorely tempted by such a fascinating array.

I do hope you have enjoyed the book as much as I have—those of you who sensibly started at the front. As for the rest of you—let us walk slowly backwards through its myriad delights. Who knows—we may eventually bump into Mr J. B. Priestley, waiting, at the front of the book, to tell us how much we are going to enjoy it. Then we can say, with a superior air—"We know— we've enjoyed it already."

*Stamps, Coins, Postcards, Books, Adverts, Programmes, Bathing Beauties, Lantern Slides, Valentines, Old Toys, Games, Cigarette Cards, Scraps, Souvenir China, Playing Cards, Bottles and Saturday Books. [The miniature models of Bathing Beauties above are from Ronnie Barker's collection, about which he wrote in No. 32.]